THE BIGGEST GANG IN BRITAIN

Stephen Hayes

Grosvenor House
Publishing Limited

This book is published by
Grosvenor House Publishing Ltd
28-30 High Street, Guildford, Surrey, GU1 3EL.
www.grosvenorhousepublishing.co.uk

A CIP record for this book
is available from the British Library

ISBN 978-1-78148-606-1

Members of the Biggest Gang In Britain in action..... sometimes it was necessary, on other occasions it was questionable. Police activities during the Miners Strike and at Hillsborough have been questioned for decades. It may be that this book helps with the understanding behind what happened and to ensure that it should never be allowed to happen again.

About The Author

Stephen Hayes was born in 1946 to two hard working parents Harold and Betsy Hayes. Having left Ducie Technical High School, Manchester with five O Levels but no advanced education he continued with his unskilled Saturday job - preparing supermarket bacon for sale - on a full-time basis. Having O levels in Mathematics, Building Construction and Surveying as well as English and Geography had initially indicated a route to being an architect or similar, but such professions no longer appealed after passing the examinations

An application to join the RAF as a pilot progressed to a four day selection process at RAF Biggin Hill, where Hayes's yet to be revealed cavalier attitude to life was discovered in a myriad of aptitude tests. This led the review officer to dispense with his proposed services with the words "would love you in a war old boy, you are mad as a hatter and we don't need you flying under London Bridge for kicks, which is inevitable."

Back to cutting bacon, then much to the delight of his prison officer father, he joined the cadets of Manchester City Police at the age of 17 and a few months. The progression through the cadets onto Bruche police training school in Warrington, Cheshire, resulted in a shiny new uniformed police officer to be stationed at Bootle Street Police Station in the City centre and let loose on the unsuspecting populace of Manchester with so many other such recruits.

The early years quickly proved that the training manual and classes at Training School bore no resemblance to reality and he was immediately thrown into the mire of dishonesty, corruption and fabrication which was actually a police culture and not just that of the city's criminal element.

Despite the general alarming culture he became a genuine servant of the Queen and the Manchester public, preventing and detecting crime, protecting the weak and vulnerable and whilst doing so enjoyed the life that such a 'dedicated profession' provided.

His natural aptitude ensured that he quickly passed through the uniformed ranks, into the civilian clothes of the Street Thefts Dept, the Vice Squad, the Drug Squad and the CID in three locations throughout Manchester. During this service in so many departments he experienced the many suspect and sometimes criminal practices which took place on a daily basis in the guise of police work.

This book moves through the early years with many unbelievable incidents accepted as the norm, all illustrating the inbred culture of dishonesty and evidence corruption in its various forms. A culture which led to the unbelievable police belief that 96 deaths could be written off as the fault of the tragic and unfortunate victims in the Hillsborough Conspiracy and beyond with several such high profile incidents during recent years.

In short, the author, also a victim of fabricated evidence on a number of occasions has had enough. It is time for a change in police training and management, properly supervised and monitored. Not by politicians with too many of their own skeletons, not by the dangerously biased IPCC and certainly not by the police themselves.

This book is written with honesty and humour and is the first of a trilogy - which will hopefully open the door to such improvements, blow the whistle on so many in bred bad practices and hopefully gives food for thought.

Anyone wishing to report police bad practice can log on to the author's website at www.biggestganginbritain.com, twitter address SteveHayes@BiggestGang. Email address stephenhayes@thebiggestganginbritain.com and website www.thebiggestganginBritain.com

Introduction

It is almost 50 years since I joined the police force in Manchester as an eager 17-year-old cadet. To be honest, while I was fresh-faced and bristling with youthful enthusiasm, I hadn't got a clue what I was letting myself in for. At the start I was still naïve enough to think that the boys in blue played it straight in their bold battle against crime. I was so green I even thought that Z Cars and Dixon of Dock Green were realistic.

I really believed that every police officer was honest, upstanding and true and that they were perfectly happy to risk life and limb to lock up dimwitted criminals in between more mundane jobs like handing out time-checks to adoring locals. I'd like to say I joined the Force because of a burning desire to serve my community and make the world a safer place, but I think it was a lot more to do with a deep-seated conviction that lots of women fancy men in uniform. So at least I got one thing right!

From an unpromising start I had a colourful career as a copper, which brought me everything from a commendation for bravery that I deserved, to a criminal record that I most definitely didn't. It also brought me a hilarious hands-on education in the ludicrous lawlessness and horrendous hypocrisy that inhabits just about every level of the British police force.

I've been musing over writing my memoirs for many years, but what booted my ageing brain into action was the report of the Hillsborough Independent Panel in September 2012, which finally concluded that South Yorkshire police had lied and altered statements to deflect the blame for the 96 tragically needless deaths from the Force onto the fans.

The police concerned attempted to blame 'rogue elements' for this callous deceit. I knew this was another pathetic lie because I know how the police work.

The Hillsborough Conspiracy has shocked the establishment, the media and the general public alike. Whether it has shocked ex police officers of the Sixties, Seventies and Eighties is very doubtful. It certainly didn't shock me. I've written such reports, as did many officers - particularly those in the CID. Thanks to my creativity I was known as Enid Blyton and having been there and done it, I suppose I am not surprised I have a criminal record and men of my era with Hillsborough have been found out.

Such was the culture during my police service and on through so many years thereafter, that fabrication of evidence was a daily occurrence at various levels in a variety of situations. The culture of dishonesty and invented evidence was always present and widely accepted at all levels of the ranking system within the police and from these ranks within various forces throughout the UK came the leaders of the South Yorkshire Police, all of whom are now reviled and recognised by the public at large.

What must be accepted and realised is the fact that these are not a 'rogue element'. They are 'just the lads, at it again' but this time they have been found out on such a scale and in such a dramatic and amazing manner. They were using the same methods of statement-taking and evidence concealment which has resulted in the imprisonment of many innocent people over the years, all in the name of justice and the protection of the good old British public.

For decades cops and criminals all knew the rules of the game and how it should be played. All manner of gangs of villains have tried to carve out empires for themselves using the most unscrupulous methods imaginable but in my experience the police always won.

The dictionary definition of gang is interesting 'a group of criminals or hoodlums who band together for mutual protection and profit' – try telling the families of the Hillsborough victims those behind the cover-up were not part of a gang and that band of brothers I once belonged to is the biggest gang in Britain.

Put simply my advice to wrongdoers is, 'Don't Get Caught' and if you do, hold up your hands and certainly do not take on the 'Biggest Gang In Britain'. The popular television programme, Life On Mars whetted the public appetite, shocked some, amused others but in the present day such blatant corruption is shocking. The main character in the hit television show, Detective Inspector Gene Hunt, was very much alive and well in my time in the Force and the antics he and his colleagues were shown getting up to on the small screen only scratched the surface of what actually went on.

I want to draw back the veil on the reality of 'old fashioned coppering' in the 60s and 70s when corruption, when lying on oath, 'verballing' a suspect, giving someone a 'smack' or 'fitting up' a known villain was an everyday part of policing.

At the time the good old 'salt of the earth' public didn't care how we got results.... just that we did and it did not involve them. In such illustrious days, the police were everyone's pals. They had a laugh, a pint and even a shag in a shop doorway. They never, or at least rarely, did you for parking, drink driving or fighting. They never locked up their own grandmothers and if a member of the public assisted in an arrest and battered the prisoner it was all part of life. The police didn't hurt 'Joe Public', they were there to be respected.

OK, we pulled a few strokes to catch the bad guys, bent the rules and used tactics which today would have politicians and police-bashers screaming from the mountain tops, even more so now after Hillsborough. But you can't say we weren't effective. Unorthodox yes, but we got results and put the bad guys where they belonged - behind bars.

This is a true record, cover to cover, pole to pole. And yes, I feel my judgments important enough to publish, to risk your assessments in spite of what you may think of me, in spite of what label you may give me when it's all done. I've been called worse, a lot worse. But nothing I've done has been anything like as bad as the conspiring 'leaders' of South Yorkshire Police.

For better or worse, this is simply my report, my analysis of the world I came from, and the world as it is - the world from which the Hillsborough Conspiracy was born. And I'm going to reveal all the little spots and blemishes in between. For there are things here, as I have written them, that cause me untold amusement and embarrassment to this day. Somehow chronicling my days gives me a certain authority over them and the right to share them with anyone interested.

Those who are interested can read on...but be warned it's not a book for the faint-hearted. It covers every aspect of being a cop, from copulation to corruption and even a spot of crime-fighting. It may shock and amaze on every other page, but probably not if you're a policeman or have at least encountered out treasured legal system. One thing's for sure, I'll certainly be interested in the verdict.

Beginnings

The summers were always sunny, or so it seemed to us back then. Days lasted forever with rich rafts of sunlight, flowers blossoming, birds singing, and not a paedophile anywhere in sight.

A Little History

I remember my childhood as being happy and carefree. I have no real complaints and no entertaining psychological traumas to reveal. Just the same as thousands of others kids born into the ravaged aftermath of World War II, I faced a life that was relatively peaceful even if it was far from being financially stable.

My father had been a Commando in the war and I entered the world in 1946 just after the end of it all, when the dust had hardly settled. Like many born in those months after the war, I too was a product of those loving, and yes, sexy times. My mother was beautiful. My father was called Harold and he was, well, my father. His tastes run in my blood still. He was polite, he was a chauvinist, he suffered fools lightly and yet he was fair. As it has happened with me a generation on, people sometimes mistook his generosity with stupidity and lived to regret it. He had returned from the conflict physically bruised and mentally scarred and eventually got a post in the prison service. He seemed to have lost the will to fight and quietly put up with all sorts of bureaucratic problems and day-to-day problems. For many years he just 'did not want to know' and avoided all confrontations until later when irritations were repeated and he would react angrily. He was never violent, but he could be loud and frustrated. It was clear he would rather kill the people he clashed with, as he had been used to as a Commando. As he was promoted through the prison service his reputation was as a fierce disciplinarian - who was admired by his bosses and feared by the lesser ranks. He was fair and would always give people a second chance, unless they were guilty of dishonesty. My dad was a straight and honest man.

My father had a clear destiny to join the army. He enlisted at the age of 17 when he was too young for anything but training. As soon as he was 18 he joined an infantry battalion and at 18-and-a-half he applied for the Commandos. After an arduous medical and interview process he was accepted. The officers concerned clearly recognised the family trait that I apparently inherited; he was a mild-mannered psychopath, capable of anything, but always on the side of good, or at least as interpreted.

He was trained at Achnaccary in the wild highlands of Scotland then posted to Number 6 Commando. He discovered that Commandos had to find their own digs and was paid 6/8d (33p) per day to do just that. There were no officers' or sergeants' messes, no soft numbers at any rank. There was an easy relationship between officers and men with no raised voices and total self-discipline. Each man had to be totally self-reliant.

On November 8, 1942 as part of Operation Torch with Number 1 Commando they put paid to the German defence of Algiers leaving it to the infantry. They were immediately transported to Bone in Algiers to take the port with members of the Parachute Regiment. They were 250 miles ahead of any reinforcements and yet took and held the docks and airstrip. They took heavy German bombing until fighter cover arrived.

'Stealing' a goods train, they moved along the coast and took Tabarka, where they seized control of the docks. They were held back by heavy rainfall until March when they moved inland conducting many hit and run missions.

The coveted Green Beret was first issued in January 1943. The Commandos were then still 70 miles in front of the main army when they literally bumped into a brigade of Herman Goering's seasoned troops. It would have been suicide to stand and fight so they split the 350 men into smaller groups and attacked from all changing directions giving the impression of a much larger force.

In this action my father was wounded and taken prisoner as a stretcher case. The following day started sunny and the damp from the all-night rain caused a heavy mist. My father and two others escaped, and my father was carried by the others for five hours until reaching British lines. One of these men was later killed in action and throughout my childhood and years later I remember my father sending money and presents to his saviour's family as a gift of gratitude.

All Commando units had seen action in Norway, France, Italy and North Africa and were hardened warriors, known by then to the Germans as absolute lunatics to be shot on sight, never to be taken prisoner. In 1944 the first Commando brigade was formed under the command of Lord Lovatt. Now in an action featured in so many war films, it was D Day and the Commandos landed on Sword Beach and headed for Pegasus Bridge near the village of Benouville. They held the bridge losing 30 men and then when relieved moved downstream to check on a further bridge. It had already been demolished by the Canadians and rather than transport the explosives back they booby-trapped everything in sight, for the Germans to fatally discover.

In attempting to return to British lines they were cut off from radio contact and surrounded as they dug in. They held the position for 83 days, fighting furiously, before getting back to the lines. Before returning to England my dad was one of a small group of men given the relatively easy duty of body-guarding Monty. Posted to Holland they attached themselves to whatever regiment needed a bit of heavy help. The Commandos fought in many actions and even moved into Germany destroying a U2 rocket factory. In the Fatherland resistance was strong with German Marines attacking at every step, which often resulted in savage fighting and hand to hand bayonet charges.

Continuing through Germany leaving a trail of death and destruction they even reached the Baltic Sea. He left the Commandos with three stripes in November 1945 when the regiment was disbanded to be replaced by the Royal Marine Commandos. He wrote in a diary "Our roots run deep into the very being of every regiment in the British Army. How could we fail with roots like that?"

He was posted to training new recruits and then six months later to a military prison to secure court martial cases. He described it as the PIT. The men it secured were cowards, thieves and liars and he didn't like it. They were not men as he knew them and in reality that strong opinion of inmates remained with him during his years in the prison service.

My dad was a good and proud man with six medals to show for such dedication and valour. How could I live up to that? I suppose I was a disgrace initially and he must have had severe doubts, but never said anything. He really had had enough and if he had a difficult son then so be it. As I have matured and had the chequered success I have, I now know I owe so much to my Dad and throughout I am sure he has given me strength to carry on. My mother on the other hand had enough fight for both of them and again I owe her so much. She worked hard at three jobs to help provide for us.

I was born in Grimsby, Lincolnshire at my grandmother's house. We were staying there because we had no home of our own. Times were very tough; unemployment was high and money scarce. Shortly after I was born we moved in with my paternal grandparents, Tom and Alice Hayes, who had a small semi-detached property about 10 miles from the centre of Manchester. My father found a job with Burton Tailoring, a company that manufactured men's clothing. The factory was built in the shape of a sewing machine and was one of the few places, actually the only place, where jobs were available. There wasn't much else in the way of employment. To a proud man like Harold Hayes it was an insult rather than an unfortunate phenomenon of post war times. But it was a job and it meant that he could provide for his wife and son.

There is a certain enchantment about a man in uniform in times of conflict. Favour seemed to follow the return of the native, especially in full tunic. Each little badge or medal added another elevation, not only in rank, but in the eyes of the beholder. Such honours gave them respect with whole troops of men who shared their daily habits, men who dressed every day as they did. In the non-military world, in the days before the fighting, they might have been school teachers or barristers, clerks or salesmen. They may have been men of low, or high esteem in the community, doing what they did, going about their lives, but put a uniform on them, send them into battle, put an ounce of brass on their chest with honours, and something else happens altogether.

War proves a man. When the blast of war blows all about us it can take a quiet reserved peacetime man and make a hero of him. It can take an Earl or a man of substance and means and show him to be without spine. War and soldiery levels the playing field. But back home, after all battles are over, after the national neurosis is quieted on some foreign front, these same men take off their uniforms and resume their place in the England they were called from. And, all that honour, all that respect, all the glory earned on the battlefield too often fades in importance when war is no longer the pressing issue, when the blast is long silenced. A medal, or a war wound, means little to the factory owners, to the man who wants an honest day's work, or the man at the bank who holds a mortgage on your house. Here was my father, six foot two, a capable man, a courageous man, a decorated war veteran, a hero who had been shot at more times than he could remember. He was a man who had killed for his country (sometimes with a knife, as if to make war personal) and had seen his friends killed, a man now reduced to the charity of his in-laws. This was an insult that wounded him deeply when war itself couldn't touch him.

Eventually, he took a job in the prison service, a job that came with accommodation, a benefit that he and my mother had disagreements about. The first prison was called HM Prison Sudbury, near Derby. It was a low security open prison, occupied mainly by simple first-time offenders who were not likely to escape the confines. For children of parents in the service, Sudbury was a playground. With countryside and woodland all around us, we would just disappear for the day. Paedophilia, while I'm sure it existed and was practiced somewhere in the seedier places in the kingdom, was unheard of in those times.

Our young days were not spoiled by such problems. We did as we pleased. Picnics were the common treat, with sugar butties and water. We roamed the countryside all-day and returned only at meal times. We even mixed with the prisoners, particularly the ones on gardening duty. Or we spent time in the cookhouse sustaining ourselves on the dessert of the day, the taste of which was little better than a sponge, a strange heavy sponge tasting of nothing in particular. Served in four-inch cubes, it looked more like the sort of sponge you would use to wash the dishes with. Unfortunately this dessert of the day was the dessert of every day!

The summers were always sunny, or so it seemed to us back then. Days lasted forever. My memories are full of beautiful rolling green hills, narrow lanes, and friendly farmers. Winters always had snow for sledging. We were allowed access to all the surrounding fields. My father was a keen photographer and today the museum of Foston Hall, in nearby Sudbury village, still displays his work that appealingly captured those times with silent images. I'm sure it's a phenomenon of the memory, or perhaps of love itself, and though I feel it necessary to record the history that shaped me, there is nonetheless a price to pay to take myself back to those times.

Sudbury village in my childhood had its own pack of hunting hounds, which were a welcome source of pocket money. Hunting was the sport of choice for the gentry, and for gentlemen farmers. I still remember the red-coated riders who usually got pissed on the traditional stirrup cup. The dogs were large, and though they were vicious with the foxes, they were friendly towards us. Whenever hunting parties were about, we captured stray hounds and later 'helpfully' returned them to the hunt. This brought us a few pence reward and we felt like masters of the world with money in our pockets. It was not difficult.

The hounds were easy to walk with a short piece of washing line. Being fairly stupid animals and easily distracted, they strayed often from the pack and got themselves lost. Of course, we took advantage of the situation. We were industrious. We were young and we were fearless. We used invention to fill our pockets, being smarter than the dogs, or for that matter, the owners of the dogs, who in reality were too pissed to care. There were five of us. We hid in the hedgerows and distracted the lag dogs, the tail-enders, with treats. We would lasso them and lead the poor 'lost' creatures back to the hunt. It was lucrative employment, which utilised my enterprising spirit. I suppose the same could be said of my later career as a policeman. Some of the animals were just as dumb, just as lost, and, of course, there was just as much of the spirit of enterprise, only older and, more refined. Life was about two things back then: adventure and daring. Well, maybe three things - adventure, daring and putting a little money in our pockets.

Hunting took a back seat for a few weeks one summer when an American fighter from a nearby air base crash-landed in a field near the prison. The pilot survived, but until the plane, or what was left of it, was removed, a sentry was stationed on 24-hour watch to guard the wreckage. Our only previous experience of Americans was on war films. In real life they were relaxed and friendly, giving out chewing gum and stockings to humble locals like us. We had a lovely scam with the guards. We made each of them believe that the previous guard on watch gave us more sweets, so our bounty increased. We could have opened a NAAFI had we not hoarded everything for ourselves. At 10, I was Robin Hood, or at least had leanings that way, especially toward other people's property, but only in mild circumstances such as this. It wasn't exactly stealing but perhaps a good impression. During these days it was unthinkable for a child to have been arrested for 'Obtaining Property (in the form of sweets from the generous airmen) by Deception' which, sadly, today would have attracted police attention to boost detection statistics. The media is often highlighting such triviality where police officers arrest women with children, pensioners and rowing neighbours purely for the statistics. I just had this talent, this ability to convince the owners I deserved the use of the chewing gum, sweets, pens etc.

My first school was a small classic building in the village nearby. A daily walk of about a mile took me past Vernon Hall. My clearest memory of school is of getting really sick by eating raw honeycomb brought in by a local beekeeper. Milk was free and in winter it would freeze in the one-third pint bottles.

On rare occasions we travelled to Derby on a family day out. We walked around the shops, and I would set my eyes and my imagination on the puppets that enchanted me through the window of the toyshop in the bus station. My folks had little spare money and we never really bought much. The high spot of the day was a fish and chips lunch before returning home by bus. One last memory of those days includes the Saturday matinee at the nearby town of Uttoxeter in a small cinema, known to us as the 'Bug Hut.' The entertainment consisted of cartoons, Zorro, Laurel and Hardy, and others. This was our only contact with Americans, until the plane crash.

The prison service shuffled staff about the country after a few years at a prison, in theory to prevent friendships with long-term prisoners. I was about to sit my 11+ exam when we returned to Manchester where my father was reassigned to Strangeways Prison. High security Strangeways certainly lived up to its name. Where Sudbury was soft and bright, with sunshine and good memories, Strangeways was, well, strange. It was like the difference between Peter Pan and Pandemonium. I'm just glad I was then a little older. In April 1990 Strangeways was the scene of intense riots and rooftop protests that lasted 25 days. The prison was wrecked so badly it had to be rebuilt. Pressures within walls can build up to dangerous extremes. It is pretty much a fortress today and yet it is easier than ever to smuggle drugs into the prison. Of course it would be when they are transported through the main gates by a minority. My father would have had everyone arrested. He had no friends when such dishonesty was involved.

We lived in a flat on an estate of houses for prison officers. The kitchen was large, and it had to be. The bath was in the middle of the room, along with everything else. The bath was covered by a lid and surrounded by a curtain.

I'm not sure who designed it this way. It just added validity to the name of the place. But kids don't much think about these things. Strange though it was I had a good childhood. We had no real money, yet we had a holiday every year, usually at my grandmother's in Grimsby, close to a holiday resort called Cleethorpes. The east coast is notoriously cold and I don't recall that many sunny days there. Our holidays progressed to Butlin's Holiday Camps where we saw many stars of the future spending their entertainment apprenticeship as Red Coats.

I took my grammar school exams at Sudbury, then moved to a junior school in Manchester for a short time. I did well enough to go to a technical high school, which was a lower standard than a grammar school. I studied surveying and building construction, along with the usual subjects and a language. We all started with French, but our teacher was weak and easily influenced, so we made him teach us Russian instead. The Cold War was on, Sean Connery was Bond, and we all wanted to be spies. It made perfect sense. We couldn't have cared less about the exams that were to come later. We didn't think about later. Now was much more interesting. It had more immediate returns. Still, the headmaster found out about our intrigue, fired the teacher in question, and we were back learning French, a year behind.

Literature was another thing. Well, it was a kind of literature though not the kind offered in schools, except maybe in secret. Like many sexually repressed, curious, and naïve pubescent males, I took an interest in dirty books. I had no experience to understand much of it, only what aroused my nether parts. Technical school demanded two bus journeys and a wait in between at a bus station manned by an inspector. Though I never acted on it or reported it, I nonetheless thought it strange that he seemed to consistently request my help at tidying his shelves. To accomplish this, I had to stand on a stool whilst he supported me by holding my buttocks. These were the days of short trousers and innocence. When I descended the stool, his hand would playfully and somewhat conveniently slip, only to run his hand up the inside of my shorts. What would be obvious to anyone more experienced than myself was not obvious to me. It was merely a slip of his hand. When I grew into long trousers the requests for assistance stopped. It was only much later, when I was at Police Training School that I realised what had occurred. On returning to the bus station years later to confront him about his offence, I discovered he had retired, and died. The offence didn't die, of course. I'm not sure they ever do. Had he been alive I hope I would have arrested him, but I might have been too worried about the ridicule.

At school there were several teachers who had a proclivity for boys. Of course, when you're one of the boys you don't notice until all that strangeness is imposed on you. Even then you're not sure what to do with it. Your understanding of things is still small. Your time as a child so far has taught you to trust adults. Fortunately most of us were not acquainted with betrayal of that trust. Some teachers spanked boys quite vigorously, and for the most minor offences. I know now that two of the teachers were indeed homosexual and gained satisfaction from the little event. One taught maths, the other physics. The maths teacher got particular enjoyment from inflicting corporal punishment with both a cane and a large heavy leather strap. Though at the time we weren't exactly sure what it was, his erection gave him away.

Having a particularly attractive backside, I was usually bruised in that area. It all seemed normal in those days, so we didn't say too much about it.

One of the two teachers had red cheeks, which never changed colour. When my father was at Wakefield, a very high security prison in Yorkshire, he ran a wing of that prison which was populated solely by what were known as nonce cases. That meant they had committed crimes like child abuse, rape, or a sex murder. Each morning they were paraded outside their cells in a line for inspection, and despite the fact they were all different ages and sizes my father noticed they all of them seemed to have strange rosy coloured cheeks, a ruddy circular colouring, similar, I suppose, to Enid Blyton's Noddy. That makes you wonder about his relationship with Big-Ears, but that's a tale that Enid Blyton never told. I only recently discovered that she owned the Isle Of Purbeck Golf Club in Dorset during her writing days.

Already in life I was capable of making money from a variety of sources and situations, finding advantage when it presented itself whether I created them or whether they just seemed to come to me somehow. I trusted no one, even those with a healthy complexion. I was still a virgin and remained so until I was about 18. I was in training to be an architect, a surveyor, or a civil engineer, careers I thought were for me. But I did this with little, or no interest, even when I passed all the examinations at O level standard. Successful completion led to further schooling, and A levels, which would have led to university had I continued. I didn't fancy more education.

I was quite the little entrepreneur, even then. One of my intrigues, while dishonest, seemed quite innocent, or at least it did back then. It was a response to opportunity, that's all. I still have an eye for such things. I was appointed a dinner ticket monitor. Dinner tickets were sold on a Monday to pupils who desired school dinners for the week. The money was collected by the teachers, and the tickets were then given to the students who handed them to the dinner ticket monitors before entering the dining hall. Several hundred students ate school dinner, so a few tickets recycled to friends by a pal and I at half-price appeared harmless. The sheer numbers of young and hungry bodies, the noise, the clanging of plates, allowed me to keep my crime somewhat unnoticed for quite a while. This fruitful little practice continued until the catering manager noticed that inadequate funds were available to feed the overflowing dining hall. The fact that there were several others collecting tickets saved the two of us involved from being found out.

At 16 I completed my basic education and had passed four O levels, acceptable at the time. But I had failed maths. I intended to take it again whilst studying A Level Economics and maybe something forgettable. At last, I dropped out of school altogether. I thought it simply a waste of time. I am now a great believer that everyone's life is mapped out, and that nothing will affect the determined route. This development period in my life, my procession through the British school system now almost seems to have had some odd sense of planning about it, and perhaps subconsciously I knew to simply let the currents carry me along. I was 17, partially educated, and ruefully unemployed. I was shaving and still a virgin. But I had a social life of sorts and was learning to drink alcohol. And was there ever a decade like the Sixties?

The Sixties. We Were Young. We Weren't Stupid

I knew nothing of the notorious Sixties until 1964 when I became a uniformed officer. Before that, all the excitement we found was in a coffee bar called the Jungfrau. It was in Manchester which is about 40 miles from Liverpool, where the Sixties found its voice. Four of us frequented the Jungfrau and, eventually, helped with the door security. My father bought me a set of weights and though I may have looked like a six feet, nine stone weakling, I had an undoubting vision of myself and wrongly believed working a coffee bar door was well within my capabilities. But who cared? There were many illusions in those days. The word 'failure' was not in my vocabulary, then or now, and I made it work for me. The Jungfrau was a large dance and cabaret hall that featured groups like The Hollies, The Beatles, Freddie and the Dreamers, Wayne Fontana and the Mindbenders, and many more. Even Screaming Lord Sutch appeared. All these groups became hugely famous much to our surprise.

Of course as they became more and more successful our door charge increased. My lessons from the School Dinner Ticket Monitor scam led me to a much more lucrative scam charging for re-entry into these clubs as I 'monitored' the door. The money I earned from this enterprise allowed for some light gambling at the many local casinos. Winning was not uncommon and in spite of my unemployment, I was able to give my mother adequate keep. No one really bothered about where it came from, in spite of my father's profession.

I will always remember The Beatles honouring a date they had committed to before their rise to celebrity, at a small coffee bar called the Three Coins in Fountain Street, Manchester, on January 27th 1963. This was after their first single 'Love Me Do' released on October 5th 1962 had become a major hit. This kind of thing happened all the time at the Jungfrau. The area where all these clubs clustered together was full of old warehouse properties, 19th century buildings once used in the cotton trade. They were separated by a web of narrow entries and alleyways and most of the clubs were in dank basements. They were the type of dark alleys you'd use to film a Jack the Ripper movie, cobbled streets and all. The only illumination at all might be an occasional light from a window, a light left on by mistake. The offices are secured at night. The cobbled walkways were dark. The doorways, and there were many, were darker. And as the evening's entertainment turned steamy, the doorways became occupied with couples making wanton with the night, having sex under the cover of darkness, making good use of the stone steps to adjust for height and optimum penetration without the knee ligaments collapsing, or a disc slipping out of place.

I intended to pass maths at night school and then apply to be a pilot in the Royal Air Force. Six O levels were necessary as an entry requirement. Whilst my application was being processed, I continued to work at the supermarket that I had begun while still at school.

I was 17 and had no real interest in girls at this time in my life. Don't get me wrong, the desire was there, it just hadn't been duly processed by time, seasoning, and experience. It just showed itself by aggravation, an energy that needed wearing down. I attempted sex for the first time while we were on holiday at Butlin's Holiday Camp. I made two attempts actually and both were disasters. I became part of a pedal cycling racing club after that. It kept all my wheels occupied. The movement was much more predictable. All my money went on accessories, not girls.

I eventually went to Biggin Hill Camp to be assessed as a potential pilot. I faced tests, took leadership courses, and tried flight simulation. After four days I was summoned to the review officer. He was a typical RAF officer from the Second World War with a large handlebar moustache, a cravat and the sort of exaggerated dialect you'd hear in a war movie. "Well, old boy. You're fabulous," he said. "We would love you in a war. You are absolutely as mad as a hatter." After laughing at his own joke he continued: "Can't have you though. You would be so bored, you would be likely to fly under London Bridge." Around this time, two fighter pilots actually pulled off such a feat. It was hard to take that they had arrived at such a decision about my character so soon. I was still pretty much a nine stone weakling with spots and no real personality. I certainly never had a wild streak, outside my school mischief. It would take a few years to prove the many evaluations right. As it turned out those military psychologists really knew their job.

So I went back home. My small wage didn't really hold up my end of things. My parents were both very hard working especially my mother. At one time she worked as a clothing machinist, with hard women who cursed with more talent and venom than most men. My mother was a very attractive woman and my father was the only man she had ever been with. The job was difficult for her, but she endured it for the sake of her family. I was clearly a passenger in my parents' home, and the drastic option I chose to remedy this was to become a policeman. My father loved the idea.

The Young Arm of the Law

Passing all the required exams and medicals, I joined the police cadets in Manchester. There was no real consideration of public duty. My young conscience didn't quite stretch that far yet. The money was trivial, not yet laughable because I didn't know any better, but it was a job and my father was quite proud. My 19th birthday was approaching and now I was a cadet. About this time my father was transferred to Wakefield. Before leaving, he was delighted seeing me with my 'short back and sides' haircut. All my talk about the suffering I endured during cadet training was a real source of entertainment for him.

Part of my 'suffering' was an adventure course in the Pennine Hills, that rugged range from the Midlands to the Scottish border which separate Yorkshire from Lancashire. It is wild country and walking was difficult. It was the police hierarchy's idea of a cadet's survival course and the object was to toughen us up and build camaraderie and character as we walked the soggy peat bog known as the Pennine Way in a week. My memories of this week are not good ones. We had hardly any sleep with fierce gales blowing the tents on one occasion with us inside them through a flock of dozing sheep into a shallow river. We had to spend the rest of that night sleeping upright in the rear of a support police van on wooden slatted bench seats. We were sure the expedition would be abandoned because of this, but the instructors were adamant that it would not. They insisted that, despite the severe weather that continued into the following daylight, we were to complete the planned mileage and use the same pre-planned campsite. We walked about 25 miles a day, sometimes 30, and it was only much later in my career I found that wherever we had camped, a pub was just within walking distance. The Pennine yomp was actually a week out for the instructors and they were not about to relinquish this easily, despite near bouts of hypothermia, sleep deprivation, bruises, sprains and the occasional outburst of, 'I want my mum' from the assembled and most uncooperative band of adventurers.

We were not quite in the wilderness we thought we were. Having arrived at the erected camp and eaten, we were knackered, so knackered that we retired to bed. We did this without any encouragement whatsoever. Of course, the instructors went straight to the pubs and drank into the early hours. The following day, at breakfast, we took down the tents, leaving it all to be packed into the van by the instructors. We saw them again at lunch, and again headed off into the wilderness armed with another map reference for the night's stay, where we found the already prepared campsite. There was never any real likelihood of us getting lost because the Pennine Way is marked with surveying trig points at regular intervals along its length, and we only came down from the peaks to find the camp every evening. What we didn't know was that the hours of walking between the camps was maybe an hour's driving time. The camp was erected with its six tents, even before lunch. Our instructor heroes had ample time to get in the lunch period at the pub.

This entire expedition was a holiday for them, and the last thing they wanted was for it to be abandoned. Whatever went wrong and however bad the weather and conditions got would only add to the training. Looking back, I suppose it may have actually helped build some character. Prior to the expedition I broke in some walking boots under the direction of my father, who was quite experienced with such things and appeared to enjoy the pain and suffering of the build-up. He had me walking miles every night after work to find the weak spots in my feet. Then he'd have me soak them in methylated spirit to harden the skin. This was invaluable, but due to the fact I trained on a flat roadway the problem with my ankles and tendons never became apparent. By the time I returned home, my ankles were the same thickness as my lower calf and the pain was considerable, requiring medical treatment. I ruptured the sacks around the tendons up the side of my lower leg from below my ankles. Even today I have trouble breaking in new boots and shoes, neither of which is now used for walking any distance. I suppose the character-building Pennine Way, the continual walking in sodden footwear has attributed along with rugby and amateur wrestling to my present state of invalidity which has resulted in two new knees and a replacement hip.

When my father met me on my return he was beside himself with joy as he saw me hobbling about and covered in grime from a week's absence of bathing. He was totally in agreement with all the hardships and reminded me that he had completed four years in similar conditions as a Commando sleeping in holes in the ground, without the 'luxury of tents', during the war and in fear of his life through most of it. What can you say to that sort of experience? Of course, my father got a real belly laugh out of my whining. In the War serving in the Commandos meant being in a unit which was so feared by the Germans that members faced being shot on sight by the SS. He had spent four years soaking wet, wounded, and under fire, being wounded by a fighter plane once, so he loved what I was going through. To him it was a jolly jape - never mind my personal pain.

A Police Cadet

Cadet training was very ineffective. The quality of the policeman on the street depends on his individual aptitude for the work, and, perhaps, whatever instincts he may possess to do the job. Experience and education are also vital elements. Men with service experience always seemed to stand out from the university types that filled the numbers in later years. They differed in appearance, bearing and in presence. They differed in response and invention in difficult situations. They differed in the earning of respect from rank and file officers on the streets. As they did their duty, they often relied on supervisory officers for advice, and on a daily basis, depended on the senior officer more and more, down to the filling out of reports.

I was required to complete 18 months of police cadet service. What was called a training school was a collection of about six classrooms, situated on the top floor of the D Division headquarters. One classroom was used for a body of cadets which included about 20 men and eight women. Serving police officers having various classes through their service also attended the training school. During the first two years of service every constable was regarded as on probation and accordingly, had regular updates on what was supposedly learnt at Bruche, during initial training.

All this was headed by a superintendent. The usual ranking structure was down to several patrol constables. I think the qualifications for instructor depended on one being rather piss-poor at being a policeman and not safe to be allowed on the street or, as in the case of one or two people, you were so problematical you had to be stationed somewhere, out of harm's way, and everybody else's.

At the time of my cadet training the instructor was Sergeant George Kirwin, a man I loved to be with. He always had a sparkle in his eye and a practical joke to perform. He was the exception to the rule in many ways, especially as choice of supervisor for the training school. He was a policeman and, through his exemplary service, was promoted to the rank of superintendent. He finished his service at Stretford, which was part of Lancashire County police when I first joined. Stretford was swallowed up as Greater Manchester Police came into being. I remember George being so proud when his son joined the police. I didn't have a great deal of personal contact with him, but I remember him as an industrious officer, rising to the CID, but falling foul due to some internal investigation which forced him to resign. I cannot recall the detail, but I recall he was 'sacked' for some 'there but for the grace of God go I' scenario involving some bent practice we all indulged in to improve society in our honest, but sometimes misguided endeavours, and methods of administering the law when in the CID.

I was, of course, very keen. My new American Marine haircut pleased my father, but cost me a girlfriend. She wouldn't be seen with me and it got me into a fight in a Chinese Restaurant with a piss taker. I had it cut this short only once. In the cadets, I used to socialize with a gang of lads from Salford. This is when I worked the door at the Jungfrau with Eddie Woodward. Extra work like that was totally forbidden by the police and would have meant instant dismissal, if discovered. We were travelling along Corporation Street, driven by Geoff Swain, a real jack the lad and the only one of us with an actual moving car. Also with us were Spas, Eric, Chad, and someone else. We then saw one of our friends. We stopped and threw him in the car and sped off. I was in uniform and this little 'joke' was reported as a kidnap. I was called to Superintendent White's office for an almighty bollocking, which nearly proved to be the end of my police career before it had even started. We never saw much of each other after I joined the Force, that is, until I was walking along Cathedral Street in full helmet and uniform and caught Mr Swain breaking into a car with a screwdriver. How lucky for him he was allowed to run from the scene. I never saw him again, but I am reliably informed he has taken over Southern Spain.

I enjoyed marching drill and even gave team displays in my white gloves at open days and the like. I look back and think: "How the hell could I do that?" Many people I know will believe I have lost my marbles admitting to this and the pleasure I got from it. The only hint of police work we did in the cadets was known as Christmas traffic in the city centre. We paraded at Bootle Street Police Station with the real policemen. We were lectured in the art of avoiding any confrontation and incident. We were instructed that should a confrontation prove unavoidable, to phone for assistance immediately. I do not recall any real incident worthy of relating, as all we seemed to do was stand at road junctions in hailing distance of a police officer, and herd Christmas shoppers across in conjunction with the traffic signals.

As with the drill, it all seemed so very important at the time. There were many drunks about the city centre. This was probably due to the many Yates Wine Lodges and the small amount of Blob it took to render an existing alcoholic uncontrollably pissed yet again. Blob was a combination of Australian white wine of such strength and bitter taste that it needed sugar and hot water to assist the consumption. The unfortunates were only arrested if they couldn't stand, or if they remained abusive even after being kneed in the balls.

I remember being impressed with the way a police constable wearing a raincoat or overcoat could lean forward as though whispering in the ear of an offending drunk and as the open coat fell to the sides of the offender, knee him so effectively that he normally took the advice and hobbled away with the shopping public remaining totally oblivious to the instant justice just having taken place. While it wasn't too commonplace in the police cadets, I was to learn later in service what an important part instant justice played in the day to day performance of prevention and detection of crime, as they would refer to it at training school.

The remaining months of cadet service were spent washing up and brooding on various detachments about the Force while learning the operations of the support departments. I remember I left the exhibits room in the Fingerprint Department cleaner than it had been for years, but I am not sure what benefit I gained from this as my service progressed, other than being able to perform Reserve Man duties at Newton Street Station.

A feature of cadet training that has remained with me throughout my life, is that of keeping fit. We went to the YMCA on Peter Street twice a week for physical training and swimming. I particularly enjoyed the physical aspects of the self-defence, the boxing and the general fitness training. The instructors also came. Budget, the reject from the streets, suitable only for training, bumbled about in khaki shorts, the worst you had ever seen, in a manner that certainly made you think of mercy killing.

One of the instructors was Granville Walker, a man I remember most from the Pennine Way expedition. He was only about five foot nine inches, which was short for a policeman in those days. Today it might be considered quite tall. He played the part of instructor perfectly. He was always immaculate, barking orders with a gravel voice, playing a great part with the instruction in the gym. I have not seen him since those days, but I am told his marriage broke up. He took to drink and the last I heard was totally homeless, living in cardboard boxes somewhere in the city. This was an immaculate man with a lot to offer, at least to the likes of the cadets, and yet he went totally off the rails to become everything he once clearly despised in humanity: unshaven, unkempt and dirty.

I have never failed to be amazed at the course one's life takes. I truly believe it is already mapped out, that even if you manage to deviate from it you are quickly dragged back on course with an astounding helping of good, or in my case, bad luck. During my childhood I nearly drowned in a static water tank at a prison where my father was stationed. Perhaps because of the trauma, I never took the opportunity to learn to swim and remained frightened of water. It was drilled into us non-swimmers that if we didn't learn to swim, and if we didn't pass the life saving examination at training school, we would fail the course. I learned to swim by being forced to run off the diving board into the deep end and somersaulted into the water. This character building method of instruction worked to a degree because as I surfaced, in spite of my disorientation, I had to get to the side of the pool or drown.

When I joined the police, the majority of serving officers of all ranks had completed some form of military service and the discipline that had been instilled into them remained. In turn, this discipline was passed on to the 'sprogs', such as myself. Other than a few exceptions, these people gained our respect and it became an excellent working unit. Today there is no such atmosphere in the police force. Morale is at rock bottom and at the heart of the rot is the decision of Margaret Thatcher when Prime Minister to recruit university graduates.

There were many constables who would do nothing in the police, and nothing really in life as well. One officer who couldn't be said to fall into this bracket was named Kirwin, though he was no relation to George Kirwin. This other Kirwin was rather pompous though he did have some real police experience. He had been stabbed and won the George Medal for bravery. He was also quite acrobatic and could do an 'ear stand' on anything. An actual ear stand, which is just as daft it sounds, was basically a head stand performed at an angle on the ear. George Kirwin might say: "Do an ear stand, Kirwin!" And up he went. He'd do it on a chair back, on the corner of a desk, and I suppose up his own arse if he could. It was an impressive feat, but strange for a man on light duties, being a hero and all that and now serving as an instructor at the training school.

Another was a real big bumbling waste of space, who shined less than bright at training school. He was one who fell into the category, 'better kept off the streets'. At 6ft 3in, he always seemed to wear a uniform tunic so small that the belt at the rear was always in the region of his shoulder blades, and his trousers so short with his braces at maximum tension, that it showed off his Doc Martens. It was the practice then to teach pride in your appearance; short hair, pressed trouser creases, and a must for maximum effect, bulled (polished) boots. This was so highly regarded that a class was actually held for instruction in boot bulling. When one looks at today's excuses for Manchester's Finest, it is clear such classes have ceased to operate.

Of course, it was bordering on the ridiculous to go to those extremes, but I think over the years it has proved to be one of those things you never really forget. And it does make you a better person. I am still conscious of my appearance and it was only the teaching of this time and perhaps my father's influence. He was an excellent role model. And whilst the Commandos were not well known for their bullshit appearance, he did know about 'bulling and creases' from his early Army life. He took great delight in showing me how to melt polish with wax and then put it on the boot toe cap with the rag, using a small circular movement, assisted by spit and hence the term 'spit and polish', followed by more serious polishing with a soft duster to see your face in the finished result. Creases in the trousers stayed in with little effort by running Evostick down the inside of the crease to hold the two sides together. I didn't do this in all my trousers because the end result resembled broken glass running the length of the crease, and this proved very impractical in certain situations especially when kneeing a prisoner in the balls or having sex in a car. I'll say more about it later, but sex in a car was how we imposed immediate 'fines' on unsuspecting and yet willing female transgressors. I was surprised in the beginning to realize just how many 'fines' were settled this way. During my induction period I obviously believed that the police were the good guys, and that the public was there to be protected. Any orders and guidance from the officers above me were based on a wealth of experience and had to be obeyed.

Bruche Training School

I was 19, and still brainwashed by the character building I was getting - the damaged legs, the near drowning, the rhetoric, the repetition, watching the old guard with a sense of awe, and being taught the way of the 'police world' by bumbling instructors who could not be allowed on the streets. But I was given admittance into this odd world, into the real police thanks to three months training at Bruche, the police training college near Warrington, Cheshire.

The old saying goes: "If you can't do it, teach it." My father's pride was large, doting and misplaced. He could not have had a true knowledge of the company his son was keeping, nor been aware of the abysmally failing training standards imposed upon his stripling child. He only saw his boy going off into the big wide world to live in dormitory conditions and endure further character building hardships. The accommodation was actually smart shared rooms, in a newly constructed block.

Bruche had once been an RAF camp. The majority of the large buildings had remained unchanged since the war, but our accommodation had been newly-built and was of a good standard. Dressed in my gleaming new uniform, my ill-fitting helmet and my reflective bulled boots, I was ready for my first parade with about 100 other recruits from Forces as far away as Edinburgh, but mainly young hopefuls from Manchester, Cheshire, Merseyside, and Lancashire. We were a motley crew but there was a brighter side to it all - female recruits. And not all of them were the well-built lesbian types of police caricature, though neither were they the little dollies of today. My present day analogy of the type of woman who was attracted to the police during this time is that of a fitness instructor. They appear attractive but lose points as you get closer. Incredibly they all appeared to believe they were attractive and not recognising their own failings practically threw themselves at the male instructors.

The majority of instructors were totally forgettable and clearly drawn from the ranks of failure in the various forces. The leading and most unforgettable personality, perhaps for the wrong reasons, of all my career was the drill sergeant, Luke Alpin, who we were to find later was not even a sergeant. He had been given this honorary rank to go with the job, which allowed him to strut about and scream at all and sundry as the typical Sergeant Major seen in a variety of comedy films. His tall thin frame was topped off with a flat military style cap with a peak set flat on his face in the style of a guardsman, apparently so he could put his face up to yours and yell obscenities at the top of his voice, as he must have seen on screen somewhere. He was supported by two of the oldest, shiniest bulled boots ever seen and, as the weeks went by, a kind of competition started between a few of us to stand "accidentally" on the toes of his boots. Of course the boots were an accident waiting to happen. On many occasions plans were hatched to 'accidentally' stand on a boot, ruining the amazing reflective finish, acquired from many hours of bulling. No one actually had the nerve for such a deliberate act and eventually such an act was unnecessary as fate took its turn.

The canteen was full, the queue enormous and weaving and rolling with its own momentum as most of the shower involved reverted back to schooldays where a bully, or a Dennis the Menace type, would push unexpectedly into an individual who in turn pushed three others and so on until the queue ahead reversed the pushing action and so the rolling wave continued. That is of course until Alpin gleaming from head to foot, upright, with marching stick under his arm, cap plastered to his puce face, veins bulging over his starched collar entered the canteen screaming all sorts of Sgt Major obscenities to bring the queue into order. This screaming, strutting vision of discipline had an immediate effect. The queue instantly attempted to form into three ranks leaving unfortunate individuals in its length squeezed out into the path of the screaming Alpin, by now at full strut and partially sighted due to his hat. Peter Burgess equally blinded, but with panic, tried to push back into the orderly queue only to be ejected again by the throng and yet again with childish amusement only to turn to seek another entrance only to collide with Alpin. The blind leading the blind comes to mind.

Initially only the men in the queue on the edges saw the perfect Tuf Boot logo impressed by Burgess's heel onto the gleaming left toe cap of Alpin's boot followed by a horrendous scuff mark on the right as he attempted to move away. The initial gasps turned to a whisper and then to a grumble and finally a full blown deafening conversation as the tale of Burgess's demise was passed from mouth to ear of all gathered. Just as quickly, silence befell the canteen as Alpin, beside himself with rage, looked about to have a heart attack as he raised his stick to strike the apologetic, but terrified Burgess and then immediately realised the list of criminal offences he was likely to commit in the name of 'bulled boots'. The silence was broken with early laughter as he stormed from the room. The noise of mirth reached an amazing level as all realised the consequences of the rolling queue disorder. Alpin never forgot this incident and Burgess was a marked man throughout his training. His exemplary drill results clearly benefited from the daily one to one training he endured.

The training was generally boring but the social life was exceptional for both of the right reasons – beer and females. The media over the last few years has regularly featured examples of the quality of training and the training officers involved. Several trainees have died of gunshot wounds, CS Gas inhalation and even from such a gas cartridge striking an officer in the chest with fatal consequences as occurred when Manchester continued to uphold its dismal training and leadership reputation. The actual result of one such 'circus' was Chief Constable Peter Fahy appearing in Court as a result of a Health and Safety prosecution.

We endured much simpler and less arduous practical demonstrations related to the investigation of complaints. We were taught what questions to ask and how to make an arrest as a result of 'dilligent' inquiries. The parts of the villain, the complainant, and, of course, the police officer were played by trainees, all under the guidance of an instructor who had probably never arrested anyone in a real situation.

The simulation goes something like this: "This man has stolen my purse, officer. He took it from my handbag whilst I stood at the bus stop."

"Is that so?" the officer asks the accused.

"No sir, I just brushed against her bag with my hand," answers the villain.

"I do not believe you. I suspect you have stolen the purse and I want to search your pockets," returns the officer.

A search was made as the villain holds his hands above his head to help. The officer then removes a purse from his pocket, holds it up and asks, "Is this your purse madam?"

"Yes it is, officer."

The officer takes hold of the arm of the villain and says, "You are being arrested for the theft of this lady's purse. You are not obliged to say anything unless you wish to do so and anything you do say will be put into writing and given in evidence."

The villain replies: "Oh dear, you have caught me. I am sorry. My mother is ill. Will I go to prison?"

And this is England, the birthplace of modern theatre no less. Such performances were portrayed in the training classes as if that was the way they would occur in real life and how they would be resolved. All the numbers added up. Everything was tidy. Even some of the instructors believed this. They were often from county forces and had pitifully little experience of any real big city situations. There were many such examples play-acted and believed during the three months of training. How could they send naive little boys like us onto the streets of Manchester armed with such fiction and improbability? Of course, they do the same today. The difference is that police constables are now badly and weakly led by men with no experience of life, and who themselves believe these childish scenarios. They have never visited working class areas and yet have tried, with textbook thinking, to enforce senseless laws with so many safeguards for the accused that the law is in fact impossible to enforce. Not only is justice blind, but so are those who carry out her bidding.

I was called to a similar incident to the one re-enacted above some six months into my service on the streets of Manchester. By then I had learned the difference between reality and training. A woman had her purse 'lifted' from her bag in Lewis's, a city centre store. She screamed loudly and the store detectives apprehended and detained a Jamaican running from the store. There was no doubt he had done it. I was quickly on the scene, being engaged directing traffic just outside. The dialogue in real life was rather different from the training exercise:

"This woman says you have nicked her purse. Where is it?"

"Not me, mon. She wrong. The fucking cow doesn't know what she saying."

"Why did you run?"

"I like running."

"Empty your pockets. Give me the purse."

"Fuck Off! You are only picking on me coz I am black."

"Listen you black cunt, empty your pockets or I will."

"Fuck off!" he screamed again.

All West Indians, especially Jamaicans, are very excitable and scream a lot in a threatening manner, but rarely take it as far as violence. You have to shout back and be as loud as them. This, of course, is not very English and certainly is not in the training manual at Bruche and certainly not PC for today's consumption.

Most Jamaicans of the criminal variety also smell strongly of body odour...as do many white criminals come to think of it. Restraining them was difficult and could only be accomplished whilst holding your breath. This man would not empty his pockets and as I reluctantly moved closer to do so he pushed me away in a half-hearted manner, still screaming abuse and spitting as he did. The spitting was actually due to badly spaced teeth. It would have been easier if I had the training manual with me because I could have at least hit him with it. In those days, to push an officer was considered police assault and to shout at one was considered 'Conduct Likely to Cause a Breach of the Peace'. Both were considered heinous offences and worthy of arrest, to say nothing of the theft, which had by now been forgotten in the battle for dominance before the gathered multitudes of shoppers. My perfectly executed leg sweep, and the hurling to the floor of the accused brought a gasp from the crowd, but not as loud as the one from the accused. I landed on top of him with both knees to pin him to the ground and forced his arm up his back until he screamed as I went through his pockets. I found the purse and then dragged him to his feet and marched him off to the security office to await the arrival of the van to transport him to Bootle Street Station. It was nice to hear the mild ripple of applause from the crowd, with never a hint of police violence!

It was, and probably still is, fair game for the instructors at the training school to seduce the new recruits, which they certainly did with real joy in their work. This left the dregs (the lower end of the sexual scale) to the rank and file who, in turn, did all in their power to nick the women from the instructors or, at least, ruin the attempts to smuggle them into the instructor's accommodation. I used to get my share of action. Of course, I always have throughout my police service and beyond, despite the hindrance of a wedding ring, the one on my own finger. We did not have the luxury of our own room for sex and, consequently, had to use cars or doorways. I didn't have a car. A doorway had to suffice. The camp was patrolled by the instructors who had a good knowledge of likely locations, which made it difficult for us.

Having discovered my sexual self at last, I put real energy into this new-found enthusiasm, and found the perfect spot. It was an unpatrolled area, an unlikely place for sex. I chose, for my 'interviews' the rear porch doorway of the Deputy Commandant's bungalow, situated at the front gateway to the camp. I was eventually caught, probably 'snouted up' (reported) by a colleague, who I suspected was jealous of my success with a little darling who had never actually done it. We were in an odd standing position. She was already knickerless and as optimistic and ambitious as our tryst was, I found it to be extremely difficult due to my height (6ft 1in) and her lack of height (5ft 5in) together with acute pain in various areas of my body from the trials of the Pennine Way and various violent sports, which I attempted with limited success.

Later in life I discovered (through trial and error, though I could hardly call it a trial) that bending the girl forward and doing it doggy style became an acceptable and actually preferred position, especially when with a member of the 'brown paper bag brigade' of the Plaza. The sexually desperate times involved during a 'Grab a Granny Night' and the foolish decision to always seek something 'better' throughout the evening with poor results up to the final two waltzes and settling for typical 'ten to two' material.

My punishment for this 'serious offence' at Bruche, as it was called by the Commandant, was confinement to camp for one month. This punishment could be compared to a hardened gambler being ordered to do a trolley dash in the Royal Mint, or an alcoholic being made head buyer for Yates Wine Lodges. Even before this punishment, I rarely left the camp except to do my swimming practice. I hardly went home because a great many women stayed over the weekend due to the large distances they would have had to travel to see either mum or an old boyfriend. Some things just weren't worth the trouble. After three months class work, practical demonstrations and marching in all weathers on the drill ground we were regarded as full police officers. I had trained at the swimming pool every free evening and had passed to the level of Advanced Safety Award which, whilst sounding grand, came with the warning: "Don't try and save anyone, whatever you do!" A slogan quite fitting years later to David Blunkett's hobby bobbies – or Community Support Officers to give them their official title.

We also completed a St John's Ambulance course, which included mouth-to-mouth resuscitation. I never forgot this, and twice I have tried the procedure on someone. The first time was on the top floor of the Watts Building on Portland Street, which is now the Britannia Hotel. I was outside the building when a man had collapsed on the fifth floor and the poor chap's demise was brought to my attention by a breathless warehouseman. I ran to the top of the building, up the staircase, which is a listed feature, being the longest free standing staircase in Europe and, a central highlight of the hotel to this day. The man appeared dead. Being as fit as I was, I still had the breath to breathe into this lifeless creature. The procedure is to hit the subject hard on the chest in an attempt to get the heart started and blow into the mouth to start up the lungs, and repeat the procedure as long as thought necessary, striking the chest once and blowing into the lungs about four or five times. I tried this repeatedly until the body convulsed vomit shot into my mouth. I, in turn, was sick onto the shoes of a nearby spectator. So much for soccer hardman Vinnie Jones and that Staying Alive advert for the British Heart Foundation.

Unlike the body, I had just completed a full English in the Piccadilly Café with the compliments of Chris the owner. Fortunately, the ambulance men arrived, took one look at the man without any real effort and certainly little bending and stated flatly: “He’s dead. He has been for sometime. Hard luck, son. You didn’t know. You did your best.” I was devastated. The sick incident paled, pardon the pun, and I had seen my first dead body. How sad it was too. He had been alive only minutes earlier. Death and being close to death, being familiar with it, intimate with it, knowing its personality, all this is a part of training that can’t be learned in a book or a lecture, not even by play acting. Some things have to impress themselves on the heart alone, and leave an image.

It Was a Way of Life

I knew I was going to be stationed at Bootle Street Police Station before I went to Bruche. Obviously, I had preconceived ideas of what to expect. If I do say so myself, I looked incredibly handsome in my new clean uniform and knew I would be hard for the multitudes of women populating the city centre to resist. It never occurred to me that I would look like a new pin next to any serving officer with at least a month of service. Of course, serving the public and doing my sworn duty would have priority. The social life would follow, or so I thought.

As my police career progressed, I understood how wrong my notions were. I was at last released on the unsuspecting streets of Manchester city centre, where people in the main supported their police force. I still believed all officers were hardworking, brave, and honest. I believed all serving officers felt the same, that they were properly led by higher ranks that had reached such heights on merit alone and could be followed unquestionably, in the uphill fight against crime. The sergeants, the next rank up from constable, could be followed as role models and, if you were seen to be trying, they would support you if a difficulty occurred. Of course, this support was slightly off 'the beam' as far as training school was concerned, tending to make the evidence fit the circumstances if the need had arisen, but nothing seen to be underhand of course.

Bootle Street had a double door entrance from the street. It had a reception counter as you entered, and on the counter sat a large brass bell. It was invariably never used, due to the continuous stream of traffic; bodies coming and going for a variety of reasons, from parking tickets, issued by police (traffic wardens didn't exist then), lost and found property, individuals reporting to CID, and even one of many of the local nutters reporting a flying saucer on Deansgate. A frosted glass window prevented the public seeing through the closed door into the charge office where justice was being done or perhaps, undone. Of course, the justice of the given moment depended on the duty inspector who sat at the desk in the centre of this hive. He was surrounded by his sergeant, several elderly constables, who were not fit for the streets, and the reserve man, whose responsibility was the cell area and the prisoners held there. All the staff were separated from everybody else who entered the charge office by the counter. This counter was more than 20 yards in length and faced the double doors that opened onto the courtyard, an area contained by four perimeter walls. The Chief Constable's office and his staff, the hierarchy of the force, the CID, and generally anybody else who had no real direction or office were hidden away somewhere in this building.

The double doors to the courtyard, fortunately, opened in the manner of a cowboy saloon. This allowed prisoners brought to the station in the Black Maria to make an entrance, including those wishing to fight anyone and anything. They were hurled through the swinging doors with a momentum that ended with an abrupt and painful halt, as their heads or their unsuspecting bodies collided with the charge office counter. The quiet confidence of the charge office inspector was reflected in his reaction to having the peaceful calm of his domain shattered by an outraged drunk, as the arresting officer hurled him through the doors accompanied by any passing officer who fancied a kick at the unfortunate prisoner. It was amusing to see 'the boss' simply continue to read a newspaper as though nothing had happened whilst, on the other side of his counter, a murder could have been taking place. When the time was right, he would slowly rise from his seat and bring the melee to an abrupt end by smashing a long circular solid wood ruler on the counter or on the struggling prisoner's head, whichever happened to be in his way.

Today they are on their feet in a flash, not to help with a violent prisoner, not to prevent the prisoner being manhandled, but to catch a fellow officer, one of lower rank behaving in a manner contrary to their idea of proper policing. It is interesting to note the culture in South Yorkshire at this time around the Hillsborough incident. At this time the Force had a complaints department which readily caused the resignation of young officers for a variety of minor reasons but once senior officers had their heads on the 'block', such young officers were expected to stand together and collude in such an amazing conspiracy as that now uncovered. This misuse of brotherhood is actually an aid to the prisoner complaining about his arresting officer, to the point where he could be simply dismissed and, without any consideration for the years of experience.

The cells adjoined the charge office and, whilst they were decorated in paint shades with a striking similarity to the dungeons in a Hammer Horror film, they were usually spotless and without a trace of any blood or hair, except during the early morning hours when the reserve man was also busy doling out instant justice with the rest of the shift. Paedophiles, muggers, murderers, transvestites and the entire cast of caged life, were not subjected to the instant justice doled out by the reserve man, whatever offence they had committed, unless they were unfortunate enough to be sick on his floor. There was no excuse for such a misdemeanour, even if the prisoner had been kicked up and down the charge office for daring to complain about any treatment he may have 'enjoyed' on his journey to the nick. It was a free service. The reserve man enjoyed his work. He got a real kick out of it, you might say. Or at least someone did.

From the time you joined the veterans of Bootle Street, you had to rely on your wits and cunning. When working alone, you were really alone. The only equipment was a wooden truncheon and snaps, the rigid handcuffs used for restraint. I'm sure the name 'snaps' had its origin in the actual handcuff itself, but I can't help but think that the name came from the result of its use, the sound made when the radius and ulna bones in the arm where it joins the wrist give under intense pressure, aggravated, of course, by the prisoner's wild and futile attempts at struggle. The detainee's hand would be up the middle of his back. On regular occasions, and with enough force, we could hear the "snap" of a carpal bone being dislocated and even broken bones on some of the less fortunate.

On one memorable occasion I recall one such struggling prisoner being restrained by snaps so enthusiastically by the arresting officer the metal end of the snaps was forced through the prisoner's skin and between the two wrist bones. Such exuberance even to that extreme on the part of the officer was generally ignored both by the prisoner having had emergency hospital treatment and a brew and the supervisory officers. It was just considered part of the job. Maybe, even a form of exercise. If the prisoner refused to play along, if he didn't show at least some sense of humour, if he complained about his treatment, he was then charged with Police Assault in addition to the offence with which he was arrested, to account for any visible injuries. It was a way of life and everyone accepted it. We all kept the lid screwed on fairly tightly and there was always respect, in some form or other, even if it translated as fear.

The bulled boots of training school, with their mirror toe caps and Tuf-Boot soles, were a source of amusement to the old hands. I soon saw the reason. The mirror polished finish was only achieved by lengthy periods of bulling. Such time consuming preparation soon became a waste of time, especially considering that after a few good kicks to persuade a saucy prisoner into submission, they just lost some of their dazzle. Doc Martens eventually replaced the cumbersome training school boots. Their air soles made running easy and silent. Eight hours walking a beat was a comparable pleasure and holding back on a good kicking to prevent scuffing became a thing of the past.

In my early days in the Force there were no personal radios to call for assistance. There was no CS gas, Taser, handcuffs, or accompanying officer as there is today. This is because today's officers are too small. The public has lost respect. We were all tall, fit men, able to look after ourselves on our own. There was no alternative, really. If we fell by the wayside, perhaps overwhelmed by numbers, it was common during these times to enjoy the support of the taxi drivers and their radio system. When we eventually did have radios they didn't work. During the evening and into the night, we were often assisted by club doormen who loved to join in the occasional feud, in the knowledge that they could hand out some mild violence and suffer no law enforced recriminations. Of course today club doormen are licensed and heavily supervised by the police who have now lost that useful unofficial support due to unnecessary prosecutions of doormen in the course of their own difficult work. Recently there have been several examples of members of the public assisting an officer in an arrest only to be charged with assault on the prisoner. A soldier was arrested, kicked in the back eight times and handcuffed by officers. One lied to such a degree at court that the learned magistrates found the soldier guilty despite CCTV, only to have the conviction overturned by an appeal Judge who was more than critical of the perjury committed.

Personal radios were introduced some months into my early days. These were made by Pye and consisted of two hand-held units, in a tasteless shade of pale blue. One was for receiving, the other for transmitting. The base station consisted of a unit the size of a music centre. The radio operator was chosen from the ranks of the 'Don't let him on the streets - find him a job' brigade. Several recruits were obvious selections but Eddie Bell took the position. Compare his small desk situated immediately behind the duty inspector with the communications suite you see in crime dramas on TV and you can understand what a Mickey Mouse operation it was.

All the upper ranks were happy that they could now have their fingers on the divisional pulse. The van would now be backup, rather than the only emergency response. All the beat hopping, drinking, and shagging they had heard of, but always been unable to prove, would come to an end. It was enthusiastically thought that a quicker response time would mean more prisoners and improved figures. Clearly, they had not considered the unthinkable, that we regarded the radios as an intrusion on our social existence. I think Eddie Bell was nearly sectioned, being constantly frustrated by the 'poor reception'. Unknown to him, everyone had toffee papers to rustle in the transmitter mouthpiece, and the radios rarely worked again anyway, when dropped from head height. I'd be foolish not to appreciate the benefits of the radios, especially for assistance calls, but in the main they were inconvenient to all of us who had existed for so long without them.

On the subject of officers with nowhere to go, and not being safe on the streets the police band springs to mind, excellent musicians all, but not one of them was a policeman. There was only so much rehearsal they could do, and on the days when there were no Flower Shows, Whit Walks, Beautiful Baby Competitions, and the like, they were let loose on the unsuspecting public. They were given single streets to patrol in the city centre so they couldn't come to much harm. They were always conscious of taking it easy as they often had a gig in the evening. They were all in private quartets and little bands and, when police duties, and I use the term lightly, didn't interfere, they were available for weddings, funerals, 21sts, barmitzvahs and the rest. To be fair, there were some fun members amongst them and the late Bill Oldham was a star. There were others, but the effects of age, time, and pochin (an illicit alcohol, based on distilled Irish potato spirit, capable of rendering severe brain damage on the drinker) in Moss Side has taken its toll. How different such things are today. I think the band still exists, but I am told they are not paid overtime for their evening town hall appearances and possibly the wheel has now fallen off their gravy train.

Bootle Street

Bootle Street Police Station left a lasting imprint on my life. Lessons learned during such an inspiring and impressionable period follow you, as they are recorded and fixed in the memory, whatever path you might choose and move on, in life and the police. Being stationed in the city centre became like a springboard, the momentum upon which the rest of my life was to be carried. Bootle Street Police Station had a public counter as described earlier where parking tickets were processed, dogs handed in, property reported lost and the like.

All police stations generally operated in the same manner as did the Newton Street Station, which was the Sub Division, allegedly controlled by the supervising officers based at Bootle Street. But at Bootle Street the public was not generally in fear of serious injury by merely entering the premises as often occurred at Newton Street as they were sometimes mistaken for prisoners when actually reporting a missing cat. Near the reception desk at Bootle Street were the Plain Clothes Office and the Sergeants' Office. One flight up the adjacent stairs was the chief superintendent and chief inspector of the entire division. Further, along the first floor landing was CID, officers viewed as aliens, particularly when in uniform. The CID was a breed apart, they appeared to do nothing, were always in the many pubs scattered about the city centre and usually under the influence of the many free pints they appeared to attract.

From the public desk, a frosted windowed door led into the Charge Office which served as the operations centre of the division. As well as Bootle Street (A Division), there was Willert Street (B Division), Mill Street (C Division), Longsight (D Division), and Platt Lane (E Division). All divisions had similar ranking structures and all kept the lid on these different areas, with their own particular policing problems, and in their own particular manner. Such a manner usually involved violence and fabrication of evidence but at differing levels, dependent on the 'quality' of the Detective Chief Inspector and the support one could expect if the wheels came off.

Each station had two police vans or Black Marias as we called them. Each van was staffed by two men, but often there was only one because of staff shortages. The vans patrolled the division and had designated boundaries. These vehicles were the lifeline to the men on the ground working their various beats and patrols and were expected to be available to assist. Remember, there were no personal radios at this time and, therefore, the public played a great part in dialling 999 if they saw an officer in trouble requiring assistance. In those days people still had respect for the police.

Below the Charge Office, in the basement, was the parade room and lockers. Each locker had padlocks, which were provided by the officer who used the locker, but nothing was left in them because many officers specialized in removing the locks and the property therein. Helmets were often stolen. They were sold as souvenirs to American tourists in the St Ann's Square area. Tourists loved to photograph us. The PC was evidently the very height of Englishness. "Gee, an English Bobby!" the jubilant tourists would say. Some enterprising officers just happened to have a spare helmet in a Marks and Spencer's carrier bag, which was sold for a few dollars, on top of the bung for the photo opportunity to any trusting American or Japanese visitor. All unaware of the fact that there was a constable minus one helmet still at Bootle Street being disciplined for the loss of issued uniform. That was Number 3 beat. I used to enjoy that beat. It had little trouble, a lot of tourists, all the 'fur coat and no knickers brigade' and the leggy hopefuls of Kendal Milne's, the Harrods of Manchester.

It was commonplace to be bunged a pound to be photographed with a tourist. By today's standards a pound would be an insult, but my weekly wage at this time was a take home packet of £20 per week. A coach load of Yanks, could double that. It was also, at this time, that the longer serving, more experienced earners amongst us would sell a colleague's helmet. To prevent this everyone took their helmets home with them in a bag. Wearing a civilian overcoat over their uniform made concealment much easier. On my first day at Bootle Street, I paraded with pride, my short hair and shiny boots, my immaculate uniform, the ruddy and well earned sparkle on my face. This stood out, not only by the pomp in my stride, but against the image of the others, the rabble of long hair, dirty boots, no creases, and beer guts. I feared this could be me in the future. What was obvious from the outset was the size of these men. They were all big men and my height of 6ft 1in was fairly average. They also carried considerable presence, which is half the battle on the streets. Each of them seemed to have a sincere interest in the job, a pride for being just what they were, policemen.

Of course, initial impressions can be wrong ones. My first day saw me paired with an experienced officer so I could be shown the realities, the actual wheels and pulleys of police life, details I had been denied at training school. After having the piss taken out of my bulled boots, I was told I could forget most of what I had learned at Bruche, that is, except how to drink beer and shag. One of my first instructions was about the image of a policeman in the eyes of the public. Many women, I was told, love the uniform, especially the helmet. Women love the helmet. I'm not sure why. I'm not sure they could tell you why. Maybe it looked like the head of a penis, who knows? One sanctioned by the Queen. Anyway, wearing this singular bit of apparel was part of sexual arousal. The helmet alone was to be worn during the act itself. I thought this fanciful speech, first day banter and all, good ribbing. I was wrong. Now get the mental picture - two naked bodies, and one helmet making its odd up and down movements, and in rhythm. It gave new meaning to the word Bobby.

The days passed quickly enough at Bootle Street, and not one of them went by that I didn't learn something new. Some things were worthwhile and others, well, weren't. I couldn't really afford a car and, indeed, didn't own one for many years after joining the Force. Amazingly, I seemed to have a full social life in spite of my carless existence. I was amazed at how PCs could marry, have kids, and a social life on such a wage. Soon I was to learn how these wages were 'supplemented' in certain sections of the Force as my education continued.

When I returned from Bruche, my father was promoted to Principal Officer in the Prison Service and was moved from Strangeways jail to Wakefield Top

Security Prison. I remained in Manchester and lived in digs with a prison officer, his wife, and their two small kids. The lodging seemed a good deal for them in getting my rent, and it certainly helped me. I was seeing plenty of girls at this time and often had scratches on my back, which my landlady saw whenever I had a quick wash in the kitchen. She clearly decided I had something to offer and on several occasions came into my room for some reason or other, catching me in various states of undress. There was no doubt she was interested, but in those inexperienced days I didn't know how to progress the situation. I did throw a sock around the back of her neck once and pulled her toward me with the sling it made. I kissed her, then panicked. Rather than stew in my panic, I simply ended my clumsy advances, making some lame excuse like a News of the World reporter of the day.

I was shown around the division by experienced officers. I'm not sure what I expected, but what I got wasn't it. Everything I was now learning was contrary to the teachings of Bruche. And it seemed to work. I was learning and unlearning at the same time. The object of being shown around was to give the trainee practical experience at doing motorists, fobbing off the public, and making arrests, especially when there was overtime to be gained by going to court. Throughout a 24 hour period there were three main shifts: 7am to 3pm (mornings), 3pm to 11pm (afternoons) and 11pm to 7am (nights). In addition, to these shifts was an overlapped shift of 9am to 5pm (days) and 5pm to 1am (evenings). A different body of men, known as a Relief, worked each shift and during the overlapping times twice as many police were on the streets of the city centre (A division). The thinking behind this was, of course that there was twice the cover during busy periods, therefore keeping the citizens of Manchester safer. I suppose it is true to say that they were safer, but this was only due to the zero tolerance operated, unofficially, by the men on the various beats to prove they were working diligently, when in actuality they worked only a short period, enough to effect the arrest, after which they actively engaged in their own activities. These activities fell into three categories - criminal, sexual, and liquid (that is to say, alcohol).

The criminal activities varied on the shifts being worked. Thefts from cars were very popular and, it is true to say that every officer with a car had the best sound systems available, either by doing the break-in themselves, or by purchasing from the stash of stolen goods at the station, or when they met at a neutral spot after work. Breaking into premises was also popular with certain officers. It was, of course, very simple in the middle of the night. You were the only defender of the peace in quite a large area which was your assigned beat. Many officers kept a jemmy (a short crowbar) in their jackets, and maybe a hammer, or a spring loaded nail punch for breaking car windows, as part of their police trappings. This handy item was kept in special pockets sewn into the inside of the jacket. Should a burglar alarm go off, you were simply the officer on the scene. The assault on the premises was phoned in as a burglary from the attacked premises. Whilst you waited for the owner to secure the premises, you, the officer in question, were able to rummage about and take out whatever was valuable and portable, all of which would be blamed on the escaped culprit. Difficulties with this simple procedure arose when the van crew and the section sergeant arrived as backup, now competitors for the spoils, all of them taking as much as they could in the minimum time. Now justice is blind, and slow - whereas hands are quick and certain.

This behaviour was, of course, blatantly dishonest and it came as a great surprise to the rookie, the cherry that I was. It was even more of a surprise to find myself involved, not as a participant, but as a silent observer. I can honestly say I never committed an act of dishonesty such as theft or burglary during my service, but I was guilty in that I did nothing about it. This again is a culture, brainwashed into every young officer and indeed the same old-fashioned culture on which the hierarchy of South Yorkshire Police relied upon in tidying up the evidence for the Hillsborough Inquest.

When I eventually got a car, I also had an excellent sound system, gifted by a 'colleague'. But where could you turn when even the inspectors arrived at scenes of crime and not just for supervision? Everybody was in on it. It left stains on everything. But it was all so normal, so widely accepted, silence was the only response I could seem to make. Who would or could I tell? In bringing down one, you bring down all. And that wasn't my style and I suppose in truth I just did not care enough.

I remember, on one occasion, many months into my service, driving to a 999 call because a shop window had been broken near Manchester Cathedral. The shop was a tobacconist's and had a display of lighters behind the security grill. The officer of the beat stood with his truncheon in his hand and his back to the hole in the window, keeping back two other officers from adjoining beats, who wanted to empty the window. It is an odd but nonetheless common occurrence to consider while learning on a daily basis and in reality one to be merely accepted as life in the Queen's Police. Putting to use what

I had gained through my informative learning times at Bruche, at last it was time for me to enjoy the experience of making an arrest.

The easiest arrests were 'sleepers,' that is homeless persons who were sleeping in a shop doorway or a rear entry. There wasn't the volume of sleepers then as there are today. Generally, they were much older than me, and often ex-servicemen overtaken by drink, having lost everything, washed away by alcohol. They were actually happy to be locked up, especially in winter, because they got a warm dry room for the night, a meal, and, hopefully, prison the following day if they were an habitual offender. I remember one very cold winter we were importuned by many of these unfortunates to lock them up to get them out of the cold. But we had been given a directive from above to stop arresting these opportunists because the cells and the courts could no longer cope with the extra volume. We then had to explain to them that sleeping out was no longer serious enough to be arrested (but breaking a window was). The city was then deluged by itinerants breaking shop windows, sometimes in the daytime, and standing at the scene of the crime awaiting arrest with a beaming smile. Soon, most of these enterprising souls were in prison, and there were only a few left to practice arrests on.

On a warm summer night we found a poor creature whose name I will never forget. He was called David Leather. He was not cold. He was not hungry. But he was quite annoyed at having his beauty sleep disturbed in a rear entry of a building, as he claimed he was doing no harm to anyone. I was the third man in the van. The driver Jim Rimmer, who I was to learn later was a 6ft 7ins waste of space, told me to arrest the bundle of rags.

In true training school fashion I marched to the ragged mess and shouted: "Come on! Get up! You can't sleep here!" While also relating some Act and Section that I can't remember now – at which he mumbled something colourful back at me. I cautioned him as to his foul language and again told him to get up and move on, all in true Bruche form. He only got more agitated. The van crew got more amused. Realising, even with my tender time of service, that Mr Leather was likely to have sleeping tenants of his own (surface parasites or other creeping things) I tried not to touch him, but with the van crew goading me on, there was little I could do to avoid this and I pulled at one of his arms. I could not have been more surprised at the speed in which he jumped to his feet and in a whirl of his six layers of holed jumpers and overcoats, matted hair, and decaying teeth, yelled abuse at me, picked me up, and hurled me at a pile of dustbins. My sparkling new uniform and bulled boots didn't fare too well from this, and the bruises didn't disappear for well over a week. The laughter, cackling and howling from the van made an odd music with the rolling dustbins as I stumbled to my feet in total disbelief at what had occurred. It was all too swift and I was all too unprepared, too ridiculously unaware. I don't remember being taught this scenario at Bruche, or anywhere else.

In that one exchange I began to catch on. I too, was to become a quick learner. Still, in those moments, my head was whirling at the offences committed against my youth, my training, and my pride. Murder rose in my heart, but as I went toward the guy, Jim Rimmer shouted and yet with little emotion, and not that loud, but as you would with someone you know: "Get in the van David, that is enough for tonight." At this, Mr Leather turned away from me and opened the rear door to the van and got in. I was told to leave him alone and forget the incident, that is, unless I wanted to be known as the man who charged David Leather with police assault. He was charged with the vagrancy offence, appeared at court, and was let out again onto the streets shortly after. It was a well trodden path and all concerned knew he was merely part of a training exercise. David didn't care. He lived just to eat, to survive the misfortune of his life. Food and a mattress for the night, he slept well. I'm sure of that.

I learned two things that night. One, I didn't like Rimmer and it was a strong sentiment that lasted an entire career. And he has never yet proved my first instincts to be wrong ones. Several events proved he was just a badge with no interest in being a real policeman. And two, I learned quickly never to pull, or even attempt to pull someone from the ground. That is what a good pair of Doc Martens are worn for. You just kick them hard, then stand back. If, in turn, they move quickly, you kick them again, and punch them at the side of the head as they are just about at kneeling position.

Violence was always close by. It kept a strong and active presence amongst us. And we respected it. But it wasn't a violence that took the shape of a gun, or a knife, as it does today. One rarely sees a fair fight nowadays. There is always a weapon involved. During my early police days, weapons were rarely used. During this time, there remained the idea that you never even drew your truncheon. It was a sign of weakness. It was a real Dixon of Dock Green attitude, in total contrast to the tear gas and riot sticks of today, common gear that appear to be used at a whim. The truncheon was only used on rare occasions.

I recall one day walking through Smithfield Market at about 3am on my usual beat out of Newton Street Police Station. In the shadows I saw an individual trying car handles. Having satisfied myself that his intentions were criminal, I quietly approached him, but he saw me coming and ran away. I was very fit and able to run at speed for considerable distances. Outside the fight or flight response, I couldn't understand how this thin, 5ft 8ins individual had the goods to keep a real distance from me. We powered through the back entries and streets of Shudehill with abandon and raw male tenacity. I suspected he was tiring, so I rallied and ran at full speed around yet another corner, only to be kicked in the balls, causing us both to fall to the ground on impact. Not having his balls in his throat, he was able to get up and run again. With that characteristic breathless, deep, spasmic, and disabling burn that only a kick in the balls can render, I struggled to my feet. The pain defied the best of words, even bad ones. I got up and ran after him again. He was certainly tired by now and had a slight limp probably from the earlier collision. Running now, my convalescing testicles allowing me to breathe again, I was able to come up right behind him.

I had adrenaline and danger pumping through my veins, and yet, being reluctant to suffer the earlier indignity again, I took out my truncheon and struck him about the head from behind as he continued to run. I struck him several times, each time he shouted in pain, and whilst slowing, he didn't stop until he ran into a nearby cul-de-sac used for the parking of two wheeled market porter's barrows. He ran as far as the dead end wall and held up his hands in a breathless gesture of surrender. Having already learned the lesson of the vagrant, Mr Leather, and my balls having the quick memory they tend to have, I was not prepared to give this guy another chance at them. It was clear he still had fight in him as I took a porter's barrow and rammed it into him several times until he fell to the ground totally deflated. I was able to restrain him with my snaps.

He was 'restrained' all the way back to Newton Street, there weren't many people about and, in every deserted entry on the route back to Newton Street, he was kicked and punched and every squirm, on his part, was greeted with a twist of the snaps. Charged with loitering with intent and police assault, he appeared at court the same morning and was given three months. No mention was made, by either the prisoner, supervising officers or the magistrates about the prisoner's clearly beaten state. He was guilty of police assault and that was that. Can you imagine the identical scenario, with today's standards? I would have been suspended from duty, the prisoner would have been afforded every courtesy as he made his statement. No evidence would probably have been offered to the court. I would have been charged with assault and dismissed from the service. This man had many previous convictions and was already wanted on warrant for another matter where he had been granted bail and then failed to return to court. This must have been the only time I would rather have gone to bed than to court to earn the overtime. My balls were the size of melons and I was white as a sheet. But I got my man. It's what cops did in those days. Then they went home and soaked their balls.

I won. Sure, it was a petty crime, but nonetheless, I won. That mattered to me. One of the few perks of the job, though sometimes you feel you're trying to push back the sea with one hand. The bad guy understood and made no complaint despite his several real injuries which required medical treatment. The cuts to his head were significant. He had been struck with a solid piece of wood, a piece of wood designed for that very purpose. The truncheon deserves the credit, well that and, perhaps the porter's barrow. Again, he made no complaint about the injuries he sustained. He lost and he took the consequences.

Sometime later, whilst working a beat out of Bootle Street, I called into the lodge at the Dunlop Rubber Factory for tea with the night watchman. He had a little sideline going making rubber truncheons. These perfect imitations were the same size and colour as the issued variety, with one really nice advantage. You could inflict all the pain you wanted and it wouldn't cut the victim's flesh. It would give him an incredible concussion, but the rubber staff when bent around the head left no trace of itself, no blood. The use of the rubber staff meant that there were no cuts and its use could even be denied if necessary. The rubber truncheons became the fashion and many field experiments took place. Heads, arms and legs were beaten and it was quickly established that the need for butting, kicking and general punching were now unnecessary to subdue a prisoner. These wonderful implements inflicted the most incredible 'dead legs' and concussions that little else was necessary. Of course, we still had the occasional psychopath in our ranks who was not content with merely restraining but still had to feel the crunch of a punch and hear the resulting cries for mercy.

Bad Guys

Early in my career, Manchester was invaded by Glaswegians, who thought it was the land of milk and honey. They brought a certain instinctive violence with them. And, as to be expected, things turned ugly. It was a particularly violent time for the city and they remained the thugs from Scotland with no regard, whatsoever, for our rule of the sword. Not only that, they told their friends who also came, and with a particular brand of violence that often involved razors and knives. They tended to frequent the all-night cafes in the Piccadilly area.

Officers from both Bootle Street and Newton Street were fully occupied ridding the city of these vermin. They were obviously well versed in avoiding arrest and had the strange notion that if they didn't have stolen property in their pockets and were not found committing any offence, they were free to roam the streets in whatever extremes of drink, in whatever measure of disorder, and with the very mistaken belief that they were exempt from detention. They had arrived from sunny Glasgow with a strut, a level of cockiness that was not in keeping with our standards of law enforcement and one which had to be quickly brought into line. This arrogance quickly dissipated when arrests were actually made, when they were charged with an assortment of fabricated offences, anywhere from drunk and disorderly, to burglary, thefts from cars and, of course, the good old police assault, two words that were repeated again and again. Any vagrant Scot walking the streets was approached and if his breath smelt, not necessarily of alcohol, just objectionable, he was arrested on a drunk and disorderly. I have actually never met a Scot whose breath didn't smell of alcohol, nor one who didn't get disorderly when arrested for nothing other than walking the streets. They had the strangest notion that they were allowed to drink, provided they behaved themselves on the streets. We had no tolerance for such arrogant attitudes and fanciful thinking.

It was like a sport. And there were winners and losers. There was no discernible reason why a Scot should walk down a side street full of parked cars. There were no pubs or cafes on these streets, so the call would be loitering for the intent of stealing from these cars. Despite the darkness and poor street lighting, there was no mistaking their efforts. Having the inevitable short temper and no sense of humour, they became so irate that an assault was inevitable. Parked cars do cause terrible black eyes when collided with in a struggle in the darkness.

Such minor arrests were common, but usually inflicted on the rank and file of this wandering horde of thieving nobodies. There were, however, a small nucleus of villains who were capable of serious assaults and muggings on the citizens of Manchester. This obviously deserved much more sophisticated attention. These were deliberately targeted, harassed, cocked up, beaten up and generally discouraged. They migrated from the town centre and burgled houses in the suburbs, returning to the city only to sell the proceeds from their labour. These villains were known to us, but we always had difficulty finding them actually in possession of stolen items.

From this they drew confidence and added cockiness which had to be snuffed out.

We had intelligence about the city so we could find them in a short space of time, if necessary. H Samuels Jewellers on the Piccadilly Plaza had its window broken by a passing drunk, but nothing was stolen due to the metal grill on the inside. The window was probably broken with no crime in mind. An officer would attend until the key holder arrived to arrange the boarding of the window. Standing with your back to the hole in the window, smiling your best, often pissed civic smile at the passing Mr or Mrs Public returning home from an enjoyable romantic night in the city, it was easy to put your fingers through the grill and pull out a couple of watches. Such an action was often made simpler, reaching further in the window for more watches, with a wire coat hanger which happened to be in a pocket, usually to assist in getting into Fords, but it worked equally well for this purpose.

Then, with a quick radio or telephone call you established the whereabouts of the main Scottish contingent, obviously suspected of this offence by virtue of the fact that they were here and Scottish. Six of us blazed into the Snacktime Café near Piccadilly and grabbed the ringleader. We told him he was seen near the scene of the burglary at H Samuels where watches were stolen. Cocky Scot, surrounded by pissed-up admiring cronies, gets to his feet, denies ever leaving the café and offers to be searched, smirking from ear to ear he spreads his arms to enable the search. This is our moment. The watches are palmed and 'found' in his pockets, and in a flurry of flying crockery, tables, and chairs, he is arrested and unceremoniously marched from the café in full view of his admirers.

During this time, magistrates were hard on these Scots who, in most of the cases, were often wanted elsewhere. They were inevitably sent to Crown Court for a longer sentence. Prison resulted. This type of rough justice was the only thing these people recognised and it was only a relatively short time involving such incidents that resulted in the herd of Glaswegians leaving Manchester for easier pickings elsewhere, leaving only a small hardcore element who were much easier to control without the use of such manpower, verbals, coat hangers and the like.

In dealing with the Glaswegians we had to use all our resources. Men who would be dealing with other matters such as other disorderly behaviours and general street thefts were all committed to the Jocks. Coat hangers were the equipment carried to hook jewellery out of shop windows where the window had been smashed, but the inner grill remained intact preventing a full size hand from sneaking in evidence. While a way of life to a degree, verbals and planting of evidence on the Jocks were everyday occurrences and always carried some risk of detection if we became too blasé.

I'm not sure why Manchester was in the sights of this type of life, but it was. At one time, Manchester was at risk of being taken over by organized crime from London. Due to the lax licensing laws enforced in his own way by Chief Superintendent Alec Dingwall, Manchester had a good nightclub presence. London had an existing protection racket operated by the likes of Frankie Fraser, the Richardsons, and the Krays. They argued between themselves and clearly the old town was not big enough for all of them and other areas were examined. At the head of the nightclub league table in Manchester was the Cromford Club, run by Paddy McGrath, who later sold the gaming license for the Cromford to the Playboy Club organization. Whilst writing this book, Paddy, who was a good friend, died and it is with the greatest of respect that I mention his name here and the part he played in the running of Manchester clubland. The Cromford was patronized by many of the magistrates who sat on the City Bench. Paddy did his bit by casually mentioning the plague of Scots and the dangers of leaving his dark entrance. On hearing of such other incidents elsewhere in the city, the learned magistrates did their bit.

The other club was the Cabaret Club on Oxford Street, operated by Bill Kerfoot. This club did not have a gaming license, but had a clientele, which enjoyed the company of prostitutes, paying excessive prices for champagne and the general flash ambience of the club. Whilst Paddy was known as a hard man, a man with a boxing background, who enjoyed connections with the Blackpool underworld, a guy who would not lay down if leaned on by the Londoners, Bill Kerfoot was seen quite differently, well worthy of a "frightener."

What they hadn't taken into account was getting past Albert Jeffrey, without doubt the hardest doorman in Manchester. Frankie Fraser sent his best men to Manchester to shake up the Cabaret Club. One of his men, in particular was feared by all in London and was regarded as the best fighter they had. Several of the Londoners rushed into the club and before Albert and the other doormen could react, they were inside and amongst the members and diners. Albert appeared to be struggling with their best man as they wrestled about the club until they piled into the kitchen, out of sight of the members. It was established later that Albert was deliberately trying to contain the situation without throwing a punch in the club area. Part strategy, part instinct. It was merely the appearance of difficulty, like misdirection, when all he was doing was steering the man to the kitchen, a man who clearly believed he had Albert well beaten. Once in the kitchen, the man realized what a serious error in judgment he had made when Albert dispatched him with a couple of blows to the floor. Albert then broke one of the man's legs over his knee to give him 'something to remember' from his visit north. The Londoners left the city and clubland remained peaceful for a relatively long period of time before the London gangs decided to have another go at the lucrative Manchester club scene.

A popular version of a Manchester legend is as follows and generally believed by the police to be the truth amongst many other versions. The next attempt by the London mob had them travelling by train to Piccadilly Station, then taking up residence at the Midland Hotel. There are many versions of this incident about the city all making various claims. This one appears to be the nearest to the truth. Classic cartoon gangsters in striped suits, black shirts, white ties, they spoke in their whingeing southern accents. There were about 20 of them, and they thought they owned the place. They had come north to show us 'hicks' what London tough guys were all about. One oversight, though. They were not aware of what awaited them when they got here, or that we had our own interpretation of the law. There were hardly enough spoils in the city to be pillaged by the locals, the police in particular, so our guests could not be allowed to stay. The practice in London was for them to be as bad as they liked, provided the tame Metropolitan Police were suitably rewarded at whatever level such a 'taste' was necessary.

Into the bar of the Midland Hotel marched the best of the Manchester CID - cheap suits, dirty shoes, and beer guts hanging over unpressed trousers. With them were the pride of the Regional Crime Squad, the Serious Crime Squad, and a sprinkling of the A Division CID dragged from the bar at the Abercrombie public house next to the Bootle Street Police Station. They were greeted by the deriding Londoners with wolf whistles and music associated with PC Plod and Noddy. What was strange about this crew was the two heavy briefcases being carried by two detective sergeants accompanying two detective chief inspectors. The remainder followed behind looking tough. The time was about midday. It was Manchester's version of High Noon – yet the guns were currently out of sight.

"There is a train to London at 2 pm. Be on it!" Chief Superintendent Dougie Nimmo announced.

"Piss off!" replies one of the whinging southern voices above their laughter. "We have come for a break in your city. We'll stay as long as we like."

"The only way your lot will stay is in custody," barked 'The Boss'. The comments and laughter didn't last long. The briefcases were speedily opened to reveal an assortment of revolvers, knives, and razors. "If you don't get on the next train, we will find one of these on each of you. Now you fuck off! And tell the Met what they should be doing with you shithouses!"

Would a senior police officer of today even leave his cushy office and indeed with so many witnesses stick his neck out like that? I don't think so. Well not until the Hillsborough co-conspirators decided to hide their incompetence in the belief that they were answerable to no one and could adapt the law to their own requirements whatever the circumstances, even 96 deaths.

There were two individuals who tended to shine above all others, in their extracurricular pursuits about the city centre. Bob Davenport and Barry Good (not his real name) - they were my idols in the shagging department. In true Life On Mars style there were unofficial departments and leaders in their field in each. The departments tended to fall into five main categories, namely, shagging, drinking, peeping, Mr Fix-its and thieving. By way of a brief explanation, the shagging is obvious but tended to be performed in police cars, personal cars and even those of the lucky female, usually married and on a girl's night out in the Big City.

Drinking would appear to be an obvious choice but there were rules, which scored 'more points'. The drinking would normally be done on the next beat and with no payment. This would then lead the licensee to believe he had 'paid' his 'rent' for the night and when the actual beat officer called the free element was no more, causing the maximum aggravation to the beat officer and the maximum amusement to the 'neighbour' who was by then, hard at it reaping the drinking spoils on his own beat as quickly as he could.

Peeping was a sport which required a special type of pervert, often non-drinking, even non-shagging but a man who could silently move about the back streets, from alleyway to darkened doorway until a pair of 'lovers' were found. His pleasure was then to watch the blissfully unaware couple copulating and get off on the grunts and sighs. Around the Smithfield Market area were several live-in pubs and strangely the landladies got off on providing a peep show at bedtime in the knowledge that the local servant of the Queen was watching nearby. At the time randy landladies, and there were several, were a constant source of supply to the shagging department, the drinkers and, of course the peepers.

The Mr Fix-it's tended to know everyone and everywhere and whilst they did little in all the departments, they knew all the best venues for drinking and peeping. They also knew who was handling (placing stolen property) what and for how much.

The thieves in the police were tolerated. Everyone bought a few nicked items but equally the thieves were forced back onto their own beats to commit their offences as the surge in crime figures often reflected on the actual beat officer, blamed for not working efficiently but, who was doing nothing more serious than a little peeing under the influence of free alcohol. Sergeant Roy Nichol, a good friend, and now a practicing canal gypsy, should be highly commended if rosettes were awarded for his observations (peeping) of licensed premises via the back door, the front door and even the bedroom window tended to confuse the issue and himself for that matter, to be perfectly honest, due to the copious amounts of free beer he acquired during his supervisory duties. He tended to lose track of the reasons he had for being in any particular area and whether he was actually supposed to be shagging, drinking or peeping.

Bob Davenport was the envy of all. He was never seen with the same woman twice, even policewomen. On occasions Bob even gave his wife, an attractive girl, an airing at certain functions. He was often found sitting in a car on an adjoining beat, in at least a passionate embrace, usually with one of the section's leading peepers in the shadows, awaiting the action. Peepers seemed to have radar and certainly knew of every spot that such activity was likely to take place. Bob was a strikingly handsome individual. He had croupiers, club waitresses, shop assistants and even nurses at his fingertips. His entire shift was taken up with visits to the various establishments involved and, indeed, he had a roster, a whole roll call, depending on the time of day. Obviously, clubs were only open at night, and shops in the daytime. Sometimes it was a cup of tea in the back of a shop, at other times a pint in the back of a pub or club. He was always able to arrange some sort of sexual liaison in his travels, even if it meant in his car or anyone else's for that matter. And I mean on or off duty.

On one occasion he was in the back of his car with a young beauty in a dark spot when the car was broken into by a short-sighted individual who proceeded to try and start the car, an activity that came to an end on being strangled from behind with the girl's tights that were free of her. The arrest took some creative writing. Bob was supposed to be on the beat next door and in his own car, so the complainant had to be fabricated as being someone from Scotland, leaving the country the same day so he could not be telephoned by the CID as the usual PR exercise as was the practice.

Bob's thief-taking skills were also legendary and while the legend according to the bosses differed from the truth and amazing luck he experienced. On several occasions he came out of a pub or a club back door only to walk into some unfortunate villains breaking into cars or adjacent buildings. Other officers crept about the back entries and saw nothing night after night giving the impression that Bob was always working. All the time Bob was appearing on the arrest sheets, he was seeing more women and drinking more beer than any man alive.

And then there was Barry Good a man with similar gifts as Bob, similar aptitude for conquest, similar appetites. Barry entertained many of his women with an Italian meal, or that is how he described it. We English love our euphemisms, especially when they're naughty. It was actually a hamburger at Tony's mobile café on Victoria Bridge, opposite Manchester Cathedral, but the image was worth the wait. Luckily, Tony was Italian. Even such immediate disappointments didn't keep these girls from repeat performances, from coming back for some more. What was that line from Henry the Fifth? "A little touch of Barry in the night." Anyway, is there a better name for a male sexual predatory hero and gamesman than Barry Good? It's just a question. Characters like this are to be found no more in the police service. Strangely, morale is quite low as a consequence.

Bob Davenport died very young of a heart attack. So did Barry Good. Barry's shine sparkled just as bright and burnt out just as quickly as Bob's. I'm sure they both went down smiling.

Uniformed police duties in the city centre always fitted a set routine and there was always crime present in some form or other. In the daytime, shoplifters were everywhere and I was always curious why a hard core of older detectives were always happy to deal with such a mundane matter. Shoplifters were rarely caught on their first excursion and it was the practice to search their homes before they were charged with the offence. Often, volumes of stolen property was recovered and brought back to Bootle Street to be kept in the property room for evidence. The prisoner was interviewed at length and eventually, admitted to many such thefts. A guilty plea was not unusual and officially the property would be returned to the stores concerned via the store detectives with whom the CID officers had a good working relationship.

In the end, none of the property actually found its way back to the store. Every one of us had modern food mixers, radios and the like. And the CID had an excellent detection rate. I suppose this was hardly better than the offence committed by the prisoner, but with a little Robin Hood thinking it was not seen that way. The system of disposing of property after an arrest has always been and still is open to abuse. For example, a man is arrested and found in possession of a great deal of valuable antiques and jewellery. Clearly these items have come from burglaries from a wide area. In the interests of justice and proving as much as possible against an uncooperative prisoner, the property is advertised to many forces and CID offices and put on display on a specified evening.

Complainants of burglaries could attend the showing and sometimes identify their property. But many of the recovered items remained unidentified. At the end of the case, the prisoner safely behind bars, it is then the duty of the arresting officer to dispose of the stolen property. If it has not been identified, it is sent to the Police Property Office where it remains from three months, then it is auctioned to dealers. This was, and I am told is still, seen as a terrible waste, and many of these valuable items would look more at home on the detective's wife's arm or displayed on the sideboard. Back then Woolworths always had an excellent selection of cheap figurines and cheap gold metal jewellery. These easily replaced the expensive items during their trip to the Property Office, and no one was any the wiser. Many detectives were, and maybe still are, so adept at the transfer of property that only old bikes, broken washing machines and, indeed, anything that will fit into the back of car ever found its way to the Property Office for disposal at the auction.

Burglaries in the city centre were frequent, but rarely detected, unless the culprit was actually found committing the offence and provided it wasn't the beat officer. Often a burglar alarm would activate and we were on the scene, the culprits still in the building. The training school theory was to surround the building to prevent the burglar(s) exiting the scene of the crime. However, such a crime fighting practice did not then allow the opportunity for a little Robin Hood activity. Burglars were often found hiding in cupboards and had to be locked in the cupboard until the 'official' pillaging had taken place. It was often the case that so many officers were on the scene that they all accepted that the criminal had been removed by someone else and on one occasion I knew of a man who was found by the office staff the following day. The police had attended, locked him in the cupboard, pillaged, departed having arranged a locksmith, who secured the building with the owner of the premises in the middle of the night. With no one returning until the normal work hours when the culprit was discovered yet again. A touch of imaginative writing, or as we called it, a little bit of the 'Enid Blytons' would of course make a further appearance and indeed a detective of some considerable experience with a 'flexible' supervising Chief Inspector was necessary to write around such an event.

This is a Civil Matter

My early days in Bootle Street were full and fascinating. Initially, every new recruit walked out with an experienced officer who was generally chosen by the section sergeant for their experience, level head and general presence on the streets. Not all serving officers were psychopaths and not all did absolutely nothing. There was a happy medium and these were chosen. However minor or insignificant many of the instances related actually are they certainly show how easy it would be with such a corrupt culture to expand on the initial principles of being bent and move onwards and upwards to greater pinnacles of corruption, never being questioned and never being caught. Such little acorns eventually reach such unbelievable proportions so much so, that the Hillsborough Conspiracy appeared at the time to be the obvious route for all the officers with such a basic education in their early days.

Standing traffic offences had been lecture subjects at Bruche Training School, and now they were put into prosecution practice. At this stage of instruction we were never shown the practice of instant fines at which certain senior members with years of experience were adept. The parking tickets had no counterfoil or proof of the original ever being issued. Old hands tended to know many of the businessmen in the city and often tickets were put on their vehicles and their friends' apparently quite innocently, but in the confident knowledge that 'a little earner' was in the air. There was some background knowledge, and the ticket was to be withdrawn on receipt of a 'thank you' in the form of cash equivalent to half of the existing fine. In these days a fine would be about £5 to £10 depending on the offence. The offender always had to attend court with all the accompanying inconvenience if he didn't pay. These 'tips' were always welcome during the late Sixties to supplement lowly paid probationer's pay. As experience blossomed, other little earners became apparent, the opportunity for many remain to this day. Such as the allocation of a motor garage for collection of accident damaged vehicles and the backhander offered to the officer for their call.

One department which had instant fines down to perfection was H Division. This was the transport division where the staff drove the white and red striped traffic cars. All blue lights and sirens, they often answered emergency calls but, in the main specialized as they do today, in prosecuting motorists. In the Sixties it was common practice for a driver to have a £10 note in his driving licence, which he opened when stopped for speeding. The officer simply took the note and the driver happily drove away. The men of this division wore a specially manufactured tie depicting a bent H. As good fiddles do, it all came to an abrupt end and the ringleader Rolly Barnes was sentenced to a term of imprisonment. He was later seen driving the governor's car on a visit from Strangeways Prison to police headquarters as the jail chief's chauffeur!

Being a probationary officer was supposed to last for two years when, in theory you were fully experienced and able to deal with any eventuality in the mistaken belief that all were fully trained and primed for action. Of course certain officers behaved as though they were still on probation with 15 years' service when their knowledge and expertise was put under the experience microscope. These officers never saw an angry man, never made an arrest, but knew every pub back door where it was the unwritten law for the officer to be supplied with two pints, free of charge, usually consumed at the rear amongst the empty crates and barrels.

Only Bob Davenport stood at the bar in his civvy coat always kept nearby, often leaving with a casual female pick up. Also on the 'free list' were the Indian restaurants which were everywhere in the city centre but mainly close to Piccadilly Railway Station. These premises supplied all the curries we needed in the knowledge that they had a host of illegal immigrants, or even an illicit casino in the back, that would remain untouched. Not to be missed in the pillage stakes were the stallholders at Smithfield Market, the butchers' shops in the same area and indeed the wholesale jewellers on Shudehill. They all provided their version of 'wrap ups' which effectively was cheap gear in the case of jewellery or absolutely free meat and veg. Such officers were a pain to the working majority who also expected the spoils of pillaging but mingled with actual police work.

The city centre was divided into small areas known as beats. Each beat had four corners and, obviously joined with the next beat. Each beat was patrolled by one officer on foot in either a clockwise or counter clockwise direction, making each point at a designated time, usually in 40 minute intervals. Each point, was a busy road junction and was supposed to be calculated so that officers on adjoining beats never met at the same point. The officer patrolled into the depths of the area surrounded by his points, which were always at junctions on the perimeter. To ensure the beat was worked effectively the section sergeant visited points unannounced, and woe to any officer who was missing, for whatever the reason. On nights, the sergeant hit the pavement with his night stick which was part of his uniform. He carried it with pride, similar to Alpin at training school but with some real and earned authority. The sound resonated throughout the beat, and the officer was expected to respond by hitting the footpath with his truncheon, a method used to summon assistance from officers on adjoining beats.

This wonderful, wireless means of communication tended to fail on occasions when colleagues were investigating offences in the pub back doors or engaging in some freelance burglary which was more common than ever supposed. Of course it could also be that the servant of the Queen was engaged at the moment, having a little masturbation session with a passing prostitute paying her rent. Prostitutes generally loitered around the Gaumont Cinema and frequented the Gaumont Long Bar where they met only with the weirdos who actually entered the premises. They were therefore forced to walk on the street outside, leaving themselves open to arrest for loitering or in lieu of a quick wank for the beat officer in the nearby back entry. In addition to the Gaumont they frequented Listons Music Hall, Lewis's Arcade and the various Yates Wine Lodges. Each location required the need for walking to one and then the other leaving the 'young lady' open to ambush and instant fining whilst on route giving the lads on adjoining beats an unexpected 'bite at the cherry'.

Everyone worked on their own initiative. Radios were not missed because they were not thought of during my early years and yet we rarely came to any real harm. The safety on the streets was a direct result of the zero tolerance we exhibited and the violence we used to enforce this zero attitude. We were all big men, we could fight and did so often with relish. In addition to the beat officers, the main streets such as Deansgate, Market Street, and even Piccadilly, had an individual officer patrolling only that street and the alleys adjoining. These were patrolled alone during the daytime and early hours of the morning, but in pairs during the evenings and early nights. Two Black Marias patrolled the entire division, one serving Bootle Street and the other Newton Street, but each supporting the other as the need would arise. There was a good sense of camaraderie in those days, clearly an element missing today.

On the early shift, the day started with an early morning bacon butty at anyone of many Greek cafes dotted about the city. They were always called Greek when, actually, they were owned by Greek Cypriots, very proud of their ancestry, people who objected, albeit quietly, that they were known as Greeks. They were all pro-police; they were very generous with nothing to gain other than our support during difficult times when all the scum of the city chose to frequent their establishments through the night. I have many happy memories of Nic's on Oxford Street and Chris of the Piccadilly Café, who I still see today, usually in the Circus Tavern, Portland Street and the Abercrombie on Bootle Street next to the nick and now operated by 'Crazy' George - a man of Cypriot origin who has lived and worked in Manchester for 30 years and I still cannot understand him. George had a party trick where he would be standing perfectly upright and then suddenly collapse to the floor as though he had been shot. Hence the 'Crazy' name. They all still attempt to buy me undrinkable amounts of booze, because of our many years of friendship.

On duty once I was standing outside the fish and chip shop, next door to the famous Nic's café on Oxford Street at about 3am. It had been closed for a couple of hours and I suddenly realised I could still smell cooking. Seeing smoke coming from the glass window vents I called the fire brigade. In their usual Attila the Hun fashion they broke in and, with the usual maximum of damage, found the chip pans were still on and the oil was about to catch fire. Nic attended and somehow didn't appear quite as pleased as I had expected. It occurred to me that the place may have been in need of a refurbishment and this was about to be an insurance claim. In any case he bunged me £20 and at that time the equivalent to a week's wages for me and a few bags of chips for Nic.

These were the days before any real traffic congestion, days when the main road junctions were controlled by the beat officer dressed in his ankle length white rubber coat or white pull-on traffic sleeves, when the weather allowed. I used to get a strange pleasure from this duty. It was easy to get to know the people who crossed at the same time every day. I enjoyed many cordial and memorable good mornings. I was there every fifth week if the same beat was assigned. It also provided an excellent introduction to passing females who were then seen later in the day near their work place, perhaps leaving or returning during the lunch hour. Several initially lukewarm relationships started in this way, only to blossom into lunch time and evening tremblers in the girl's car or the rear of the office building, thrusting on cold concrete steps, trying to keep some dignity in keeping on the helmet by request whilst banging away in true doggy fashion, but nothing firm or lasting. Sex had a smaller jurisdiction over me in the beginning. It wasn't a priority but very welcome under these circumstances.

Such sexual activity was cheap but quickly came to an end with each victim as they realised I was not to see them as a serious relationship. My wages didn't allow for serious entertaining, so I became somewhat obsessed with being supremely fit. I became a regular at the Manchester YMCA, where I joined the Amateur Wrestling Club. This sport necessitated an incredible level of fitness and I trained every day if possible, often for three hours a day, skipping, bag punching, weight lifting, and, of course, wrestling. Whilst I went into several competitions, I was never particularly good by YMCA standards. Still, nobody could touch me on the streets. The incentives were different, I suppose. Today, I have no photographs of the muscular definition I displayed back then. I wrestled as a middleweight, at a maximum of 12 stone, 12 pounds. It is another one of those sad reminders of age, another thing I can look back on and compare what was with what is, even if the thing is me. I'm in relatively good shape today because I still attempt some daily exercise but such dedication to such a sport has necessitated the replacement of two knees and a hip. There is no comparison to those rookie days when my body responded quicker and to more of my demands than it does now in every department. I look back at the times when I wrestled, played squash, played rugby had sex every day at home and with at least four little strangers a week with fond memories. I look at four mile hills I ran up which I cannot now walk up with so many fond memories but with little present ability. Thank God for Viagra.

I knew I could restrain anybody. I could catch anybody if they ran. I could carry them over my shoulder if they "tripped and banged their head" during an arrest. I had the necessary fitness to chase a 20-year-old, seen breaking into a car outside the Odeon Cinema on Oxford Street. I chased him through what is now China Town, past what is now the Piccadilly Hotel to the steps of the Grand Hotel on Aytoun Street. This chase was a distance of about a mile, taking into account the tortuous route chosen by the one in flight. By then, exhaustion caught up with him. And I would be next. On reaching the hotel steps, he turned, raised his hands in kind of a limp breathless surrender, only to get the benefit of my YMCA bag work. Unfortunately, at the same time, the revolving doors of the Grand spilled out several couples adorned in evening wear, which was not that common in the Sixties. Initially, startled by the scene before them, they managed a: "Good evening officer," as they disappeared, laughing, from my view. One of the divisional vans was called from the back door of a local hostelry by the concierge to commit to some actual police work and on the journey back to Bootle Street we stopped at the doorway to collect my helmet, which was still there. Today, it would have been kicked up the street in a fit of ever decreasing respect for the wearer, not only me, but anyone like me. That is, the man in uniform.

They were heady days in Bootle Street. Everybody from the Superintendent down had secret liaisons both on and off duty. On nights, there were more police cars on car parks, rocking from side to side than there were patrolling the streets. Most had a female on every beat, some had the same one and, as the old saying goes, a change is as good as a rest. If a beat boundary had to be crossed to achieve "the end" both in criminal and sexual activity, so to speak, then it was. The job got done, in a fashion, the figures showed some effort and everyone was happy.

The Sex is Jolly Good Too

What an amazing day of news, as I write. The Law Lords, in their infinite wisdom have decided that the police were wrong to reject the application of a transsexual to join the Force. If he/she should ever be a serving officer, one of the many difficulties he will face will be to search both women and men upon arrest. But there is always an excellent blow job to look forward to, perhaps by his companion on nights. From the experiences I have had and witnessed, the fact that the transsexual "came out" is the only difference, considering that policewomen have always shagged other policewomen and policemen. Gay males have shagged all they can, and anywhere they can, even fellow officers, for as long as I can remember.

On the lighter, more hetero side of sex, many officers made an art form of seducing the female inhabitants of the city centre. If that wasn't an option, they might engage in the 'peep,' known in school as the voyeuristic arts. I remember a nameless colleague being disturbed. He was fully naked, with an equally naked young lady in his car on the site, which is now Piccadilly Station. The vehicle with him inside was fully concealed and he had even cleared his presence with the security man, telling him he was taking observations with a lady in the car for cover. Peepers with their own rules and their own unbelievable radar knew that no such act of serious policing ever took place. Colleague and lady friend, with a full head of steam, and well into the act, suddenly realized they were not alone. Colleague was happy to continue, but his lady friend was not amused, and having unscrewed and separated themselves with some difficulty in such a small car, they started to get dressed. It was only when he undressed at home to retire to bed, with his wife watching, that he realized he was wearing the lady friend's knickers. The knickers were very similar to Marks' gent's underwear, but with the artistic addition of lace on the legs and waist of the pink apparel. Wives were much more trusting in those days, and she accepted the explanation of hubby following through after a curry at the Piccadilly Indian, which was common, necessitating the dumping, so to speak, of the original underwear and wearing a replacement pair obtained from the night security at Marks who appeared amused, for what appeared to be an unknown reason. Now that I write it down and report it, it seems beyond belief to me. Are wives, like Lady Justice, really that blind?

The most extreme example of peeping actually occurred during my service in the CID at Didsbury, in South Manchester. I accompanied a fellow officer who now is employed at the Police Museum in Newton Street, Manchester who wanted to show me the best peep on the beat, immediately behind the station. This was a residential area of terraced houses with high walls, garages, and rear entries. The best peeps were to be found through bedroom windows. I declined the offer when I realized I was to climb over and balance upon several walls, sneak through private gateways, over fences and finally balance on a garage roof to gain the perfect vantage point. Obviously, some were much simpler, and in certain circumstances the female was fully aware of her audience, and got obvious pleasure from the show she was starring in.

I had limited success with policewomen, although I did actually marry one. But that did not hamper my success with the opposite sex. It was quite a simple matter to stop women driving home. Some were married, and usually very drunk. There was no such thing as the breathalyser at this time, and enforcement of the law relating to drunk driving was very relaxed, leaving the enforcement to fines in the form of sexual favours, usually in the back seat of the offender's own car. On one occasion, I remember two females driving past a colleague and I. We smiled and waved. It was obvious just how pissed they were. They waved back. The driver didn't notice the Stop sign. She passed over the white line and collided with a Post Office van, which was hardly damaged. The postman was happy to leave his details and vacate the scene. Although very drunk, the driver was not impressed at being distracted. We wrote up the accident as 'no fault' because the Stop sign was actually broken and it was not illuminated. Well, that was the case after we hurled a couple of bricks through the illuminated plastic casing. Instant fines followed. Once again the painful vertical version came to the fore but needs must. Copulating cops or to be precise two happy constables, carrying out their civic obligations with two model citizens, giving their best to the law. I actually saw the passenger on three other occasions, until her husband stopped her coming home so late from town.

Female shop managers were also a favourite target. I had the pleasure to know a few. I suppose I knew them in a King James biblical sense as well. One such lovely managed a branch of a well known national name that will remain anonymous. Many happy hours were spent during the evening patrol of Market Street after closing time, in the rear stockroom. As I have already alerted you, I was expected to wear my helmet, studded collar and tie, but nothing else. This seemed peculiar at this inductee stage in my sexual career, but it was no stranger than other lessons I was learning at the time. I came to accept the helmet bobbing sex, but perhaps lost a certain fondness for it in my later years. She was eventually promoted to area manager and the stockroom was no longer available. We then met at her home in Bolton and did so for many years. I think this wonderful arrangement floundered when my entrepreneurial ambitions were on the rise. I asked her if she would put me into a situation where I could purchase seconds of the clothing sold at the shop. It didn't happen. And neither did any more tremblers.

I recall once being on point duty in Piccadilly with its junction with Market Street, outside Lewis's. It was hardly a taxing duty, standing in the centre of the road, directing traffic to my right down Market Street and to my left towards Oldham Street. The duty was to stop the traffic and allow pedestrians to cross both lanes. To my right was a continuous barrier fence to direct pedestrians to the proper crossing point. I saw an elderly lady collapse on the other side of the barrier fence. I could easily have walked the few yards to the gap in the fence but chose to dramatically vault it instead. It would have helped if I had not caught the top rail with my right knee, which moved my kneecap from its usual setting and rendered my leg unusable. I appeared to be tending the old lady, whilst seated on the pavement, the perfect picture of the caring policeman. When the ambulance arrived, I had to explain to the crew that I could not stand. Still laughing, they helped me to my feet and assisted me into the rear of the ambulance to be transported with the old lady to Ancoats Hospital. The crossing remained unmanned until the regular day's elderly constable returned from his lunch. Nobody was run over, no accidents occurred and everyone was able to cross the road safely. It occurred to me at this time that the duty on this crossing and three others in the city existed only to keep these men in work until retirement. There was nothing else they could do with them; they had no initiative, no promotion visions and really no interest in the job generally.

Each division had a crime prevention officer and the main office of this group of stalwarts was situated in the headquarters building. An inspector and a sergeant ran this fine group of men who visited premises which had been burgled throughout the city. Their objective was to explain to the complainants how poor their security measures had been and how to improve them to prevent a future incident. Such improvements usually included an expensive burglar alarm system and luckily they had the contact number for the local representative. The reasons for such a reference was obvious to all except the complainant, who, in paying such a price, was including the CPO's bung. On retirement from the police, Crime Prevention Officers were usually found employed at their favourite suppliers.

Enterprise was there for the taking. One just needed to watch and listen carefully. One needed only the necessary ambition, because the opportunities were everywhere. Enterprise and invention always seemed to find its way to gold. One needed to listen to the right voices above them, and to the side of them, and to develop instincts. It also helps to have the right male gear. Brains and balls is a good combination. Maybe we're too close to the bad guy. That in pursuit, in the art of the chase, it becomes an imperative to think like the quarry itself. Being close, this often causes a contamination, an infection of sorts. To defend against this is difficult at best, if not impossible. As I said earlier, everybody was in on it. And then some – there were cops with yachts for hire and mistresses to match and other cops with Rolls Royces servicing weddings on their weekends off. Cops with homes that cops can't afford, bought at the price of common and fruitful infractions of the very law they are sworn to uphold. I tasted the goods. It was a taste too sweet not to.

And then again, the sex was jolly good too. There were many friendly women visiting the pubs and clubs. The Ritz dance hall was very popular. It served as a venue for the BBC programme 'Come Dancing' on regular occasions. It was also the 'grab a granny' headquarters and has remained so to this day. If you didn't have sex of some form or other in her or your car, you had to be gay or too choosy, which was never the case with serving police officers, especially the married ones. These elderly queens performed the act as if it was their last. I wouldn't be able to explain it then, but there was always a small hint of desperation in their sex. It made the work a bit easier, with the exception of the work it took just to engage at all with them. To a sexually inexperienced individual such as myself, the rewards were immediate and cost effective. An education that by far compensated for the nostril offending perfume and the masses of Boots Talcum Powder in their generous gussets, damp with excitement.

The First Word in Copulation is . . .

Cops and clubs go together well. Manchester had all sorts and they all had their great characters. There were the many Greek Cypriot owned clubs, opening just before the shift finished. These clubs buzzed long into the night, past the normal licensing hours. Dino's, The Garden of Eden, with its ornamental baby alligators, Mister Smith's, The Auto, and indeed, The Continental, were all situated a stone's throw from Princess Street with many more, perhaps, smaller and less well known establishments. And, across the city was a whole new breed of seedier clubs serving the less well-heeled populace.

The introduction of the breathalyser and various other licensing difficulties quickly caused the closure of the smaller clubs. They were usually populated by the older end, who drank spirits until they had to drive because they couldn't walk. These veteran inebriates also recognized the need for generosity to the constabulary when stopped for their questionable driving.

Dougie Wellsby operated The Queen's Club on Queen Street, which later moved to a back street behind The Playboy Club. Dougie was one of the old characters and a very hard man in his day. A mixture of villains, Magistrates, Police, businessmen and their female companions frequented the club in total harmony. Fighting in Dougie's would be like fighting in someone's front room. It just was not done whatever the animosity felt at the time. The only sin which was ever committed in the Queens was when anybody of whatever standing actually said "Fuck" in a sentence. You would think Dougie's world had come to an end. He went hysterical claiming an apology for swearing in front of his equally elderly barmaid who just happened to be his young lady also.

Another legend was Les Sim - who was then number one man in the city, with the legendary power and reach of a Godfather. Les had several nightclubs, all of which he ran with a rod of iron. In addition to his regular premises, he also had a late drinker (in the early days the extended licensing hours related to hospitality he provided in various forms, to the local constabulary, forms he reluctantly parted with. I'll come back to Les later. From Chief Superintendent down through the ranks there was a scale of bungs to 'keep the city vibrant.' All we enjoyed at the pointed end was a couple of pints with the doorman, a chicken leg, or maybe a smoked salmon sandwich with the chef which would have been a left over from an earlier reception. Another by-product of the flexible licensed hours, promoted by Mr Dingwall, friend of the Greek club owners and model for the suits originating from the Greek tailors of the city, were drunk drivers wending their way home through rush hour traffic after a night's revels until the daylight hours.

Early one morning I was conducting the traffic at London Road and Whitworth Street. I signalled for the cars heading out of the city to stop. I waved a bus to turn right from Whitworth Street also going out. The bus shuddered to a halt before it was able to complete the turn and a loud metallic bang resounded from the other side. I walked around the bus to see a Ford embedded in its side. The offending driver was still at the wheel, uninjured but bemused. Opening the door I found him to be dead drunk and totally lost, having intended to drive out of the city. Unfortunately, he was travelling in the opposite direction. Such a situation would attract a number of solutions during the night, but in morning rush hour the possibility of an 'instant fine' was out of the question. The driver was unconscious through drink, not the accident and was arrested.

All the non-drivers on my shift tried to finish at 10.45 pm, so allowing time to catch the last buses out of the city before the unreliable all-night service started an hour later. After 11pm there were many buses parked in Piccadilly, lights out and doors wide open. The buses provided a way of unofficially testing new officers. It was a simple matter to remove the light bulbs from the parked buses, and the experienced officers would do this. They would then follow their pathetic prey (the young unsuspecting officer) into the alleyways, keeping out of sight, darting from one dark doorway to the next, often throwing the light bulb which would explode near the officer being watched. They would watch what followed, usually with amusement. Such tricks tended to bring out whatever stuff the stripling officers had in them, show what they were made of and how reliable they might be. As shiny new probationers came from Bruche, many tests were thrown at them to ensure their bravery, loyalty to comrades, and general balls for the job. During these days it was unthinkable to tolerate cowards, liars, and informants in the ranks, unlike today when such things are encouraged, in the form of training school indoctrination regarding various PC levels and expectations.

Manchester, during these times, was a warren of back entries running from Cannon Street to Market Street and in the opposite direction to Shudehill. This is now the site of the Arndale Centre, once known as the largest toilet in Europe, due to its tiled exterior. That is, until the IRA blew it up on a busy Saturday in 1996, breaking every window in a square mile, though miraculously causing little or no real casualties. These were the testing fields for the fledgling heroes. They patrolled these lonely backwaters, seeing moving shadows in their minds, only to be hailed with the occasional exploding projectiles in the dark. Then, such a 'training' exercise would be accepted for the joke it was. Today, such a prank would just be more ammunition for a report to the inexperienced senior ranks, resulting in prosecution for criminal damage or some other form of disciplinary action usually resulting in dismissal. This sort of supervision encourages cowardice and indecision at every level. Taking the easy way out is the only option and such attitudes cascade down to the daily dealings with the public, in the form of 'Not a police matter' etc. It encourages selfish, self-promoting behaviour, with no respect for anyone, and with an attitude that is then reflected when dealing with the public. It undermines confidence at all points.

Having grasped most of the working practices, official and otherwise, I was able to tackle most things that were presented to me. Processing this information, I quickly developed my own form of law enforcement. I think there were also many others who did as well. As the breathalyser became more widely used, I still resisted its use. Most of the old school continued with their life-long values and using a breathalyser would have been a major hypocrisy. The majority on afternoons and nights drove home pissed to some degree. Creeping into some of the sections, fresh from training school was a nervous new breed of police constable. Brainwashed and polished with the PC views of the academic hierarchy they tended to stay on illuminated streets, issuing traffic tickets and breathalysing as many unsuspecting motorists as they pleased (and probably a few pedestrians as well). They did this for the numbers, purely to appear in the figures and stay out of harm's way, without ever seeing an angry man. The real work, the real trouble on the streets came later, in the afternoon shift, or early in the night shift when the streets were at their wildest.

I gave only one person the breathalyser in my entire career and this was only after two strongly worded cautions. I can still remember the incident and I suppose I still feel some regret for the action but, genuinely, had to administer justice to consider the safety of others on the road. I stopped a car that was being badly driven along Sackville Street. I spoke to the driver, who was incapable of answering in anything other than some slur, although it could have been English. I pulled him from the car, leaned him against a wall, moved his car to the kerbside, and wrote on a blank parking ticket that the car had broken down. I then walked with the staggering driver in the direction of the Piccadilly taxi rank. I returned his keys having established he had sufficient funds for the journey to Cheadle in Stockport.

I continued with my crime fighting, drinking, seduction, and peeping duties (all in a day's work). I did all this with the confidence that I had done well for a fellow human being, an inebriated fellow citizen with the same values as my own. As I whistled my way back to cross Sackville Street I saw the silhouette of a head in my new friend's car. Thinking it was being stolen, I sneaked up to the car, threw open the driver's door, grabbed the culprit's hair, and banged his head into the door pillar before dragging him onto the street to slip him into the snaps. The movement was swift and deliberate. In these situations there is always a measure of risk involved, therefore, I do not negotiate. I simply act. It was an understatement to say I was surprised when I realised it was 'my pal', the one I had sent on his way via the taxi rank. I stood him up, dusted him down, accepted his profuse apology, and told him not to take the piss and pointed him at Piccadilly. I fully believed the bump on his forehead would have reminded him not to repeat the process. It didn't. He did the routine a third time, and again I treated him with the same ungentle touch. It was only when, having sobered a little with the shock treatment, he swung at me, told me to: "Fuck off!" and leave him alone, did I exercise my powers of arrest. The charge office sergeant remarked on the bump, but was happy with the explanation that the ungrateful little bastard had tripped. It was all I needed to say. By this time in my service they had come to accept that if a prisoner wasn't bleeding profusely and could still walk, then I hadn't restrained them with the vigour of the YMCA wrestling section. 'My pal' was not charged with police assault. This case was worthy of arrest. The driver was obviously very pissed and didn't have the sense to take advice.

There are many people suffering a 12 month ban and a possibly ruined career, wondering how it all happened.

The truth is, they have been the victim of a random breathalyser. It has always been boasted by various MPs and senior police officers that such a situation does not exist. Drivers are always said to have committed a moving road traffic offence. A moving road traffic offence includes showing no lights, a rear light out, going through a red light, weaving about the road, using a mobile telephone, etc. Some of these offences are the arrested's word against the officers. When stopped, you are immediately asked to take a breathalyser because of any of the above cocked up traffic offences. The driver is in a difficult no-win situation. He gives the test and, if it is positive, whatever the arresting officer says about the traffic offence will be believed. Should the driver refuse the breath test, he then commits the offence of refusal and is banned in any case, whether the traffic offence could be proved or be believed anyway. Traffic police, keeping up their figures, use these methods daily throughout the country. The Traffic Department is despised by the rest of the serving police. They are arrogant and impolite to the public to the point of real aggression. They will prosecute fellow officers as soon as they would a drunken labourer.

Apart from minor incidents such as simple drunk driving, which I didn't pursue anyway, I was becoming very adept at arresting car thieves, as well as individuals stealing from cars. It became embarrassing when the thief proved to be a cop from the next beat. I found on more than one occasion, I had the need to physically caution the perpetrator to keep the crime figures down on my own beat. It was never a consideration to arrest or inform on him. I had a very good friend who I still speak with today, caught on the B Division near to the CIS building, testing car windows with his truncheon and removing property therein for "safe keeping," or at least that is how his poor defence read, before his conviction and dismissal.

I was having such success with my skills at detecting street theft in its various forms, that it wasn't difficult to appear on a different level to most of the others. I suppose my wrestling skills and daily training, gave me a level of supreme confidence on the streets and no situation held any real fear and, perhaps, I proved to be too cavalier on occasions. I remember patrolling Market Street with another officer of a quieter but competent nature to myself. There were five stocky, clearly capable young men walking toward us, shouting lewd comments at passing females. They weren't touching them or causing any real distress to anyone other than me. I had already developed by then a low tolerance to unnecessary rowdyism. Walking past them in my Marshal of Dodge City mode, I said "Keep the noise down lads, leave the women alone." They went quiet. We walked on. But clearly they were festering in drink and one of them came up behind me and punched me in the back. I immediately turned, and as I did I jabbed him at the side of his eye with my gloved hand. He fell to the ground and later I found out that I had fractured his cheekbone with a perfect punch. It was a dividend for all my YMCA bag work. The others were reasonable, but had to be arrested, nonetheless. They had pushed and jostled us and clearly would make better co-accused than defence witnesses, or so I thought. Later, at court, they admitted to being a bit rowdy. They also described me as belligerent. As a master stroke worthy of some of my prosecution evidence which became a work of art later in my service, they produced a doctor who stated that such a skull fracture was not possible with a hand, and it must be, as they were all saying, that I had used my truncheon. The magistrates dismissed the charges against them all. Dismissals such as this never really mattered; it was six of one, half dozen. We all knew magistrates to be in cloud cuckooland in any case. They had no grasp of reality, so how could they dole out realistic convictions? Back then, even as it is today, magistrates were political appointments, friends of friends, or in the post for a variety of other reasons, so how could they give fair judgments, not really knowing for sure just what would constitute a real offence.

Generally, they supported us as did John Bamber, the new Stipendiary Magistrate, a professional full time appointment. Due to his legal background and training he sat alone. Other magistrates sat in twos or threes. Mr Bamber rarely or never sent anyone to prison. He seemed to support us in his quiet way and I know of several officers, not as verbally skilled as myself, getting into difficulties and being saved by 'Uncle John' from the aggressive clutches of a defence solicitor bent on a perjury accusation.

One lunchtime when driving a police van I saw 'Uncle John' stagger from the Reform Club, which then was an exclusive Liberal establishment for the legal and business hierarchy of the city. He had clearly had more than sufficient drink and it was apparent he was in some difficulty walking the half mile back to court. He needed little persuasion to get into the van and I drove him to the magistrate's entrance, which then had several flights of steps to the rear of Court 8. His legs still appeared to be arguing with his brain and the rest of his body as I supported him up the stairs to the rear of the court where his bench was situated. Out of sight of the assembled masses in the court, I supported him through the door and he walked the three paces to his chair, where he sat in judgement for the rest of the afternoon displaying the usual legal countenance we were all accustomed to. He never mentioned this incident again, except to thank me for getting him back to court. I could tell he always supported me in many ways throughout his term in office.

And, of Course, More Actual Police Work

Late evening and night duty increased the opportunities for all our excesses and 'extra-curricular activities' during my uniformed days. Making arrests on the late shifts always ensured court the following day, and with it the overtime rate that prevailed. The rate for a court appearance was the equivalent of five-and-a-quarter hours, however long you stayed at court. This became a source of income that I came to rely on in addition to the instant fines and gifts that improved with my experience. Overtime was an art form, so more about that later. Burglaries were commonplace in the city centre. Of course, there were many burglaries that were not committed by serving police officers.

I recall attending one where the burglar had climbed to the second floor on the outside drainpipe. At this time there were so many very old buildings with equally old attitudes from the owners to security. Not all premises even had burglar alarms and those that did covered only the ground floor and if particularly security conscious the first two floors of buildings which could be five storeys high. Drainpipes ran the height of the building without the sticky paint and barbed wire of today. Being aware of such thinking, skilled burglars, as our subject of the moment would think nothing of such a climb. What he didn't consider was the age, the corrosion and general lack of maintenance on the drainpipe. As he climbed to the fourth floor and an easy window to force, the aged drainpipe suffering from the added weight and corrosion slowly came away from the wall as the corroded mountings and screws collapsed and as they did so the pipe leant back into fresh air, creaking and groaning, pulling out lower mountings allowing gravity to join in and leaving 'our hero' silhouetted against the night sky as in a Felix the Cat Cartoon at a 45% lean but increasing in speed all the time.

Luckily, his accelerating fall was brought to an abrupt end by a large wire reinforced skylight on an adjoining building on the ground floor, separated only by a narrow entry. The skylight shattered, leaving jagged edges of wire mesh in the shape of a flailing body, star shaped and perfectly formed around the climber's outline as he had hurtled through the glass. As one would expect the sharp broken ends of all the wires lacerated all his exposed skin and his clothing. The crimson pool on the floor indicated the serious amount of blood he had lost when bouncing off the floor and was probably still losing as he staggered about the darkened room into which he had fallen. Despite having fallen two floors and having the ignominious fortune of his fall being broken by the wired skylight, he was able to stand in the darkness of the office and in his panic, have the sense to search for the light switch. To climb the drainpipe he had removed his gloves for a better grip. His bloody handprints were visible from the many attempts as he paced his hands along the walls, to find his way in the pitch blackness. Successful at last, clear from the blood smeared all over the light switch, he eventually illuminated the way and made his exit from the office onto the darkened staircase into the warehouse of the building on the ground floor. In doing so, he activated the burglar alarm. To add to his already near fatal injuries his ears then suffered the onslaught of an internal deafening siren and loud alarm bells on the outside at all corners of the building. We attended in the van, called as an emergency 'thieves on' but couldn't find a forced point of entry, and thought it was a false alarm.

The owner quickly attended and felt it could not be a false alarm and allowed us access to the premises to conduct a search and joined us. We locked the door from the inside and moved to the staircase having quickly looked around the ground floor, examining only the large boxes and any obvious hiding places. We didn't really take the search seriously and didn't believe it to be a genuine alarm call. The owner turned on all the lights and we then saw all the blood which led us to a ground floor toilet where this bleeding mass of shredded clothing was trying to hide and by this time remain conscious. The owner examined all the floors with me as my colleague watched the prisoner deteriorate further from shock and blood loss until an ambulance arrived. We quickly found the point of entry. But whilst there were traces of blood in the warehouse, we felt there must have been an accomplice but we couldn't find anyone else. A police dog was called and whilst he had a hell of a time slopping about in the blood and following various trails, they all led to the downstairs bog. The prisoner was admitted to Ancoats Hospital for observations and serious reconstructive embroidery.

Nights were different. There were hardly any rules and instant justice reigned. Depending on where you were in the ranking structure nights had differing values. The dregs, Police Constables, headed off into the night with only beat points to make whilst Sergeants sometimes made the points but were generally engaged with keeping warm in the charge office for a couple of hours before venturing out for a pint and a curry with a couple of supervisory points on the way. Inspectors were a different kettle of fish. If it was the Cathcart brothers both Inspectors on different shifts they would be out there, drinking, eating and even arresting when the need arose, alone and without company other than the beat bobby they stumbled across moving between pubs and shags on his beat. Inconvenient yes, but it kept everyone happy.

In the main Inspectors were nervous of the public, villains and even us in case they got 'involved'. They were usually accompanied by the section Sergeant, pissed off and bored. It. seems like everyone had their own version of work and all it stood for and in the winter, differing standards of dress, dependent on whether you were a worker or a socialiser .Bob and Barry dressed for the summer whatever the weather, in the knowledge they would be much too hot and excited in a mini. I used to dress for warmth in winter. I drank little, because I trained seriously. I was always struggling to make the twelve stone, twelve pound fighting weight as I was 6'1" tall and such a fighting weight usually applied to men of about 5'8". Being a late starter at wrestling I had to use this advantage of height and reach to give me any chance at all and even then I often lost but at least I survived. Amateur wrestling is a hard game and so I was lucky to survive without any serious injury or sprain. Curries were few and far between. Friday and Saturday nights were always a madhouse. The city was full of the public visiting the cinemas, the thieves stealing from their cars, drunks, the residue of football matches and of course the daily scum of chancers waiting to nick anything or fight anyone. Even the likes of Sergeant Roy Nichol were seen in the melee, often pissed but there anyway and of course in the absence of the patrolling Inspector who had just found a load of writing he had to complete in the warmth and safety of Bootle Street.

I remember once walking down the steps of Piccadilly Gardens gent's toilet, which was always a fun palace at the best of times. Outside paraded prostitutes and the odd importuner looking for a likely wank. Inside were the sleepers trying to get warm, the drunks too pissed to climb the stairs out onto Piccadilly and the usual teenager crying for his mum, pissed and wallowing in sick, shit and piss all of which had evacuated at the same time as he coughed. As I confidently descended the stairs I was struck in the chest by what I later discovered was a stolen briefcase in the hands of a drunken Jock who in the alcoholic haze thought I had caught him red handed with the stolen loot.

I never moved. The blow was cushioned by a thick sweater, beneath my lined winter weight tunic. Over that was a quilted raincoat liner beneath my heavy greatcoat. My legs were adorned in lady's tights, purely for warmth; my sexual distortions had not yet really shown themselves at this time. Such heavy armour was good for warmth but made throwing a punch somewhat difficult. The 'Autumn Honey' shade of tights, however, caused no restriction whatsoever to kicking the Jock in the balls, and with such accuracy and ferocity that he didn't touch four stairs as he hurtled backward into the wall at the turn in the stairs. Such was the acceptance of police behaviour, that the law abiding populace continued to make their way in and out of the toilet, business as usual, stepping over Jock as necessary, some offering assistance, and most showing mild amusement at his writhing on the floor and his attempts to dislodge his balls from his throat.

How many do-gooders and barrack room lawyers today would have assisted in complaining about the police violence before them? And made a few quid at my expense? In addition, how many police today would actually have put themselves in such an aggressive situation? As I have already stressed, very poor supervision, coupled with the inexperience of senior officers, hardly makes any effort worthwhile, even for the few. We were on our own, no radios and no contact with base. If you didn't win such a confrontation then apart from the total embarrassment you could easily be injured.

I was grateful for the non-existent supervision of the old days, particularly when I found a night difficult to get through without a nap. This was totally dependent on the quality of sleep I had through that day at home. Screaming neighbours, noisy children, dustbin men and the like could disturb daytime dreaming. I wore earplugs and an eye mask but even then sleep was difficult.

It was summer, I had wandered about all night, had a couple of unusual pints and even a snack and it was just getting light when I chose a large cardboard box behind the Refuge Building - now the Palace hotel on Oxford Street - in a warehouse loading bay. With the gigantic box on its side, I was able to crawl in and fall asleep. I have always had a good body clock and needed little sleep in any case. The beer and burger must have had a sleepy effect and I didn't wake as I intended and my sleep continued after the 7am finishing time of the night shift. I awoke in bright daylight, I could hear pedestrians and rush hour traffic. It was 7.40am and it was always critical that the station was informed of any such delay. As far as they were concerned I was a missing person, possibly badly injured somewhere so I phoned the charge office from the nearby rail station to assure them of my safety. Being so concerned they had kept on the night shift and instructed the morning shift to search my beat with them, but I reappeared before the search was well underway. The boss knew I wasn't a malingerer and accepted my truthful explanation. The rest of the shift knew it was 'there but for the grace of God go I' and went home a little late with no recriminations at all. Now that is the camaraderie and supervision that is missing today. True fraternity is self-evident and requires no further explanation.

Having shown my worth at catching car and property thieves, I was put into the Street Thefts Department which meant I worked with another officer all the time, only with differing priorities. Overtime was not a prospect on this duty and by then, the Police Prosecution Department, had been formed which meant there were no following day court appearances.

Early evening starts meant training every day at the YMCA. Yet before this, I was booking in my partner and showing him present on the Division whilst he remained at home or with his girlfriend as she left work. Sometimes he proved to be a little overdressed for the darkened streets but the partnership worked. To him it was like a promotion to the CID and accordingly he turned out in full three-piece suit, complete with waistcoat and raincoat and looked every part the policeman. But it wasn't really the dress of the day for 'street thefts' where we were supposed to blend in.

Despite this we often found that we stumbled over a 'baddie' breaking into a car or building as we walked in civvies from pub to club to eatery. Whilst it sometimes interrupted our social life, we were still able to affect at least one arrest every day for the month we had this duty and, as a result, we were commended, which meant a lot in those days. I never failed to be surprised by the gall of these thieves as they smashed car windows in plain view of passing pedestrians, which sometimes consisted of us. On other occasions we would see a man walking slowly along a darkened street, peering into parked cars for property, coats etc left on the seats. They would try the door, they were often left open and if locked smash the quarter light with a screwdriver they were carrying. Should they walk up and down, too nervous to actually commit the offence we grabbed them in any case and arrested them for loitering with intent to steal. A touch of the Enids with a dose of the verbals usually did the trick.

Every arrest meant we had to parade in front of the Chief Super and relate the circumstances. Strangely it was a proud moment and from those times I never looked back as far as my 'career' was concerned. Duties continued to differ and whilst court overtime ceased, there was the opportunity to police football matches on Saturdays as overtime. This meant point duty before the match, when I would conduct the traffic at Princess Parkway and Wilbraham Road the A5103, main thoroughfare into Manchester from the airport. I had officer assistants at every crossing at the four-way junction and conducted the entire exercise like the Normandy Landings.

I had traffic crossing from all angles, stopping as commanded in a waiting position and then flowing at speed through the junction without any trace of congestion on the side roads, manned by my troops. I remember how sad it was that an inspector found it acceptable to compliment me on the expertise I displayed. He should have gotten out more. After this 'exacting duty', it was into the ground and on the touchline in the days of no barriers between you and the crowd. I do not recall any crowd difficulties in those days. I am sure there were some, but they were outside the ground. I was always impressed by the ferocity of football at such close quarters and often had the likes of Mike Summerbee in my lap having missed one of his crunchers on some unsuspecting forward.

This of course was at Manchester City. Manchester United was policed by Lancashire County in my early days and we were confined to the City matches. The players were well-known names then, even to me, a non-football fan. Colin Bell, Francis Lee, now a passing friend, from holidays in Barbados since leaving the police and having a few quid to throw around. Mike Summerbee, also a friend today, and many more who I don't think got any real trophies but were great to watch. Sitting on a bench on the touchline left no doubt how hard the tackles were and the ferocious speed at which they were made. Being a rugby player, I still believed them to be 'mard arses', a good Lancashire term, from the annals of my father, witnessing the unnecessary writhing on the pitch to obtain a cheated decision from the referee.

On the other hand police rugby was a different game. The violence dished out on the streets was repeated during every game. Being a very poor ball handler, I tended to confine myself to "shaking up" the opposition and could go a whole game without handling the ball. The team manager was Detective Chief Superintendent

Tom Butcher. A legend in the force, he had many unorthodox methods of conducting a murder inquiry and was highly respected by all genuine hardworking uniform and detective officers, alike. His rugby team management skills were honed to perfection in the bar after the match, but on the touchline he left a lot to be desired, especially as far as the match referee was concerned. On at least one memorable occasion he was barred from the touchline, but continued to hurl abuse at the opposition and referee alike from the 100 yards limit he was exiled to. This was the lighter side of one of the force's true detectives. I still see Tom Butcher in a pub when I call in on occasions near to the Manchester International Airport. It is always a pleasure.

I was playing rugby when I first met Bob Sharpe. I liked his sense of humour, his fitness, and his overall size. He dished it out on the field, as well as the streets, and was respected for it. Later in his career he decided to grow a beard. There was nothing in Police Regulations to prevent this, provided it was tidy. By this time the Chief Constable James Anderton who was happily living in his strange politically correct world - never having been criticised by the "crusading Manchester Evening News". He was later known to me, for his close attention to prostitution and pornography which I regularly saw him vetting. Anderton ran GMP for 16 years between 1975 and 1991 - crusading whenever he was able against the many dirty bookshops and, later, saunas in the city. As the detection rate was falling because of the poor morale and refusal to work due to attention from the Y Department, who by then were picking on every detail under the instructions of Anderton. At the bookshops we would seize, pin-up books, salacious novels and porn films which in those days were cine films. They all had to be vetted and sent off to the Director of Public Prosecutions with the appropriate pages marked for easy reference so that the DPP staff didn't wank themselves to death reading them all.

We took to this duty with some considerable alacrity leaving us to later desperately seek any 'granny' at the Ritz for a serious scrotum emptying or a passing brass for an instant fine off the wrist. God's own servant, leading Methodist and righter of all wrongs would personally 'assist' with this film vetting, not with the lads but tucked away in his office, door secure leaving only the sound of a whirring projector for us to form the obvious conclusion.

And among all this from his secure office, Anderton decided to engage in a crusade against Bob Sharpe's beard. Bob refused to shave as he was entitled. Anderton had a fit at having his authority ignored, and having the backbone he later displayed in so many areas, ordered Bob to be on regular nights until he shaved. Bob was moved off the A Division, out of the public gaze somewhere on the east of the city. Devout Christian Anderton was known as God's Cop and pontificated about officers being smart only to later validate the hypocrisy he became famous for, in his newspaper interviews, his conduct of the Force and later in the removal of John Stalker and so much more. Unbelievably, and so very him, he grew a beard of such unkempt proportions that he looked every part of the cartoon character. He became famous for his AIDS pronouncement in 1986 that homosexuals with the disease were 'swirling in a cesspit of their own making.' God's Cop's own daughter eventually came out as a lesbian.

But the mention of Bob reminds me of seeing him on Elizabeth Street in Cheetham and he didn't have a beard then. On the same street was the main garage and workshop of M&N Autos. I don't know if he had been there. It was a garage which tended to be preferred by police officers throughout the Force, all 'bung seekers' and it was used for their own vehicle repairs. The management who charged favourable rates for officer's own cars also encouraged officers from every division to persuade unfortunate drivers involved in road accidents to have their vehicle collected by M&N Autos. Their undying gratitude was calculated on the damage to the vehicle and shown in the form of crispy oil stained notes. Some things have been corrected it seems. Today, there is the presence of a list of approved workshops which are supposed to be used in rotation. The rotation one hopes is rounded and fair, but certainly reflects the attitude of the poor, ill informed police management of today to the 'bunging business.'

I took the police driving course and spent a month driving about the Cheshire countryside with two other officers and an instructor. I did not have a driving licence at this time so there I was in full police uniform with the others with L Plates on the car. We took it in turns to drive throughout the day and I quickly became quite proficient. Passing the test meant everything to me and I advanced on to driving the divisional van. This can only be described as fun-on-wheels, but meant I only handled other people's arrests and answered emergency calls. Attending so many calls, I met and saw a variety of officers at the pointed end of arrests. It was quickly apparent that the quality of men on the beat was falling at an alarming rate. I witnessed many frightened men and, on many occasions, had to leave the driving to my partner and get 'in the back' with the arresting officer and his prisoner. On many occasions prisoners were hurling abuse and profanities despite being told to shut up through the grill, which separated us. The arresting officer was sitting in the back with the prisoner and was clearly very nervous and in fear. The task was to take command of the situation back there, to help remind the arrestee just who was in charge as was always the case on the wild streets. Complaints of police violence were becoming more common, but were still not being taken too seriously by the station supremos, provided there were no broken bones. Any cuts warranted the police assault charge, which was added on with more regularity. Where is the rubber truncheon when you need it?

During these wonderful days, terrorists were unheard of. The IRA didn't exist in England, so a 999 call regarding a suspicious package outside the third floor offices of the Italian Consulate in New Brown Street didn't cause any real alarm. At this time we even thought it may be a bit of found property yet to be misappropriated before being auctioned. I had always visualised bombs as all red sticks connected with curly wire and batteries. This 'bomb' was a brown foolscap envelope, filled with bath crystals and a brown solid tube. For ease, we transported it in a dustbin to another call at the Market Street Yates' Wine Lodge, where we loaded four fighting Paddies into the rear with the dustbin and me. We were driven recklessly to Bootle Street where the Paddies were unceremoniously unloaded, knocking over the bin as we did so and I was still fighting the Irish as they were hurled through the swinging doors into the unmovable force known as the counter.

The inspector continued to read his paper as was the custom of the 'been there done it' brigade of confidence, whilst the Paddies were put into formation to await processing for Drunk and Disorderly. All were processed and charged, the paperwork completed and a cup of tea taken in the canteen. An hour later we remembered the 'bomb' in the bin. We shook it to the upright position and dragged it from the rear of the van to put it on the ramp which led to the basement parade room. Procedure took over and the efficient way of dealing with a suspected bomb was followed to the letter, or at least what applied during these years. The bin was left on the ramp for about two hours whilst the bomb disposal squad drove from their Chester base.

I will never forget the Major examining the package: "Well you have a bomb all right. How did it get it here?"

"Well," I spluttered, genuinely shocked, "in that dustbin, in the back of the van, kicked all the way by a bunch of Paddies."

The Major was not impressed and having dismantled the components, he explained that the crystals were weed killer, the tube was explosive and, buried in the weed killer, was an eyedropper bottle containing a concentrated acid. The procedure to an almighty explosion was simple actually. The acid would burn through the rubber of the upturned bottle, producing a heat reaction with the crystals and causing the explosive to detonate. Had it exploded, the remains of the van would have been the engine block and the six of us would have decorated Cross Street. It would have killed many others as well. By one chance in a million, the rubber of the dropper had a fault and was too thick, thus preventing the acid eating through. I couldn't believe we were not to be commended for our bravery, even as clueless as it was, or that we were not disciplined for reckless stupidity.

I wasn't commended either when I climbed scaffolding erected on the tower of the Manchester Town Hall to rescue a reveller one New Year's Eve. He had climbed up to the clock face, stood on the fingers, stopping the clock at 1.10am. He then climbed to the roof of the spire. He could not have known there were holes in the roof for the distribution of sound, and he fell through onto the wooden beams of the roof and bell supports. The fire brigade was unavailable, committed on real emergencies. Volunteers were asked to climb and report if he was injured. Being the worse for a couple of 'sherbets', I volunteered. Heights were never a problem for me. I climbed for what seemed an eternity with another officer. We found the reveller strewn over the beams, moaning, drunk, but apparently uninjured. He shouted a bit as we lifted him over my shoulder and continuously as we carried him down the scaffolding. Not surprising really, he had a chipped vertebrae. We were supposed to render only first aid, not carry him down. We could have killed him, or permanently disabled him. A commendation for this act of bravery was not in my immediate future either.

With these and many other cavalier actions, my days at Bootle Street were numbered. My behaviour and that of the other originals when I joined, was becoming more politically incorrect to the degree that Duty Inspectors of the nervous variety paled as we threw yet another bleeding prisoner at the counter. In addition and at every turn was the new breed of supervisory ranks creeping in like a dose. Several colleagues, all of the old school, including myself, were constantly being referred to the Y

Department that dealt with complaints. These were being taken more seriously and were even being investigated, but still by officers with some real field experience and sympathy for our style of working.

I was doing my job out in the field and, for a reason I now forget, I had a prisoner in tow when I was summoned to the Y Department. No excuses. 'Stop what you are doing', with no consideration for real police work, 'and come immediately'. The excuse for a real policeman doing the summonsing over the radio clearly felt everyone hid behind a desk and wrote all day like he did. Thinking of 'bringing my work home' and giving this desk jockey a surprise of his own, I declined the van crew's offer of minding the prisoner. Instead, I handcuffed the prisoner to me. We marched into the Y Department offices, wrist to wrist. To see the look on the face of a man who had never seen a prisoner, and certainly not an angry one, was well worth the effort. My 'partner' complained profusely that the cuffs were too tight, and I think the Y big shot was actually in fear of being assaulted. When my new partner 'accidentally' collided with the desk and stamped about in agony the Y guy nearly pissed himself. He could not believe he was now a witness to a typical 'accident' involving a struggling prisoner. How sad, and what a travesty, that a man with no backbone and no real police experience should have the right to criticize me, and worse, to fabricate his report, putting my career and my name in jeopardy. The power over me was unearned and undeserved. I don't really remember the rest. I can't say I was even remotely concerned at the time either. My aggravation was too present in my thoughts. And whatever he was investigating, whatever he thought he had over me wasn't proved. So it all went in such a way, forgettable and childishly stupid, the 'blind leading the blind couldn't care less' brigade. It's almost sad, not really boasting but a fact and even pathetic, to have to make such a confession, but nonetheless, for the record, to the day I resigned, nothing was ever proven against me.

Little has changed with the Y department. Even years ago, the detection and arrest rate within the uniform branch and the CID was visibly falling. An attitude of 'Why should I stick my neck out, and risk dismissal?' was becoming even more common, especially as the Y Department was becoming staffed with career jockeys who only wanted to progress through the ranks. The 'offender,' the poor beat cop at the pointed end, the man with wife and kids to support, was given little consideration at all. Most of the men on the ground had little or no higher education, only a few had passed the entrance exam to the police and then with some difficulty. Therefore, they had little other employment options. The exam was an insult to anyone with a semblance of intelligence and remains so today.

Courses were offered to the politically incorrect, by the inspectors who were rapidly losing interest in writing creatively around our exploits. In truth, they were scared and wanted to see the back of us. But we were getting the results. Newton Street nick was thought to be the ideal exile because the inspector visited rarely and the station sergeant ran it like a Beirut outpost, with few rules and excellent results. It was always fully staffed and there was an unofficial waiting list, not of volunteers, but the bent psychopaths dotted about on other sections.

John Cooper: Legend and Servant of the Queen

During my days stationed at Bootle Street Police Station I had always been considered for relocation to the Siberia-like, outback of Newton Street by various duty inspectors who, were, basically fed up with writing around my violent and often suspect misdemeanours. They spoke of it as though I would be sent there as a punishment with the thinking that, if they were scared to even visit the nick then I would be as well. To me this was like a promotion, I couldn't wait.

I was delighted when there was a vacancy at Newton Street Sub-Station. It was known as the Dodge City of the A Division. Boasting its own esteemed Marshal, Sergeant John Cooper, on my shift and others less legendary but equally off the wall in their interpretation of the 'law of the land' on other shifts. John Cooper was without doubt a legend and a name which when mentioned in Bootle Street, caused the duty inspector to pale. I had only seen John Cooper on rare occasions when he appeared at Bootle Street, much to the duty inspector's dismay. Sergeant Cooper loomed through the door and aggravation wrote itself all over Mr Duty Inspector, anticipating a sudden spoil of his happy little existence. John Cooper never visited Bootle Street except for very serious reasons. Perhaps not serious to all and sundry but the hot water being cool, the cleaner being sick, or polish running out were horrendous matters to be discussed at a high level.

Because of his unorthodox methods and outspoken nature, which in the eyes of all us mavericks, made him the legend he undoubtedly was and we followed him unquestionably. It wasn't actually a faith in his judgement which caused such loyalty, it was the knowledge that you could be as quickly returned to Bootle Street if any of his interesting decisions were ever questioned. He was permanently exiled to Newton Street Police Station. He regularly struck fear into the supervisory ranks and tended to be ignored whenever possible, unless the wheel really came off. Nobody had the bottle to question his decisions and when they did the explanation was inevitably without fault. Newton Street station was a small building which had served as a mortuary in its Victorian past, and is now the Police Museum, alive with presence and history, and well worth a visit if only to get the feel of the following stories.

On the ground floor was the police station, open to the public via a large hallway protected at the street with large barred iron gates. From the hallway ran a staircase to the kitchen, a refreshment room where there was no staff. We cooked our own food on the large gas range, cleaned up after ourselves, and woe betide the foolish young officer who left a dirty plate. I showed far too much aptitude for cooking and, consequently became John Cooper's personal chef, particularly at breakfast time. It was my duty to deliver Sgt Cooper's compliments to the various butchers and greengrocers on the section. At this time we had the old Smithfield Meat, Fish and Vegetable Market and as a consequence the pickings were considerable. I would cook us the largest full English breakfasts you had ever seen and then the remains of the ingredients were shared and taken home. The art of such pillaging was to not take advantage of any one individual and instead share the Sergeants 'compliments' and my visits between all market operators.

The actual police station room had dimensions of about six yards by six yards. It was furnished with an immense solid wood counter easily dating from the early 1900s, and a desk and chair for the Sergeant. Another desk and chair, with a couple of filing cabinets, were the only other pieces of furniture in the room. The station was painted in a fetching pale green often favoured in Victorian kitchens. On the counter lay the Station Journal, which was a very substantial book measuring about two feet by fourteen inches and about three inches thick - it was the Station Bible. And everything that occurred on the patch was entered in diary form into the book. Strangely, in one corner and behind the desk was an array of pigeon holes, each of which contained a box. Each was numbered and was rented to local businesses. Each morning and evening the business owners either collected or returned the keys for their businesses. I never really understood why. Clearly they trusted the police with the keys. I knew there were officers suspected of taking the keys on nights, entering the premises and on occasions removing property, but I never actually experienced this on the shift I served. John Cooper was revered by these businessmen and it would have been an insult to 'The Legend's' standards to steal from his 'parishioners'.

The station was staffed by the Sergeant and one PC, known as the reserve man, whose duties were dealing with the public, keeping the kitchen clean, the kettle hot, Sergeant Cooper fed and also caring for prisoners in the cell block. This was entered through a massive old wooden door from the station room. For some reason Sergeant Cooper liked me to be reserve man, despite my tender years. It was usually an older man's job. I had only been in uniform a little over a year-and-a-half. I eventually turned 20 at Newton Street Station.

At this time I trained every day at the Manchester YMCA on Peter Street with the amateur wrestlers and was incredibly fit. The training consisted of a run of about six miles to get warm, 30 minutes of skipping, 30 minutes of bag work, some weight training, and then wrestling practice. All this took about three hours. He trusted me and knew I would support him in any action and resulting investigation. Also, he knew that due to my training I could deal with any violent prisoners easily. As we had four Yates' Wine Lodges, about 20 pubs and Smithfield Market on this small section, we had plenty of violent prisoners.

Inside the cell block were five cells, all of which smelt of a mixture of urine from the antiquated urinals and toilets and strong disinfectant stored by the gallon in one of the unused cells. The keys for all the doors were enormous. Of course, the doors themselves were enormous - thick, steel, and gloomy. The station adjoined another council building occupied by Weights and Measures Inspectors and the entire building was heated by a coke-fired boiler, the coke for which was stored in the station yard and, due to the volume, filled the entire area often making the rear entrance into the station difficult to use.

On one occasion, just as the coke had been delivered, a long serving constable from the shift finishing as we arrived was removed from the station by two senior officers on suspicion of a theft or a burglary in the area. Commissions of such offences were not uncommon, though the arrest of an offending officer was unheard of. He must have been very stupid. As he was being led to the waiting car at the rear of the station, he whispered to a colleague known to be a 'boss's man' and a snout (informant). "Don't let them search the coke." Despite our threats to the snout, it was more than he could keep secret and within the hour a team of unfortunates, 'volunteer' probationers, arrived in shiny, newly-issued overalls, and spent the rest of the day removing every piece of coke to find the reason for the whispered warning. Of course, it was a ruse to prove the unreliability of the snout to the lads on his shift. The snout's life was made a misery after that. It was commonplace for him to be locked in a cell 'accidentally' sometimes with a shitting, vomiting drunk attempting to recover from an overdose of 'blob' consumed at one of the many Yates Wine Lodges on the section. Blob should have been registered as a laxative as the results were astounding but perhaps a little lacking in social graces if an innocent was locked in a cell with a sufferer. Despite the existence of the reserve man this unfortunate officer was often called in off his beat to mop up the mess in the cells.

Such messes were a regular occurrence, apart from the normal biological workings of blob there were often misguided individuals who had put up a fight whilst being arrested and suffered a good kicking as a result who stupidly decided to continue the vendetta inside the station, out of public view. Then the kicking really happened, often resulting in an attack of nausea and bowel uncertainness. He stood this for a few weeks until he was transferred to another division by the duty inspector who was concerned about his general welfare. He needed to seek some solace before eventually resigning as a direct result of our informing the troops he was to work with and the vendetta continuing. Whoever you were and whatever the reason, you had a leaving do, you bought a few sandwiches at the Ship, a pub on Shudehill and a few beers. You had many more bought for you and off you went into the big wide world. No such thing for our hero, he was a snout, telling tales, not to get out of the shit, but just telling tales. You just did not snout and that was it.

John Cooper was about six feet tall, big shoulders and chest, with very strong arms. His hair was cut military short, his ruggedly pleasant features, and bent hooked nose, belied the power of the man. He could still do push ups on one hand. He wore a uniform issued in some other age. His shirt had a separate collar, starched of course, fastened by a stud and his trousers had a waist that covered his ample mid section to a few inches below his armpits and these were supported by army issue, wide braces attached to buttons. He talked in an army sergeant major fashion, very curt and matter of fact. He was known by everyone in the city, especially in the area covered by the station. He had a lot of respect and humbly enjoyed it.

Newton Street Station covered what was known as the Fourth Section, which consisted of Smithfield Market (before it moved out of the city), back Piccadilly, the home of Mother Macs, a drinking shrine, which exists today and along Back Piccadilly, outside, the C & A Store, which is now a hotel. We also policed the barrow boys, selling fruit and vegetables – the world's experts in short measure and all of whom were controlled by various Ancoats families, which I suppose were Manchester's answer to the Mafia in those days. What simple little lives we led.

Oldham Street, had its four notorious Yates Wine Lodges, serving blob. The strength of this drink as already mentioned was legendary and it is still served today. The brain damage, bowel movements and vomiting it has caused over the years is incalculable. Suffice to say, rather than have a fighting horde demanding a last blob they closed their doors 30 minutes before all the other pubs so, they all ran to the nearest pub to get a late couple of drinks and it was generally at these pubs that we had the most trouble at closing time.

Shudehill, which formed one side of the old Smithfield fish and vegetable market, is now a bus station. The fish market building remains today and houses craft stalls. The roads nearby were also well known for wholesale jewellers, used bookstores, and radio shacks. It was all a welcomed part of our responsibilities. It was an area populated by the hardest Ancoats people - market porters, barrow boys, chancers and petty thieves - all of whom got drunk and wanted to fight at regular intervals. They were the salt of the earth and whilst difficult, always appeared to show us an element of respect. They would assault us. We would assault them. If we lost, we came back and eventually won with more men. If they lost and they did most of the time, they were charged with police assault to cover the reason for the black eyes and cuts they showed.

They never used weapons such as knives and guns in those days and we never charged them with serious assaults, unless deserved. We always won. We had little choice. We had to be seen as the biggest gang in the city and the lid had to remain firmly in place. There were very few complaints by this population; they knew it was a waste of time. For us during those years, it was the survival of the fittest. Maybe survival of the dirtiest or the meanest, the most cunning, but you always had to win. The stakes were high. And the evidence had to fit the circumstances, so in trying to arrest someone who became unconscious, they were then guilty of police assault to cover the circumstances of rendering them in that condition. This was John Cooper's time. This was a man of some 20 years service, under difficult and trying times, times when men were men.

There should be some newspaper archive covering the time when John Cooper was charged with the murder of a man he was attempting to arrest. The man was as powerful as John Cooper and was wearing steel toe capped boots. Sergeant Cooper could not control him. He was kicking Cooper's legs causing wounds which were visible many years later by scars, from his ankles to his knees. Sergeant Cooper, who always told us younger officers to 'never draw your truncheon unless you intend to use it', drew his truncheon and, in defending himself, struck the man on the head and body several times. The man died from his injuries. Cooper was charged with murder and eventually appeared at Manchester Crown Court to answer the charge. He was a proud man, proud of his position in the police and the respect he had from the law-abiding public, from businessmen of the city and, indeed, the magistrates at court. The Crown Court was a judge and jury trial in those days.

A jury in those days consisted of genuine, honest people who were proud to sit. They were not the type jury service attracts today, consisting of badly dressed, unshaven Government employees of dubious political persuasion and social beliefs, the only people able to take such time as necessary for the prolonged trials of today. Sergeant Cooper was instructed by the Chief Constable of the day to appear at court in civilian clothes. Cooper argued that he was charged with an offence whilst performing his duty and, as such, was entitled to wear his uniform to put the charge into perspective. Despite a clear order, he refused and appeared in uniform.

When in the witness box giving his evidence he showed his injuries and scars on his legs. He then drew his truncheon and made a statement to the effect that he was performing his duty as a representative of the Crown and, whilst he was being attacked ferociously, he hit the deceased on the head and shoulders as hard as he could. In doing this, he struck the dock with the truncheon to demonstrate the force he used. His presence was plentiful and his vocal demonstration brought in a Not Guilty verdict.

Sergeant John Cooper is widely known for the stories that have followed him over the years. Characters like him seem to be great story material. To say his methods were unorthodox would make the rest of us grin or, maybe, tremble. But he was one of the most respected men I can remember when I look back now. And here is a paradox. The line between honest and dishonest was never too well-defined. All of us sort of came into the police with our own definitions and rules, defining that line with our own measures of thickness. A certain dishonesty was always present in the Force, particularly involving thefts and burglaries by some of the men on the beat. The higher you go up the chain the bigger the prizes. We use words like 'corruption' to soften the accusation. It is just plain stealing. Sergeant Cooper would have none of it. A double standard had always existed, but we all knew where his line of demarcation was and just how thick it happened to be. He thought nothing of accepting gifts from the public and would sometimes look the other way on minor issues, but only the minor. He would not be swayed on serious matters.

With the vegetable, meat, and fish markets being on our section, John Cooper took full advantage of his 'fame and respect.' He was a well known figure doing the weekly shopping about the stalls with little attention given to the passing of money. We all did this to a degree, but John Cooper appeared to be stocking a shop with the volumes he accumulated on such expeditions, often using the police van to carry the bounty back to the station. We loved him for it, and for what he was. He grew attached to me for some reason. I suppose the expenditure of words on his behalf gives me away as well. I'm not that sure he even knew my name, but there was something certain in the number he called me, a safety, a trust, a quality of understanding and good faith that we both understood. It was the way he said it. To him I would always be A186. A number he could trust!

I honestly can't ever recall John Cooper using my name. Maybe numbers were easier. Maybe they were closer to his old heart. A186 - that was me – hardly Morse of TV fame. This indicated the division I was on and my individual number. One day he instructed: "Go to the Market, 186. There is a nutter hiding behind the stalls leading onto Shudehill, jumping out on passing women and shouting at them. I don't think he is grabbing them, but they are pissing themselves with the shock. Wear your civvy coat, so he won't see you."

It was common practice to travel to work in uniform with a civvy raincoat over it, carrying your helmet in a bag. Few of us younger officers had cars and even Sergeant Cooper travelled by bus. I don't think he had a car, either. Being old school, he wore full uniform and stood on the open platform at the rear of the bus being liable then not to pay. We showed our uniform, even wearing the coat and travelled free as bus guards were pleased to have us on the bus to deal with any rowdies.

So off I went to the market, entering from Tib Street, a strange narrow street with of all things, four pet shops. Animal rights of today, would have had a fit at the conditions of these sad little animals. As I walked through the busy morning stalls, amongst the piles of crated vegetables and acknowledging the occasional stallholder I recognized from the pillaging run. I saw relief come over them for not being blagged on that occasion. As soon as I stepped out onto Shudehill to have a look around and choose a vantage point to observe from, I saw the mad man jump out of a stall entry into the path of two women - both of whom screamed loudly at his appearance. They remained rooted to the spot, standing there nearly in hysterics, as he ran away laughing at what he thought was a joke. He didn't touch the women and no violence was involved, at least until he had the misfortune to run towards me, as he made his laughing escape. I stood in his path as he came at me, running at full speed and straight into my knee, which caught him accurately in the balls. The strange hysterical laughter changed to retching, the sound of sudden sickness. I followed with a wonderfully executed Judo throw, which I used in wrestling but could never remember the name of it. I then pinned him to the pavement in an arm lock, to initially assess his strength and sanity.

From painful experience I was fully aware of the super human strength a nutter could muster. Having assessed his capabilities, I didn't regard him as a real problem so I stood him up, still holding his arm up his back and started to walk back to Newton Street Station, which was the practice. The van as usual was parked at Bootle Street during the morning shift and would have taken at least 20 minutes to reach me in the rush hour traffic. On this occasion it was not transporting vegetables for the 'Queen's defender of the peace.'

My mad friend initially had some trouble walking properly. His balls appeared to be elevated to some unnatural height due to sudden impact. It wasn't uncommon for the market workers to take the law into their own hands with people such as this, especially those who attacked women. In this case, I had to stop them from abusing the prisoner as we passed along the narrow alleys between the stalls. We were constantly so close to the porters and stallholders that, I admit, I turned my head on some occasions. We got away quite lightly. We passed quickly through the stalls and he was punched only about three times in the mid section. These blows came harder than they actually were, because he was already quite tender. Strangely he no longer found the dodging amongst the stalls quite so entertaining. I was back at the station before 8.30am and Sergeant Cooper was pleased with the success of my arrest and on placing the poor guy at the front of the counter. Cooper crowned him with the Station Journal. Because of its dimensions, it had considerable weight. It was no surprise that the prisoner had to be lifted to his feet again. He was running out of hands to hold his injured areas. He protected his balls with instinctual coverage as it seemed a waste to allow him to be at my feet without kicking him once again.

At this time, it was normal practice to charge a prisoner and have him appear at court the same day, if time allowed. We quickly completed the charging paperwork and told the van to collect him on its rounds and transport him to court. Sergeant Cooper was pleased with this result and decided to come to court as a witness. The fact he was at his desk at the time of the incident, some distance away, really didn't appear to be of any consequence to him. Number 5 Court, with three magistrates, sitting in pompous judgment; this was the select venue for this particular example of British justice. I gave my evidence, explained what I had seen and how I struggled to arrest the prisoner, falling to the ground with him, restraining him, and on lifting him to his feet, cautioned him by telling him he was not obliged to say anything, and then arrested him. The magistrates, peering at the prisoner's obvious injuries, silently accepted that they were due to the violent arrest necessary to subdue him. They sat solemnly. The clerk sitting in front of them asked, "Are there any witnesses, officer?"

"I'm the witness, Your Worships!" boomed Sergeant Cooper as he walked from the rear of the courtroom toward the witness box. His booming voice with his unique military bearing brought the court to a silent standstill. The faces of each magistrate lit up in unison and the whole atmosphere in court lifted as Sergeant Cooper pulled his bullish frame up the steps into the elevated witness box. One of the Magistrates greets him with, "Hello, Sergeant Cooper."

"Your Worships," he warmly and confidently returns.

"How is your wife?"

"Very well, thank you."

"And the family?"

"Oh, yes sir," he addressed the Chairman.

I thought they would ask him about the health of the family dog, but no, he launched into his evidence initially without the oath and was stopped by the clerk who was embarrassed. Cooper gave him the "glare." He had the floor. He took the oath, with apparent pride and totally disregarded the fact that he wasn't even at the scene.

"Your Worships, this is one of the worst cases I have had the misfortune to deal with. This man has been terrifying the female citizens of Manchester as they attempt to go about their business. This morning this man jumped and screamed into the path of two ladies. He waved his hands in their faces as he frothed at the mouth." Remember, he wasn't even there. And in any case, my evidence had already said the perpetrator had his back to me when he faced the women. These women were so terrified they screamed and ran into the road causing traffic to swerve to avoid them, barely missing a fatal accident."

Cooper, in full flow, continued: "As you know, he is charged with conduct likely to cause a breach of the peace. The breach of the peace could easily have erupted into a riot because the market porters wanted to lynch him and we were in danger saving him from this mob. I think under the circumstances he is lucky to be alive, and really I think you have to give him the maximum sentence." Meanwhile, I was beginning to think I wasn't there and had dreamt it.

The magistrates sat in a huddle, whispering and nodding with each other until they sat back and the

Chairman spoke. The prisoner was made to stand in the dock, clearly, still in some pain. The testicles have long convalescence and long memory. The Chairman then addressed the groaning prisoner.

"You are very lucky to be here in one piece, and it is fortunate the officers were there to save you at a danger to themselves." Clearly they were referring to the many market porters in the market and their lack of a sense of humour over such an incident. In their eyes it was okay to give the Mrs a smack, for discipline measures only but to attack strangers 'on the manor' just was not on. Obviously the prisoner's mental state was not as it should have been. A kick in the head can easily confuse the natural thought processes. Everything, every normal thought process, every self-preservation drive turns south. Perhaps he should have been remanded in custody for a medical, as he would be today. "We agree with Sergeant Cooper," announced the learned Chairman of the Bench. "You are a danger and should be sent to prison to protect the citizens of Manchester. We are giving you the maximum sentence of three months. Take him down." The prisoner looked in disbelief as he was dragged below to the cells. Sergeant Cooper thanked the magistrates reverently and we left court to visit the canteen for a brew and the inevitable bacon butty. Sergeant Cooper barely mentioned the incident again. As far as he was concerned, it was justice at its best, and it had been done.

"Come on, 186. We have a city to protect." I loved the way he made statements like this. There is no doubt he saw himself as the people's champion and, in his eyes behaved as some Superman in Gotham City. Maybe I felt a bit in awe myself.

Terrifying women appeared to be a popular sport to many drunks on our section. It must have had something to do with the blob at Yates' Wine Lodges. Whilst driving the police van, as I was prone to do on occasions when I was not in the nick competing with John Cooper over some outrageous act or other, I was called to an incident on High Street in the city centre, across the road from the Fourth Section. A drunk had, for no reason whatsoever and in a particularly violent and deliberate way, physically attacked a woman and her 20-year-old daughter while they were walking home from work to catch the bus on Cannon Street. The older woman had bruises to her face and her daughter was hysterical. The culprit had staggered off, they described him, his dress, orange jacket and work boots etc. We found him only a few hundred yards away heading toward Market Street and yet another Yates' Wine Lodge shouting obscenities and deliberately lurching at passing pedestrians who were forced to run out of his path often into the road, as though in a John Cooper script but on this occasion, perfectly true.

He then made two further errors of judgement. He left the main street and passed into an entry away from the public gaze. We ditched the van, lurching from an angle off the footpath and chased down the entry and caught him. We reminded him of the incident a few minutes earlier with an added knee to the balls. This appeared to aggravate him and still game for a row, he told my colleague and me to "Fuck off!" His mumbled explanation through his tears as he pulled his balls down from his chest was that the older of the two had reminded him of his wife, so he belted her. I am not really sure who hit him first, but we both did, and with such great effect he pissed himself immediately and was unable to stand, especially having had the benefit of initially a knee and then a pair of Doc Martens in the balls as he fell writhing to the ground. He was dragged screaming and frothing as he pleaded for mercy before he was thrown, and I mean thrown or at least hurled, into the rear of the van where he was kicked about until we returned to the women. We needed to make sure we had the correct person maybe a trifle late in the entire proceedings, but necessary in the interests of justice. They could see that he already looked in a worst state than when he had left them screaming in fear and in some considerable pain from the kicks and blows he had rained upon them. We explained that he had also assaulted us and that we needed to defend ourselves. Clearly, we had been assaulted by him as well.

Laying on the van floor in excruciating agony would have led a normal violent prisoner to believe that the worst was over and he had learnt his lesson. A night in the cells, court in the morning, perhaps a fine with a guilty plea, and back in Yates' by lunchtime was order of the day. But no – not for this soul as Sergeant Cooper, the Personal Executor of the Queen's Proclamation, the Defender of all that is good, and Keeper of the Peace, was on duty. He didn't like nutters or drunks who assaulted women, or anyone who merely upset the serene Fourth Section which, to him, was not the brick jungle it appeared to be. He preferred it to be a Garden of Eden to be enjoyed by all who trod its pathways, even if they did have to step over the odd 'police assaulter.'

The thick metal cell door was locked, as was the enormous connecting door from the public area. The prisoner was sequestered safely within both. It was the next best thing to sound proofing. And soundproofing was certainly necessary. Sergeant Cooper beat this man about the body with such violence that the man physically screamed and cried for mercy.

"Stand him up, 186. Come on, you spineless pisshead, get on your feet!" I thought he meant me as I winced at the torture being inflicted. There he stood, begging for mercy, crying, and wishing he had never laid a finger on the women, which of course, was the object of the exercise.

"What's that smell?"

"I've shit myself, sergeant." Sgt Cooper looked at him with contemptuous disbelief. With that, the prisoner shook his right leg and the biggest, roundest, freshest, and most intact turd fell from his trouser bottom. It just laid there steaming on the floor. The Defender of the Good was beside himself, and literally jumped back in total amazement.

"You filthy bastard, pick it up!"

"With what?"

"Your hands, of course, you miserable shithouse!" The poor whipped, shit-stained unfortunate, bent down with some difficulty, his ribs in disarray and his balls in the area of his nipples, and tried to pick it up. The slime, the ooze, the general repulsive consistency of it made this impossible. Also, by now the smell was beyond description. I had by then in my service, or so I believed smelt everything bad that was possible. I had been present at post mortems and that is a smell, I had locked up sleepers who had not washed for months and I had even locked up the loose bowelled blob drinking brigade from Yates'. Nothing compared with this. The meal I was looking forward to, well, it lost something for me.

Always there with a solution, the legend, what would we do without him, the Leader of the Brave, the Queens Servant, Sergeant Cooper asked: "Have you got a hanky?" He didn't. Unfortunately, I did. "Lend him yours, 186." Lend? Like I might want it back. My mood was suddenly more generous than that. The doomed linen a present from my mother with the annual slippers even had a monogrammed S stitched in the corner, which had new meaning now I suppose. It was a Christmas present, but at that point it could have been given to me by the Queen herself.

"No . . . please, I insist." Was all I managed. Somewhat perplexed at the need for this wonderful piece of work from the Irish lace industry. The handkerchief was handed to the baffled prisoner who as instructed by the venerable Sgt placed the hankie on the floor, carefully in perfect line with the cell bed. I think the Sgt had a touch of OCD and many things had to be in straight lines from his meat and veg to his trouser creases and now the hankie. On his instructions the steaming mass was piled on it, and with his bare fingers, of course. Again on the barked instructions of Mr Tidy he then tied it, closely directed by The Defender of the Peace, neatly at the corners. Though I wasn't thinking of food at the moment, it did resemble a steamed pudding.

"What do I do with it now, sergeant?" His voice trembled as he spoke, in total submission to our venerable leader, who proclaimed: "Put it in your pocket. No, not your jacket pocket, your trousers."

Without murmur or protest, this defeated and quite sober individual did as his commander directed. As soon as the neatly tied, steaming bundle was pushed into a trouser pocket, the godly Sergeant Cooper kicked the resulting bulge, releasing the contents out through the cracks in the handkerchief filling the pocket with warm turd. Little molten jets of oozy shit fell to the cell floor.

Cooper was speechless until he bellowed: "How dare you shit on my cell floor again. Give him the mop and bucket, 186. Don't feed him. He has a stomach upset anyway."

He was locked away at last. To all our satisfactions, there would be nothing worse than a dead or badly damaged prisoner to write around just on finishing time. We finished at 11pm and failed to mention the mess or suggest any hint of what the changing staff were literally walking into as we swapped duties. We put the smell, the sacrificial hanky with the embroidered S, and the memory behind us. We left the station and walked to Piccadilly for our buses home still not really able to consider solids, but confident justice had been done.

"Another quiet night, 186. I like Piccadilly Gardens in the evening. See you tomorrow," was Sergeant Cooper's gentle goodbye after one of the most savage kickings imaginable.

Newton Street: The Siberia of Banished Constabulary

A few weeks later I had just started duty and was standing alone outside Woolworths on the corner of Oldham Street and Piccadilly. It was a nice spring evening and I was considering sneaking off to Mother Mack's, a pub on Back Piccadilly for a pint, or to find an "overtime victim.' Of which there were many, lurching about the area.

I didn't have a radio and so I could not be contacted, which was normal practice in those days, unheard of today. Walking at a brisk but controlled pace, appeared Sergeant Cooper, resplendent in his pressed uniform, helmet on, chin strap down, and his sergeant's walking stick in his hand. "Come on, 186. There's a fight in the bus station." Fights in the bus station were not uncommon, so I wasn't that concerned. We strode out together, through Piccadilly Gardens, when we were approached from the side by a well-dressed, middle-aged drunk who wished to speak to the good Sergeant. Cooper refused to speak as he forcefully explained that he had "Queen's business" elsewhere. The drunk was insistent. He started walking backwards, at quite a fast pace, facing Sergeant Cooper as he did so. Quite impressive in view of the large amount of alcohol he had clearly consumed.

"Get out of the way - you buffoon. I am on the Queen's business." The man ignored the order and continued with his backward motion until he was struck under the chin with the handle of the heavy stick. Upon impact his feet left the pavement. In mid-air he flew over the low fence which bordered the flower beds and lay motionless there, surrounded by daffodils. He could have been dead, he was absolutely motionless. Undaunted and unmoved, the Sergeant simply proceeded onward. I turned as we walked and the man was still motionless and had made a real mess of the daffs.

To address such a situation at that moment would be pointless. It was clear that John Cooper had already forgotten about him and with a few paces more we were in the bus station where the fight had stopped, buses had left, and where it was business as usual. And there was no trace of trouble. We headed back toward our section and as we approached the flower bed, the unfortunate individual was struggling to his feet but still obviously dazed from the earlier blow.

"Get that drunk, 186. Look at the damage he is doing to the flowers. Drunk and incapable. That's five-and-a-quarter," said Sgt Cooper - the last line a reference to our overtime payment due to the resulting court appearance. There was contentment in his voice. The unsuspecting gentleman was arrested and charged. We were back on the streets in no time and with overtime to our credit. At court the day afterwards there was a guilty plea and apologies for getting so untidily pissed from the accused. My star witness, also claiming his five-and-a-quarter hours was by then all warm and tucked up in bed, having gone straight home after duty.

A full breakfast at Chris's on Piccadilly seemed in order before going home. No charge, of course. I think Chris was always genuinely pleased to see us, even when there was no trouble. It was his way of saying thank you for the quick attention during troubled nights. Even today I see Chris, often in the Circus Tavern on Portland Street, operated by another old friend from those times, another Greek Cypriot named George before his move to the Abercrombie. Even today they refuse to let me pay and, indeed, are very genuine and generous people.

Sgt Cooper ran Newton Street area and the station with a firm hand. He also had the utmost respect from the public who saw him as their guardian angel. There were, of course, the key holders collecting their boxes and, in addition the odd old lady, who would bring him a cake. If they failed to do so, their husband would call in to hand it personally to the resident 'servant of the Queen'. It was strange, however, that few of them seemed surprised to see him one day wearing an enormous six-gun in a holster with bullets around the belt. Sheriff Cooper wore his usual high-waisted trousers with the gun belt slung beneath all that brawn, the holster tied to his leg.

There had been a firearms amnesty but guns were not as fashionable in those days, and the amnesty was an attempt to recover the many weapons brought home after the war. Whoever handed this in must have fought at the Alamo. The comments from the public were all good-natured and the Sheriff was becoming quite adept at drawing the gun and spinning it around his finger. Two constables, I didn't recognize, entered the station and introduced themselves. They were from Derbyshire Constabulary and they were there to collect a man wanted on a warrant in Whaley Bridge for something as innocuous as maintenance arrears. He had been found drunk on Oldham Street, during the night, but not charged because of the warrant. To be honest, we had forgotten about him even existing, we were too busy being entertained by Sheriff Cooper. The prisoner hadn't been checked every hour as rules stated. He hadn't been fed and, somehow, had made it to 11.30am without a murmur. It could have been the unlikely comfort of the cell itself with its thick oak cots and oak pillows. The county officers couldn't come any earlier. They had been dealing with school children "onth" crossing and loose sheep "onth" road. They seemed puzzled and said no one was shagging the sheep as they crossed the road, in answer to the gun-toting Sheriff's question. They appeared nervous. There were four of us in the station, one was still drunk from the night before, and we were still amused at the Sheriff's antics, and making some noise. They saw the gun on Cooper's leg. He drew it and pointed it at the cell door.

"Are you armed for this man? They've armed us."

"No, sergeant."

"Go and get him, 186. Be careful, and let me know if you need the gun." He turned to the two white faces and said: "Once 186 is out of the cell corridor through that door, he is your responsibility. 186, I think we had better bar the front entrance to help these lads." And with that, I pretended to lock the enormous barred gates at the entrance, making it apparently impossible for the public to enter. In truth, we didn't have a key for the antique door.

Into the cells I went and opened the cell door. There sat the thinnest, weakest looking, smallest individual I had seen for a long time. Scrawny might be a word that comes to mind. He was clearly showing the effects of the night before and was not well. He suffered a green tinge, which matched the lime green cell walls in a strange but coordinated fashion. I explained to him we were having a joke with some other officers and I wanted him to make it sound like I was having trouble with him. He nodded nervously, very nervously, when I pulled out my truncheon and struck the cell door whilst I shouted as though he was struggling. The Sheriff shouted as well: "Shall I bring the gun 186?" I replied in the negative. With his hands raised above his head in the belief he was joining in the fun, the unfortunate prisoner was guided through the large door into the main station area. He was immediately seized by the county men and hurled to the ground to be handcuffed. The pressure was too much and we gave way beneath it. We broke out in fits of laughter about the station. It couldn't be helped. The gates were opened and the queuing public allowed in. An explanation might have followed for the public's benefit concerning the presence of a dangerous prisoner being dragged away, a prisoner with a perplexed and terrified look on his face.

Practical jokes were all part of the day's entertainment. We sometimes described it as work, which it often regularly became as the day got later and the populace got drunker and more disorderly. Such jokes were always at the expense of an innocent third party, usually a prisoner, often a member of the public, and sometimes even a senior officer. We had a relief which overlapped ours and they had a couple of probationer favourites for the jokes we had in mind, often cruel ones. The probationer we had inherited had little chance with our humorous 'japes'. In addition to being instructed to stand in a telephone box for the whole of his shift and take observations during the daytime, he was also quite often strapped in the phone box by a length of rope and left, until he decided to dial 999 and have the van attend and release him. Such incidents were common and always at the expense of a learning constable.

An exception to that rule was an officer who was regarded as a liability by everyone, probably because he took everything very seriously. He followed the training school manual to the letter. He was totally honest and totally devoid of a sense of humour. To us he appeared to be mentally ill. His shirt was wrinkled, his collar open, usually due to missing buttons and his tie was tied as a piece of string. His uniform was dirty, ill fitting and unpressed. He wore his helmet like a bit part actor over his ears and his dirty hair was badly cut with some form of spikey appearance, making it impossible to comb. He didn't look the part, he was regarded as a total liability and because he had nearly killed the night watchman on the site of the new Crown Courts, he was exiled to Newton Street, the Siberia of banished constabulary, where he wouldn't stand out as such an obvious leper. The rest of us were also exiled for a number of reasons, but none of us could claim to have given a pensioner a heart attack. The duty inspector we may perhaps have given a slight coronary, but not a pensioner. Despite his history, Dennis (not his real name) disappeared onto his beat with vigour. He regularly chose to wear his cape, probably to hide his uniform.

The circumstances of Dennis' exile hinged on his practice of hiding in darkened corners, concealed totally by his cape. On this occasion Dennis, wrapped in his cape, was perched on a partly built wall of the new Crown Court building. This was a new beat to Dennis, but unknown to him, the site, because of its large and open nature, was patrolled at night by an elderly watchman. The old man doing his duty tried a few locks on cabins about the site, walked below the wall where Dennis, the caped crusader, was crouched. Then came the pounce, the inevitable pounce, cape flowing behind him. A short-time later as the burbling nightwatchman was lifted into the ambulance with a suspected heart attack, he was still hysterically rambling on about the giant bat that had attacked him from the dark skies.

"Welcome to Newton Street, Officer," booms John Cooper, as he took the briefing for the night shift. It was the practice to read all notices from the Divisional Headquarters at Bootle Street pertaining to police business and any notices just for our section, which usually referred to a 'few staying behind' at one of the local pubs. The 'few' were rarely more than 50. One such notice referred to a stolen painting and Sergeant Cooper held up a photo of the picture and made a point of showing it to 'Batman'. Nothing strange about this he would think but, of course, he didn't know that the memo had been specially prepared and the painting was rolled up in John Cooper's desk, a worthless print.

It was known to be Dennis's practice to carry with him a large ball of cotton, which he used to seal off the ends of back entries. There was no real need for anyone to use such entries during the night other than to break into the rear of premises or to give a young lady a trembler in the darkness. But this type of diligence was not as silly as it appeared, and the maze of entries was much more effectively patrolled in this manner. Upon returning to an entry he could tell if that area had been seriously compromised.

Dennis came into the station for his meal at 2.15am at which time Sergeant Cooper disappeared in to the darkness in the direction of the maze of entries with what appeared to be a rolled document under his coat. He was back in 20 minutes and sat behind his desk when Dennis again took on his role as the caped crusader and left the station. His intention was to examine all his threads to ensure all was safe and wasn't really expected back until 6.45am when the shift changed. To the good Sergeant's feigned surprise, a breathless caped crusader ran back into the Station clutching 'the painting' which he unfurled with considerable care. Sergeant Cooper had by now raised his bulky frame from his chair and walked the three paces to the counter facing 'Batman' on the other side, and without a sound punched a hole in the centre of the painting. A paralysed ashen faced 'bat', was still holding up the painting when Sergeant Cooper peered through the hole and bellowed: "Get out of my station, you stupid bastard!" He could not believe it. He knew without a word it was a set up and off he went back to his beat.

"Is he mad or am I, 186?" The Defender of All sat down wearily, shook his head, and collapsed in a fit of laughter. Thank God he didn't expect an answer. Sergeant Cooper's eccentricity and pride in his section was illustrated ably when an officer brought in a young smartly dressed individual who until now had only heard of Sergeant Cooper. John Cooper looked up as he was writing in the Station Journal.

"What's this, 232?"

"Stolen car, sergeant." With that John Cooper picked up the enormous journal and hit the poor chap over the head with the book causing him to fall to his knees.

"This is the complainant, sergeant." "Thank God I only lost the car," said the complainant as he struggled to his feet and was dusted down by 232. Sergeant Cooper, surprised for only seconds, nodded, then stared at the complainant. He then said firmly, with only a wry smile: "Be more careful with your car next time." I think he meant it by then, and the poor judgement call he had made was forgotten. Again, he had instilled the words of the Defender of All That Is Good onto yet another convert.

The Newton Street Section covered Back Piccadilly, which in those days was home to about 20 barrow boys. They were unofficial and were often moved on and even arrested by probationary tossers who had nothing better to do in the guise of gaining more experience. Realistically they were doing no real harm. They treated the public as ripe for a simple scam and wherever possible short-weighed the purchases, or short-changed the customer. I never arrested any of them and only told them to move on when directed to do so. I used to examine scales and find weights hidden under the brown paper bag lining of the produce end of the scale. If I caught any of them twice, I would arrest them. I was not impressed at anyone taking the piss out of me and the champion of the public, John Cooper, who took all villainy as a personal insult.

On one occasion a mounted policeman, on the biggest horse I had ever seen, tried to arrest a barrow boy who refused to move. The mistaken boy felt confident that he could not be thrown over the saddle and taken in, especially with his barrow, as so often seen on the cowboy films. The Mountie called for assistance. He was in no danger and we were all suddenly engaged with all manner of emergencies, to prevent our attendance at this scene. Eventually after several calls for assistance we thought this was to become a nightmare situation, putting the logistics and the mechanics of prisoner transport to the test as more barrow boys became involved quickly realizing we were avoiding the area and the stranger with horse regarded as fair game. Despite being a public relations exercise, the horses were really for old ladies to give sugar to, anywhere except football matches, where they appeared to prefer to stand on police rather than rowdy supporters. The mounted officer stood firm.

He knew the horse transport wagon was in the city and requested its attendance. On arrival, the four officers who manned the giant horse box told all the barrows to move, as they were causing an unnecessary obstruction. They all refused, and were put into the horse wagon which smelt cleaner than some of them. The officer deputised one of the labourers and his mates to look after the barrows and stock which remained at the scene. It was our normal practice to arrest only one barrow boy with his cart and make him walk with it to Newton Street, which was about half-a-mile away. This was the usual discipline which was expected and tolerated. On arrival at the nick we were then able to eat the fruit whilst completing the paperwork.

John Cooper was well pissed off. His supply of free fruit was 'out the window' and he had to charge about 15 individuals with the same offence. Each address had to be confirmed and everyone had to be checked with Criminal Records to establish if any warrants or non-payment of previous fines were outstanding. Of course, John Cooper delegated the tasks to the rest of us. While doing so, he asked me why I hadn't attended to sort it out and just bring in a nominal barrow boy. I told him

I knew it was the mounted branch and none of us regarded them as real policemen. Besides, I was feeding the cat, and 232 had gone out to get milk for it.

This was an acceptable explanation to the Defender of the Peace, but regarded as unacceptable, as well as unbelievable, by the Mounted Department. The instigator told us he felt he was in serious danger and could have been assaulted. All the barrow boys, in full knowledge of the fate of those who committed police assault on the 4th section, chirped up with the theme of 'Do you think we would come here on a Police Assault charge? You must be mad. We were only having a laugh, Sergeant Cooper, they weren't yours.' They meant all of us based at Newton Street. The Protector of All, in his usual fair and balanced manner stated that even the mounted branch, were to be regarded as his officers, when on his section and that they had been deputised for this purpose. To the visible fear and then relief of the assembled hordes his judgement was that there had been some disrespect, but he would let it go this time.

Barrow boys were run by Bobby McDermott and family. He was not pleased at the loss of income and had arranged a demonstration outside the nick. Whatever he said, the barrow boys in need of employment, the following day, followed his every word. As with so many senior police officers of today, Bobby didn't actually lead from the front. Even he wasn't brave enough to come in the nick and hadn't even attended in person to register his complaint. He wasn't stupid. John Cooper loved a good siege but preferred to be on the outside doling out the grief, giving instructions to rush in and batter everyone participating, in the name of the Queen. He reluctantly gave instructions to lock the gates into the rear yard, and with the horses safe and sound, close the heavy bars at the entrance. We had no key for the massive padlock so we used a pair of handcuffs. John Cooper, loving every minute, pretending to fear the prisoners revolting on the inside, had them all locked in the cells. He explained to the startled mounted section that we may be under siege for hours, but he would call for assistance. The mounted 'boys' were more concerned that their horses would be upset by the noise from outside the yard but appeared to be quite content eating somebody's butties from the canteen handed to them by the St Christopher of Newton St, the good sergeant. The fact that the horses blocked and were shitting all over the station entrance did not bother the Sgt as no one could enter siege headquarters anyway.

The intrepid inspector at Bootle Street couldn't understand why his valued newspaper reading time had been violated and suggested we deal with it ourselves. The Sergeant explained over the telephone that there were only three of us and four mounted officers, with two horses, but could not charge the mob, because they did not have their knee caps and other assorted pieces of armour. He excused himself for a moment, kept the phone lines open, and shouted through the open door, "In the name of the Queen, I order you to disperse and desist in this rioting conduct!" The inspector was beside himself when Sergeant Cooper returned to the phone. And, of course, he was still trying to avoid the issue. "No sir, I can't do that, I have 186 and 232. I can't send them out. The cells are full already and the ambulance may be stoned when it comes for the injured," John Cooper told the Inspector. He was smiling and nodding as he listened. 'No Sir, 186 and 232 will be okay, but I'm not happy about the barrow boys."

A van load came from Bootle Street with our inspector, who had probably never seen an angry man or visited Newton Street. There was a crowd of about 30 winos, beggars, and general dropouts, recruited by the barrow boys for numbers. They dispersed on the first command. There were a couple of real barrow boys who hung about as negotiators, but stayed well out of the way and held their hands on their heads to avoid the impending police assault charge and inevitable fractured skull. The Protector of All explained in a typical Enid Blyton manner that there were a hundred or so initially and he was forced to take preventative action to protect his station and his men. When he closed the gate he couldn't see how the numbers had diminished, probably coinciding with Yates' opening time. The reinforcements knew it was a wind up, but the inspector never saw the "light." Today I think the reality is that they choose never to see the light as a deliberate act as dawning realisation about anything at all could affect their further promotion.

Dad Harold takes me for a spin on the dodgems at Butlins in Skegness in about 1950 – we had fun and it stood me in good stead for a lifetime of dodging things.

Mum Betsy on the Golden Mile at Blackpool with me aged about 11 and my younger sister Susan – we did like to be beside the seaside in those days.

Me as a baby back in 1947.

Mum and dad and me and our Susan in the pram - it's part of my history and I ended up policing the very streets I played on as a nipper.

My grandparents Tom and Alice Hayes - who we lived with in those far off days after the Second World War - I am about three years of age in this picture.

Idyllic days down in Sudbury when dad Harold worked in the jail mum Betsy, sister Susan and myself, aged about six, enjoyed the country life with fields as far as the eye could see.

My proud mum Betsy on my graduation day from the police training college at Bruche....little did I know what the job had in store for me.

Me standing proudly at the Commando monument at Achnacarry - about 15 miles north of Fort William - where dad did his training.

Me in my first suit aged 15 - a lady killer even in my teens.

The proud day of my graduation from Bruche in the centre - between two colleagues.

My dad Harold with his chest full of medals - he wore them with pride as men he fought with had given so much for our nation to triumph over Adolf Hitler and his Nazi hordes. Us Hayes' have a history of uniformed service.

Bollocks! Open the box, 186

On a brighter note regarding the barrow boys and there are many stories, I went to a call of a distressed woman down off Back Piccadilly. Initially, I thought it was a shopper who had found the weight under the brown paper bag on the barrow scales. It wasn't. It was a seriously pregnant woman whose waters had broken. She was assisted to an orange box, where she sat, doing little for the oranges inside and in obvious pain. Whilst an ambulance had been called, it still had some journey to make. I comforted the woman. The barrow boys offered her a cuppa, but suddenly all hell broke loose. She started screaming. Clearly the baby was on the way. As happens, a crowd of sickos gathered to watch, give gynaecological advice, and offer Aspirins.

We laid her on my raincoat. I deputised a couple of the barrow boys to get rid of the crowd. They were good at this, as we had discovered during the siege of Newton Street, where they certainly pissed us off. Others assisted me by holding up coats around her, whilst I dragged off the very sexless but practical knickers that pregnant ladies wear. I had been trained, in a fashion, to do this in a class. Plastic dolls, fully clothed policewomen hardly give you the experience for what comes next. I expected the birth to take ages, but it wasn't her first. Whilst I considered myself a connoisseur of the female nether parts, the closest I had ever got was a little oral sex. I often gained other opportunities by claiming that I was actually the Olympic champion until I was disqualified for greasing my ears. A joke of course, but it appeared to generate enough interest.

Anyway, I was examining the area in a purely professional, medical manner when her vagina appeared to be turning inside out. It was an amazing sight. I was in some state of shock as the head appeared. The lady clearly knew the breathing and pushing routine and just as I was holding the baby's head, the shoulders came through. My powers of description being what they are, I can only say it looked like a severed armpit. To say I was nervous was an understatement, but the baby seemed all right and was still on the move. As the last few inches made their way out of the gaping cavity, with masses of green red and smelly flesh, the afterbirth or something like that. The ambulance crew arrived and took over. We all had tears, including the barrow boys. And a great cheer went up as the baby started crying. The crowd was still being told to move on as only the lads could tell them. Mother and baby were carefully stowed into the ambulance and then sped away.

After that little episode all the damage caused by the mounted police had been repaired. We were all pals again and John Cooper was back on his weekend fruit. If I had taken the lady's address, we could have bought her a present. Probably a set of horse brasses which would appear suitable, the way she gave birth without the need for a stitch.

To digress a little from John Cooper stories, the use of the Caution brought a tale to mind that is worth relating. It exposes some of the difficulties in fabricating evidence, these exaggerations or infractions of the truth over a point that was seen as unimportant in any case at the time. It involves the public as witnesses. The old adage "Never work with children and old people." springs to mind. Or something like it. Fans of television shows such as Dixon of Dock Green, The Bill, and their contemporary successors will recognise that whenever an arrest takes place the arresting officer must say at the earliest opportunity, words which in my day were: "You are not obliged to say anything unless you wish to do so, and anything you do say will be taken in writing and given in evidence." The wording has changed slightly over the years but the principal remains the same. There is a farcical aspect of this. If you are rolling about in the roadway or happened to be having your brains cudgelled with a pickaxe handle, you are nonetheless supposed to caution the prisoner. If this is omitted or forgotten, you cannot use any conversation as evidence until that has taken place. There are other cautions for other circumstances. This tale refers to the use of firearms.

A police marksman was giving evidence at the Crown Court on the arrest of an armed robber engaged in a hold-up at a village Post Office, operated by an elderly postmistress. Acting on information, several officers were hidden about the village, with two behind the counter of the Post Office, out of sight. The postmistress was standing behind the counter serving customers. The officer was armed with a revolver and was a trained police marksman which, as in my case, may only have meant that he had fired a gun on a range and actually hit a target once, or at least once more than the others on the same course.

From the intelligence we were given, we knew the robber was black and would have a sawn-off shotgun.

He would also have a driver waiting outside. The officers placed outside saw the suspect arrive in the vehicle, then radioed the officers inside to inform them that he was about to enter the premises. The shotgun was concealed under his coat as he approached the Post Office counter. The postmistress was safe behind the armoured glass screen. An officer was to the side of it with a clear view of the door, which was some 15 paces down the shop.

At court, the officer gave his evidence: "On my radio, I heard that the accused was entering the shop, so I stood up, pointed my gun at him, and said 'I am an armed police officer. I believe you to be armed. Drop your weapon and raise your arms!' The accused raised his weapon and appeared to be about to shoot at me, so I opened fire, wounding him in the chest as I am trained to do. The accused fell to the ground and whilst still conscious, was arrested. He was then cautioned and taken to hospital."

The officer was cross-examined by the prisoner's barrister but never wavered from his original evidence. There was no reason to doubt his evidence despite the barrister's attack on every word. The officer was stood down from the witness box and the postmistress was called to the stand. Due to normal court procedure and to further illustrate that British justice was beyond fair, the postmistress had waited outside the courtroom and had not heard the evidence of the officer. She entered the witness box, took the oath, and was allowed to sit down by the judge who tried to put her at ease with the surroundings. She could only be described as a typical village postmistress from Walt Disney films, grey hair, bespectacled and smiling.

She related how the nice officers had come to protect her from the robbers and how they all had tea and toast through the morning and again what nice young men they were. They were wearing earpieces during the incident, so she couldn't hear the radio message, but they told her the man was coming and to stay behind the screen whatever happened. She saw the black man enter the doorway. She was asked if she saw the black man in the court and she immediately identified the accused in the dock. Her testimony continued with these words, "The nice officer with the gun stood up, pointed the gun at him [the robber] and said, 'Bye, bye, Sooty' and shot him. They apologized for him bleeding on the floor, but helped me clean it up after the ambulance had gone."

Now had the proper warning been issued, the officer would probably have been shot.

In Case of Nuclear War, Shoot Somebody

For reasons best known to themselves the Home Office and the Government in general decided that a nuclear war was imminent. In making this prophetic decision they also felt it necessary to select a hardy breed of law enforcers with a background of austere enforcement in the public arena. We were to train in a mobile column. The Inspectors nearly had a party. The entire body of uncontrollable psychopaths was to be shipped away and hopefully, never heard of again. We left for our assignment, but to their eternal disappointment were absent from their sight for only two weeks.

We were driven to Weeton Army Camp, near Blackpool, the Las Vegas of the north of England. The first day involved being told our purpose in the event of a nuclear war. Basically, the Government and their families would be housed in a secret, submerged five star city whilst the mugs, that would be us, would attempt to keep law and order amongst the homeless, the injured, the displaced, and the radiation poisoned public. We were to be moved to a place of safety somewhere in Scotland to await Armageddon. Of course, no mention was made of the safety of our families. Remember, these were the days of sticking window panes with white tape in fetching diamond shapes and digging corrugated covered holes in the back garden as fallout shelters. These same useless shanties would be stocked with tinned food and condensed milk.

There was definitely an air of Enid Blyton to these lectures and clearly no one had bothered to look at the pictures of Hiroshima after the A bomb had been dropped. In the 20 miles of totally flattened areas of population and razed acreage I never saw one corrugated shelter or anyone peering through a taped window.

However, we soon became more than interested when we were told we would be armed for crowd control. They never gave us guns at Manchester City Football Club, which we also policed in a similar fashion to a nuclear disaster. We herded supporters together into confined spaces, forming ridiculous queues and arrested anyone who objected for disorderly behaviour, just to mess them about and miss the match. In addition and, certainly most encouragingly, we had never been instructed to use actual violence on any cheeky bastards and here we are now being told to shoot them to gain the crowds undivided attention and force them to stand in whatever food queue we wished. That is exactly what we were trained and encouraged to do. In the crowds, already severely agitated by recent nuclear aggravation, we were told there could always be at least one real pain-in-the-ass dissenter, a trouble maker, a rabble rouser. We were given the go ahead to shoot the plucky bastard. This Marshal Law certainly had some real appeal. We just wondered why it had never been tried before in Manchester on Saturday nights. The training, whilst a little far fetched, was excellent. We were given a script which basically meant that the 'crowd's spokesman' would be given three warnings of varying severity, the final one being: "If you do not cease with the present disorder, you will be shot." Of course, it was realised that the good old cannabis smoking, left wing British public would treat this with the same disdain as the rest of the laws of the land. We were then shown how to move close enough to ensure hitting the target, preferably in the head and, of course without also shooting the man behind. It had to be worth a small war, just to try this one.

The mobile column consisted of about 20 Thames Traders, the larger seven ton vans of the day, fitted out in a variety of ways and painted in a tasteful black, sporting MOBILE COLUMN in white letters on the side. The vehicles for the troops, were fitted with bench seats the length of the van, with a table along the centre. It wasn't easy playing cards on a moving and vibrating surface, holding down sandwich bags, flasks and the odd copy of Playboy, but we managed. Other vans contained marquees and catering equipment. Others had equipment for latrines. One van was the Command Centre. This had a very fetching, important looking black and white checked design along its length so we could tell the function it served. In the event of a war, which may even have had enemy aircraft to mop up, the fetching black and white checks made the van the priority target, which would then have rendered the entire column useless. Planners who encouraged white taped windows and corrugated shelters had not of course considered this.

I suppose being the only vehicle with 20 aerials sticking out of the roof, next to the glass dome, would have given it away without the need for the artwork. The plan was to breakfast at the army camp, then parade on the drill square in front of the finest of the finest regiment in Lancashire. The regiment had their own visitors at the camp, and so they paraded themselves; brass band, leather aprons, goats, drill sergeants, and all. We would then march in our piss taking fashion, long hair, creased uniforms, egg stains and the rest, to our column of vehicles, mount up, and drive from the camp hurling abuse through the open ventilation windows at passing females, in the true fashion of the building trade, from where most of these recruits had come.

The column would then move at speed with a full motorcycle escort who ensured we never stopped as we pushed our way through towns, built up areas, and of course stretches of countryside. It looked quite impressive, really. We would arrive at our destination, dig a row of latrines, erect a canteen, prepare lunch, eat it, and have a shit in the chemical filled holes before dismantling it all and return at break neck speed to the Army camp for tea. While the day in the vans, playing cards and hurtling through the countryside was a great way to pass the time, the day didn't end there. We had the evening meal, showered, a touch of Old Spice or 'splash it all over', and we were ready for a night in Blackpool, which was only four miles away. We took one of the Thames Traders and filled the rear with all who wished to go on the piss. Being a police vehicle, we parked it on the main promenade, on the footpath, outside Central Pier where there was a perfect parking area with criss crossed yellow lines, a signage threatening prosecution and vehicle removal of offenders. Of course, such laws did not concern the likes of us who, back at our forces, made a career of breaking them.

Most nights we went into a big show bar at the entrance to the pier. We put two tables together, got a kitty going, and had a great night. We had with us the complete comedy double act in the form of 20 stone John

Whittaker and a nine stone, wet through midget, from Cheshire Constabulary, called Peter whose surname was as forgettable then as it is now. The Master of Ceremonies had a box in an elevated position so he could survey the room in his hunt for victims to embarrass between the acts. We had sent a note up to say we had twins in our party. He was over the moon and, in his totally over the top, enthusiastic manner, called out, "La-a-adies and Gen-tle-men, we have a first. We have twins! Come on now, give them a tremendous round of applause! Stand up John and Peter!" The room went wild. He appeared to be in the throes of an epileptic episode, screaming above the noise for them to stand up. All twenty stones of John and all nine of Pete stood on our tables. The room went wild. The laughter followed the cheers and the MC didn't know how to cover his over enthusiastic embarrassment.

The nights in Blackpool have long congealed together in an alcohol induced fusion, but I remember two of the party picking up a real pair of 'slappers' who were happy to come back to camp, and we all knew that the two 'boyfriends' were not to be the only partakers of flesh. The return journey in the back of the van was an education with the two women being passed about for a serious grope which they loved and which they revelled in to the point of a couple of hand jobs and a blowjob for somebody who had to lie on the table in the absence of any more seats. I have always been surprised at how many men, in their constant search for any old legover are happy with sloppy seconds.

Personally, I remember only one occasion when two of us on an early morning visit to the rear door of a Greek café for a bacon butty met with the newly arrived washer upper who was Turkish and apparently madly in love with anything in a uniform. We arranged to pick her up at 9pm when she finished and drove her to a quiet lane beside Whitworth Park near where she lived. We couldn't go to her flat because the husband was waiting. We had my mini and the two of us were both over six feet tall. We managed and whilst going second it was my first experience of a shaven muff, especially one with the lingering aroma of a full English breakfast, the café speciality which was served all day.

The camp had two Military Police patrolling, one with a radio and one with a pickaxe handle. There was not a gun to be seen and clearly this would have been a perfect team if the IRA had paid a visit. They caught us smuggling the girls in, a terrific row ensued with threats from both sides. The girls as with any contraband were confiscated, stating they were to be ejected from the camp in a taxi. In truth, the MP's both gave them one, as we discovered on our next visit to the pier. However, the trusty Thames Trader was put to good use as the evening wore on. We were not impressed with the actions of the MPs and plotted all sorts of retribution which then paled with sleep and further alcohol.

Because the regiment still had us as visitors, albeit a comparatively poorly disciplined, long-haired jumble of rejects, they gave a full parade on a daily basis. As I have already said, this was a fine regiment and at the head of the marching ranks, behind the band, were two soldiers, dressed in large, brown leather aprons. They led a goat each, beautifully groomed and resplendent in their coats, embroidered with the regimental colours and battle honours. A couple of officers jerked behind them in a manner they regarded as marching. Why is it that officers are always so bad at marching? Following on was the rank and file. Drill sergeants barked orders and because I used to enjoy drill in my younger, less informed and easily impressed days, I watched the parade with genuine interest. These were very proud and disciplined men. The spectacle was very impressive. To this day, even as I write, the respect has a certain unforgettable quality about it and more so with the constant media coverage from Iraq and Afghanistan.

The Military Police were not part of this spectacle. They were in bed by this time. We couldn't help ourselves. The temptation was way out of reach. There was no way to keep ourselves in harness and, certainly, no intention to do so. We hatched a plan, based on the morning parade. We would take vengeance for our ruined sexual excursion. Oh, satisfaction! As the MPs strutted around toward the end of their shift the following morning, we kidnapped them both and handcuffed them to the flagpole on the parade square. No one could see them until the parade was already in full flow. The regiment, massed out of sight, marched onto the square to increase the dramatic effect with the band playing, the goats strutting along with the drill sergeants. The discipline amongst the marchers held the best it could. We could hear a few murmurs, but the Sergeant Major soon silenced these. He had seen them, made attempts to ignore them and bid others to ignore them, but couldn't. We were undermining his parade. Other MPs were called to release them. They were marched back to their post, awaiting the judgement of hell whilst we simply boarded our trucks as they did so, loudly cheering and grinning out of the van windows. We left the camp that day and went home. We arrived back at Longsight station at around lunchtime and clearly a pub was calling to the dedicated few. In truth there were only about three men out of the entire group of over a 100 who fancied a pint after the week we had.

The new intake boarded the trucks with expectations of a fortnight on the piss in Blackpool only to have the fundamentals of real police work vividly hurled at them. The entire mobile column was sent to Aberfan, in Wales, where the enormous slag heap, a by-product of the local mining industry, had slid down the mountain and totally covered the local primary school full at the time of little children and teachers. The BBC reported that on 6 October 1966 "a colliery waste tip containing unwanted rock from the local mine slid down Merthyr mountain. The collapsing rock destroyed 20 houses, a farm, and virtually all of Pantglas Junior School. Of the 144 people who died, 116 were children, mostly between the ages of seven and 10. Five teachers were killed in the accident, and only a handful of children survived."

The mobile column spent the entire week digging little bodies out of the debris, choked by coal dust from the black slime. They slept in the tents we had been so amused by, enjoying no showers, and crapping into holes in the ground. On their return there were no complaints, the memories could not even be imagined and realistically that is what police work is about. You play hard, but certainly work hard when the need arises.

Mill Street

The Home Office came up with another disastrous 'bright idea'.

It wasn't enough to give university graduates accelerated promotion, raise admin sergeants with no experience whatsoever of arrests and detections to Assistant Chief Constable with special responsibility for the CID and let a crowd of psychopaths loose with guns in the event of a nuclear war, they had to go further. In its wisdom, after being told so ever since Sir Robert Peel, it was decided that the streets really were under-policed.

This perplexing informed decision was based on months of research, but in reality, all the civil servants had to do was ask any officer who had been to a pub fight alone in the absence of other officers and then kicked about the deserted streets in need of urgent assistance, which was just not there. To prove this, they initiated an experiment. Four men would work the same beat, making all four different points at the same time. This would give the local criminal populace the impression that police were everywhere and, consequently the crime figures would fall dramatically. They had not considered the fact that when officers are making points on the beat perimeters, no one is policing the jungle within and in any case during the times between such points four times the usual number had the golden opportunity to undertake extra-curricular activities.

It was decided that a division adjoining the Bootle Street, A Division with a high crime rate, would be suitable and, therefore, the C Division was chosen. The C Division boundary was roughly from the city centre where I did point duty and then out in a fan. To the left there was Oldham Road and to the right Ashton New Road or some lesser roads running parallel to these and then outward all the way to the Oldham boundary. The division consisted of very poor council housing and some cheaper private homes. The people, the pubs and the women were rough, but as they say they were the salt of the earth. Belle Vue Zoo and Speedway was on the C along with Clayton Analine a massive chemical works and Johnson and Nephew wire works. There were many scrap dealers and general thieves. It was all industry, gas works, and council housing with very few private dwellings. Several of us, all the usual 'suspects' of the mobile column and Newton Street Police Station fame, were transferred from the A Division for a three month trial. The alternative was confinement to a mental hospital, or some other devised method, to protect the rowdy public and property at large from such a horde as they 'raped and pillaged' their way through the city. The pubs and restaurants in the city centre must have seen a recognisable jump in profits. The hordes of female drunk drivers who dropped their pants at the sight of a breathalyser were to be replaced by the lonely wives of the imprisoned masses of the C Division.

Most of us took the move in our stride. It provided us with new pastures for all our general cavorting and also, according to the so-called experts, would provide endless opportunities for arrests, resulting in a visible decrease in the crime rate. They hadn't accounted for the fact that each division in the Force had also transferred all of its mavericks with their own interpretation of policing to the experiment. The beats were much larger than those we were accustomed to. Many of us saw little purpose in trekking around industrial areas which, having their own security, were largely crime free, especially at night. These areas also had no women, no pubs with back doors, or curry houses. We quickly realised that this was to be real police work which, on this division, proved to be a leisurely eight hour walk with invisible health dangers. I was amazed to see how the pollutants in the air settling from the previous day's industrial output from the Clayton Aniline factory discoloured my shiny silver buttons and badge to a tasteless yellow in a matter of nights. I'm not speaking metaphorically, either. It wasn't fashionable during these days to consider what damage our lungs were suffering and I don't think the Health and Safety people were doing anything more than lunching and taking their weekly bung.

On each beat there were so many officers in such a relatively small area that they could not be properly supervised by the original force of sergeants and inspectors at Mill Street Police Station. There was also a part-time sub divisional station of Beswick Street which was actually only a mile from the eastern boundary of my beloved A division but in reality, worlds apart. The supervisory ranks also had to supervise the other five beats as well and, thereby, were attempting to keep track of at least 24 men instead of the usual six and, in doing so, still had to be able to continue with their own hostelry and home visits, in the knowledge that their favourite pub and landlady were to be overrun by the pillaging hordes from outside. It has always been a fact that pub landladies were more accommodating in the sexual area and such favours had to be enjoyed to the maximum by the maximum.

Mill Street Police Station was a large old building faced with brown tiles on its three-floored exterior. It also used to house a fire station, but this had been relocated to a modern building nearby. In the ground floor reception area was the usual public inquiry counter, behind which, concealed from the public gaze, was the charge office. This was smaller than Bootle Street's charge office but also had a similar counter for the softening of prisoners brought in via the rear entrance from the courtyard. The sergeant sat in the charge office and, as with the A Division, ruled all. The inspector had his own office and behaved accordingly, just as the Bootle Street inspector as though they had all been on a training course in the correct manner to ignore all around them, especially an attempted murder at the counter. Even the hapless radio operator had his own stud partitioned office constructed in a brown pastel shaded hardboard with the sound proofing qualities of a Kleenex tissue. He was also on the verge of insanity, as was Eddie Bell at Bootle Street, due to the relentless rustling of toffee papers and dropped equipment as the continued protests against inevitable progress continued throughout the Force.

The Home Office, with its customary level of naivety, tempered with their idea of efficiency, had been planning the beat experiment for about 12 months. The new invention of personal radios had not been considered by our leaders in London and, consequently there were only enough for most of the regular C Division staff, but not all, and certainly not all of us interlopers. This would appear to have defeated the entire purpose of the experiment in one simple stroke of Government inefficiency. Clearly the Home Office believed we cared and that we were diligent and despite the lack of life saving equipment, would go forth alone into the wilderness and produce results. Results in an area where even the milkman would not summon help for an officer attempting to make an arrest. There were no 'pals' here just scrotes and villains who rotated through the prison system with some regularity leaving only their wives to be consoled in their absence.

The first floor of this aged building was occupied by the CID – it was once a hostel for single 'homeless police constables'. The bedrooms had all been converted to office space. The bathrooms remained unchanged, possibly because of the economics of removal. These were an important part of CID interrogation and there are many stories of unfortunates suffering from varying levels of hypothermia, from the cold water, and even near drowning for the less cooperative during interview. Victims were also paraded naked before and after the freezing bath, and great amusement was had by policemen and women alike at the sizes of tackle before and after the freezing experience.

During such halcyon days such an interview technique was regarded as quite soft when compared with other divisions and, indeed, other city forces, such as Liverpool, which realistically was a law unto itself and famed for its interview techniques now converted to law of the land as assault occasioning actual bodily harm which in effect is a couple of blows down the scale from attempted murder.

Every CID office throughout the city had its own form of 'aide-memoir' - Bootle Street, for example, had an electric shock machine, introduced by officers who will remain anonymous for obvious reasons. This device was plugged into the mains and as it was equipped with a transformer could be held onto the bare skin of an uncooperative and often hysterical prisoner as he reacted to the pretty blue flashes of light jumping from one handle to the other. Heavy gloves and goggles were worn for effect. The strength of shock could be governed with a dial, which inevitably was set to maximum. Such a machine was confined to use in the station because of the need for mains power. However today, the beat officer has a mobile version, carried in a holster with his other life saving paraphernalia. This is known as a Taser and is widely used by the inevitable midget, fearing for his life on pregnant women and blind stroke victims as has occurred recently. Again with this country following the States with all fashionable accessories, we can only anticipate further more horrendous assaults by the boys in blue on the unsuspecting public.

Longsight CID, in the D Division headquarters building, was on the first floor directly above the coke pile for the boilers of this enormous building. Visitors who were reluctant to cooperate were hung from the office windows over the coke pile and threatened with dropping. Luckily, the coke was there, breaking the fall of the odd unfortunate who slipped from the pissed up interrogating officer's grip.

Didsbury had a Scottish detective sergeant who took exception to liars and wasn't prepared to play the precursor game, of nice cop, bad cop, cup of tea etc. He went directly to full on interrogation and all the pain that entailed. He always preferred to give out a good kicking often before their name had been uttered. I had a 20-year-old in custody. I arrested him at his home after finding stolen property in his bedroom. These items were from burglaries, a serious offence. But not worthy of hanging or any form of torture. For reasons known only to myself, having spoken at length with the boy's distraught mother, I decided on my Sunday soft interviewing technique, not often taken out of the 'box' but necessary on this occasion. The good Jock could not believe my soft interviewing technique and decided he could bring the interview to a speedy conclusion and we could then hop across the road to the Royal Oak. Before I could tell him that the prisoner's mother had warned me of his epilepsy and that a fit was likely if too excited, the psychopathic Jock slapped him off his chair to the floor, then in a nimble fashion usually associated with Highland dancing, stamped on him. Despite my protestations and shouting, he regarded me as soft and bent to pick up the trembling prisoner by his clothing to 'give him another one.'

In his pre-planned manner to haul the shivering wreck to his feet, he bent down with his head within reach of the prisoner just as the epilepsy detonated. In addition to spraying the Sarge with foam, he grasped him by the hair, screaming and frothing constantly, and also kicking out. Our Scottish hero, was clearly taken aback and a trifle ruffled, shock on his face was visible as he had never experienced such an assault in all his service and because of the tight grip he was suffering and I mean suffering he was totally helpless; personally I had not been so amused at the antics of a prisoner since the trouser fouling incident at Newton Street, which by now seemed so long ago.

The room was full of the CID's finest all pissing themselves and some of whom eventually attempted to prise the prisoner's hands from the Sarge's curly but balding locks which already had the Bobby Charlton comb over. The victim relaxed as time passed and eventually we were able to release his hands, sit him down, and give him a sweet cup of tea. A doctor was called and we left the newly plucked Sarge to spray what was left of his hair in place and explain why the fit occurred with some Enid Blyton style of excuse, which of course was totally accepted by the doctor.

Other stations had their own brand of confessionals and, as a result, the detection results were noticeably striking. Today, all detentions are booked on entering the station. The prisoner's rights are read and he or she is interviewed by two officers and the conversation is tape recorded. There is no opportunity for any aide-memoirs, and when they do occur they are generally caught on CCTV in the station or 'shopped' by some two-faced little sprog in his futile attempts to skip up the promotion ladder. As a result it is common knowledge amongst the criminal fraternity that saying nothing results in a charge being dropped unless the evidence is immediately overwhelming. As a result they are often released on police bail to continue pillaging and raping, for that matter, whilst further inquiries are supposed to progress into the original offence. In other words, they can go on about business with a backlog of legal debt.

Detection rates have plummeted in recent times and while the methods we used were extreme, they worked. They protected the innocent public at large, which really was the objective. Today everyone loses. Morale in the police is very low. Officers at the pointed end are badly led and always open to criticism and even disciplinary action, which can easily result in dismissal. As a consequence officers 'on the ground' do not get involved. On television at the moment are many programmes with titles such as Road Wars, Police Camera Action, Night Beat etc. They all feature uniformed constables and sergeants, usually chasing stolen cars and arresting the drivers, most of whom are usually black, often Asian and under the influence of drink or drugs or both. Such programmes also feature incidents, where officers are the victims of unbelievable abuse and even threats, all on film and with them taking no action at all. Such abuse is a clear public order offence with a power of arrest.

Such zero tolerance was commonplace in the city but we found during the wonderful 'experiment' that the C Division generally stood for abusive banter and as a consequence attracted little respect or even fear. We continually marched such offenders into the charge office. They were often juveniles and required their parents to attend before they could be bailed. The station was often bulging with such little bastards as we had to wait for the parents to leave the pub. Because of their age they could not be put in a cell and lounged about wherever they could.

The C Division had become tired with the constant abuse from juvenile scrotes who were rarely arrested. The influx of fresh blood for the Home Office experiment included many officers not used to taking crap and so they constantly arrested them in order to give them the slapping the parents never did. It was the ultimate inconvenience for parents to come out of the pub or off the nest to collect them and as they waited they were all sat on a long bench and then the floor in the charge office.

Of course it was a ball-acher but not as much for us as for the parents who usually gave them another hiding which today would be child abuse.

Having moved all the mavericks to one division, it was hardly surprising that the crime rate rose as many of them practiced the dark arts learned on other divisions. Coupled with the lack of supervision, the streets were not actually policed any better than usual after 3pm when the local cinema opened. At any time throughout the afternoon and evening the standing area at the rear of the stalls was full of officers as were many of the seats during the quiet times. The night shift was unable to use the cinema which closed at 11pm. They had to stroll the streets until refreshments at about 3am unless they made an arrest.

After the refreshment period, the 'few' slept off their meal in the cellars of Mill Street amongst the heating pipes. I was happy walking the streets until I finished my shift. I had many arrests, purely to pass the time and the most unmemorable for petty offences and some for Disorderly Behaviour. As I have said, on the A Division, there was a low tolerance level for rowdies, drunken behaviour and cheek. The hard-pressed officers of the C Division became accustomed to such behaviour on a much wider scale and tolerated it. There were innumerable youths and young men from the council estates frequenting places of entertainment, behaving in what they saw as an acceptable manner which was tolerated on the C Division, but would never have been permitted on the A. It may have been cowardice, a quiet resignation toward rowdies, or it might have been overlooked for the sake of maintaining a presence on the streets to deal with more serious incidents. The locals saw the extra policing as an opportunity to take the piss out of more coppers.

We didn't see it that way and got amongst them, told them to move on and shut up, prodding them ever so slightly to aggravate them further. In not taking the hint, they were arrested for Disorderly Behaviour and inevitably banged their heads entering the van. Should their unruly attitude continue in the van, they were charged with police assault for the usual reasons. Our arrests caused considerable amusement with the charge office staff who were quietly impressed with our labours and team work. We were of one mind. But that was then not today.

To The Dogs: A Territorial Dispute

One early morning I declined the boiler room sleeping period and did the unthinkable. I walked through a large gypsy caravan encampment, grouped illegally on a cleared and undeveloped bomb site. They were causing no real concern. Older travellers usually caused little trouble. They travelled the area, laying 'temporary' tarmac, lopping trees which would then die, and stealing scrap metal. Pikey offspring were a different breed and were responsible for many more serious criminal acts in the area, often involving thefts from derelict buildings that caused gas escapes or flooding, as they attempted to prove their worth to their equally wayward parents.

No one was about at 4.30am except the dogs. Gypsy caravans always have dogs. Not being a Pikey, and not being another dog, they treated me with suspicion, giving me the usual inspection. Suddenly, led by one large heavily scarred dog, they surrounded me, and formed a tightening circle around me. Some were snarling. Some had not yet the courage to snarl, but the pack psychology soon kicked in and each of them showed some measure of teeth. The large scarred dog appeared quite intelligent. I guessed he had won a few battles and had earned the right to be the pack leader. He was clearly the alpha male and knew what he was doing. Plus, he had numbers behind him. With these calculations going on in my head, to say I was concerned was an exercise in understatement. I had never been frightened of dogs, but had the sense to realise that now might be a good time to start worrying. I think some of the dogs sensed this and became emboldened, snarling in practice attacks. It's something you can smell. I tried to contain my alarm, at least to keep the smell of it to a minimum. Bristle flourished amongst them. I wasn't prepared to see how bad the situation might get and decided to take the initiative, to challenge the big dog, alpha to alpha. It's not an uncommon thing in police work, to mix things up a bit, taking the occasional challenge to its conclusion, especially when you're young and challenges always have a slip of glory in them. This was a bit different. This was not a bluff. This was the testing of the great male imperative between the species.

I slowly pulled my truncheon from its hold and kept it concealed until the big dog made another lunge. His 'four wheel drive' failed to gain the necessary adhesion on the dusty ground, and reverse was not an option. The blow to the head floored him. But he made an attempt to get to his feet. The other dogs stopped in their tracks. Again, the order of things is quite simple. In an instant, I was back on the attack. I went to the ground in a normal wrestling move, grabbed the stunned and yet brawling dog by the scruff and battered it to death. I made chase on another dog and the pack scattered. I slid from the site with the residents no wiser, continued with my walk, and reported the incident at the station to the resident sergeant. I believed these dogs to be dangerous. I expected a full turnout to capture the other dogs, with the RSPCA, and armed marksmen.

"Leave it alone, son. It's not worth the trouble with travellers. Deny any knowledge, whatever they say. Well done. We all have wanted to do that over the last 10 months." Sarge uttered something else and got back into his newspaper. Days were more interesting, just because the streets were so well populated. It was easy to get to know the local ravers. They were either divorced, separated, or the old man was in the nick. I lost count of how many sat opposite me in a pub or even the station, with no underwear and responded to a quick remark, an eventual little grope and cuddle, but rarely sex in the daytime. It appeared to be a local sport, to have a neighbour burst in through the open back door in the hope of catching the local 'sheriff' in a state of undress with her laughing pal. I was caught out until a quick 'lesson'.

On the day shift I put in a request to work from the sub-station at Beswick Street. This was an interesting little nick on a council estate with all the perks. The added bonus was that it had bicycles. Not any old bicycle, but typical sit up and beg, large wheeled, black cycles of Dixon of Dock Green fame. I was struggling to get to the YMCA to train and being an ex-cyclist at Middleton Wheelers, I jumped at the chance to cycle around the area. These bikes were never used. There was no one else at the nick with any interest in any form of exercise other than drinking and shagging. I had to buy a pump and oil for the chain and, to the amusement of everyone, I disappeared into the morning mist. They even gave me a rare radio and I became the next best thing to the van, breathlessly answering the occasional emergency call some beats away.

Cycling from Beswick Street was only on the rare morning and day shifts - most of the time I was on nights and walking the beat. It was a totally boring experience on nights, but once dawn was showing, and I don't mean the leggy little Scot at number 24,the streets started to warm up. One early morning I was walking the rows of terraced houses and back entries when I heard a strange rattling noise and shouting from a nearby street. Running round a corner, with steam coming off the Doc Martens, I came upon an old man with his back to me, holding a long pole, with flexible metal lengths on the end, which he was banging on a bedroom window. I could hear shouting from the bedroom, and grabbed the culprit from behind. We nearly broke the window but that would have paled into insignificance, compared with the heart attack I nearly caused. I had never seen a "knocker up" before. I couldn't apologise enough. During these 'ancient' times alarm clocks were a luxury and this chap was paid to wake people up with his pole, if you'll pardon the expression.

The crime rate continued to soar and the experiment was coming to a failed end when we had to investigate a very unusual crime. The flamingo compound at Belle Vue Zoo was invaded by young teenagers who painted the pink birds rather fetching shades of green, blue and red with aerosol cans. The flamingos were wandering during the night along Hyde Road. With some difficulty a few of us managed to catch all five. We put the birds into the van and took them back to Mill Street intending to put them in the dog kennels until morning, there to await the arrival of the "birdman" of the RSPCA.

The rear yard where the kennels were situated was always open to the street to allow access for the van to drive in. Kids had removed the kennel doors probably to be used as sideboard doors in someone's council owned palace. This refurnishing venture didn't help our predicament and our only alternative was to put the birds in the radio room with the operator. He was already going round the bend thanks to permanent toffee paper rustling in his ears and no one to talk to. He took to the flamingos straight away and in no time they mumbled as he did. They slept a great deal of the time and he fed them on sandwiches from the refreshment room. It was a marriage made in heaven.

The serene picture of contentment couldn't continue. Into the charge office marched a local Captain Mainwearing, who, whilst arrested for drunkenness at the British Legion, had broken a window when ejected by the steward. It was only his insistent pompous attitude that got him arrested and this attitude continued at the Charge Office counter. This was not a person to chastise in the regular fashion; he was no harm, too old, and quite entertaining. His undoing started when he insisted on complaining to the 'highest officer in the station.' This was the signal for a PC to climb onto another's shoulders and put on his helmet and wear one of the very long white traffic macs to hide his support. They entered the charge office in front of the drunk and boomed: "YES!" At the same time the befuddled radio operator clutching his sandwiches, the ones used to feed the flamingos, opened the radio room door, shouting for quiet as he did so. In doing this, he disturbed the roosting flamingos, all of which had been happily dozing in the radio room.

The flamingos, in a flash and blur of luminous colour, left the room and entered the charge office floor. This animal flourish would have excited David Attenborough, but it perplexed the drunk. He was attempting to hold the giant officer in conversation and suddenly he was surrounded with a scene from Mary Poppins. There was no such thing as a simple caution in those days and anyone arrested had to be charged. This eventually took place and he was placed in a cell for appearance at Court the following day. At Court, he was sober and totally lucid, which made his complaint of a 10 foot tall policeman and multi-coloured flamingos rather difficult to comprehend. The concerned chairman and his learned bench of magistrates remanded him in custody for medical reports as a gesture of concern as a result of his hallucinations clearly brought on with alcohol or hard drugs. Indeed, custody was ordered in part for his own protection.

Did anyone ever believe him? We never really bothered to find out and continued sending other occasional 'clients' around the bend for the purposes of entertainment. Sadly like all times, the excitement of Mill Street had to come to an end. And none too soon, we were all getting bored and as a consequence were capable of anything for entertainment's sake. The pubs were fed up with being blagged for so much free beer, as were the few curry houses. The sex life remained uneventful. The local women were all so hard and capable of anything that there was the continual fear that we were being set up, on behalf of an imprisoned individual who lived in the house when at liberty. These were the same women who would stagger into the police station, bleeding from facial wounds to complain about an assault by their 'loved one', only to refuse to give evidence within the same 24 hours.

Ding, Dong. It's like a party

I went back to Bootle Street just three months later and my reappearance did nothing for the duty inspector's mental wellbeing. In truth he wanted two things: few arrests and a quiet life. He liked to be surrounded by YES men. I was back on foot involved in more forgettable moments. Arrests and incidents were unending, or so it seemed, and were becoming somewhat mundane. The concern of the supervisory ranks was that our cavalier attitudes had gotten worse due to the lack of supervision we had enjoyed on the C Division. It was clear that several of us were seeking extra thrills and taking ever bigger chances to get them, at the expense of the odd innocent bystander. They were also the same public individuals who remained somewhat puzzled at the police assault charges, which were becoming more common as extra insurance, if a complaint or investigation raised its head. The charge office supervisory officers were noticing this fact and, whilst acceptable only a few months previously, the new breed of inspector was appearing from the county forces, all of whom would prefer to discipline a hard working officer rather than support him through a cursory investigation. The rot of supervisory ranks with no real street experience was becoming a serious factor.

In the midst of it all there had been enforced local training refresher courses, which only went to reinforce the view that instructors were instructors because they were a liability anywhere else, particularly on the streets. There were also probationer refresher courses away from Manchester. I attended one at RAF Dishforth, an airbase in North Yorkshire. The instructors were drawn from several forces and it was refreshing to see that all instructors were full of bullshit and obviously incapable of surviving a throw out in a Yates' Wine Lodge with the inevitable violence. The only memorable incident on one such course was when some tosser threw an active fire extinguisher into Eddie Bell's room. It is amazing how much foam there is in one of those things and how much damage the foam can do. Eddie was an ex-merchant navy man and, accordingly took it all in stride. I felt sorry for him, he did no harm to anyone, he got on with his work and it was only his unkempt appearance and strange stooping gait which opened him to ridicule. On this intermediate course, for some unmemorable reason, the handling of potential suicide situations was covered. We were sensitively instructed on how to deal with someone who was so deranged that he/she was capable of taking their own life. Later in my life, at the age of 50 something I was to learn the depths that can be reached and how these affect one's outlook on life. Lesley my wife of only seven months and my partner of 10 years, died of cancer. I cannot describe the utter feeling of loss and finality. My father had died a year previously, but Lesley's death did not compare. Whilst I never actually considered suicide, I suddenly realised how a weaker person in the face of such sadness could easily take the final step.

It was coincidental that after finishing the course and back in Manchester on van driving duties, we were called to the site of Piccadilly Station which was then under construction. In its centre was a tower crane with a very long jib. By the time we arrived in response to a 999 call, a man was halfway up the tower and still climbing. It was possible he was drunk. His friends were egging him on from the ground to climb higher. Having more experience than the reveller and now being stone cold sober, I compared the climb to my own up Manchester Town Hall clock tower and all it involved in relation to nerve, fear and the possible consequences. I knew he would soon get scared or realise he could go no further, get cold, and come down. He wasn't committing a murder and didn't seem to be a potential suicide.

We locked his noisy friends in the van. He climbed the entire tower to the cab. He rested and waved to a growing crowd of noisy drunks. We couldn't fit any more in the van. Suddenly, he climbed to the roof of the cab and then balanced and crawled along the jib. He soon relaxed, stood upright and began walking along one of the girders of the jib in a rather nonchalant manner, waving and shouting to the crowd below. The crane was the height of a 12 storey building. He appeared to be enjoying this moment of theatre. The girders of the jib, though they appeared narrow from ground level, were clearly wide enough to walk on. The difficulty was that the jib came to an end, but his walk didn't. The crowd went quiet, then there were screams as he plummeted to the ground, landing with a sickening thud and strange squelching sound on the building site. We called for assistance to tape off the scene of the death and cover the bleeding body. His friends were locked up, initially unaware of the tragedy. This then became the scene of a sudden death and initially was treated in the same manner as a murder. But in the light of the circumstances and the fact that the CID had to be called from Foo Foo Lamar's Palace, a transvestite entertainment centre, it was quickly signed off as a suicide. Later it was ruled to be death by misadventure at the coroner's inquest.

Clearly this was not a suicide. The insurance investigators attempted to extract a statement from us to the effect it appeared it could be suicide, that the jump was deliberate. We would not do this. They hadn't offered a bung and, consequently, they had to pay tens of thousands for the accidental death to his family.

On another occasion, with a nameless colleague I attended a suicide call. I will keep the full details and location confidential. We climbed the stairs for the four storeys and out onto the roof. The miserable bastard was standing on the stone parapet, soaking wet from the falling drizzle and threatening to jump. His life had turned to shit. Or that was his assessment. I suppose it had actually. He'd lost his job and was about to lose his house. His wife was shagging away from home, probably with a uniform off the A division as so many were. We talked to him for about 20 minutes. Time was passing and we were getting wet. It was now 2.40pm and we clocked off duty at 3pm. Overtime was not paid for incidents such as this. Believing he was kidding and seeking attention, my sensitive colleague uttered the words which still haunt me and I am sure my colleague to this day: "Look mate, I don't think you want to jump. Let's take you to a doctor. We won't lock you up."

"No, no. I want to jump," he said. My sensitive colleague, looking at his watch, told him to make his mind up, that we finished in 15 minutes, so get on with it and stop whining. My colleague turned to laugh in my direction and quickly turned back when he saw the expression on my face. The poor, unfortunate bastard had gone. We were perhaps his only friends and we certainly let him down. There was no expression on his face as he turned and jumped.

"Fucking hell, I didn't expect him to jump!" said my stunned colleague. He was white by the time we reached ground level, which was more than you could say for the dead victim. I remarked that he would now get overtime just writing the thing up. It wouldn't need both of us and I said I would do my statement the next day. I went home, thinking, with amusement, how the sudden jump would be explained to the coroner's satisfaction. The coroner was actually always willing to lean toward the police report provided, of course, that he had something tangible to 'hang his hat on'.

On the subject of plausible death reports, I remember a 'queer-bashing' that had gone wrong close to the old arches of the original Piccadilly Station. There was a 'cottage' nearby. This was a fond term for a gent's urinal in regular use by homosexuals for meeting and daisy chaining, which is the simultaneous holding of each other's cocks between several little perverts and blow jobs. I have never found the smell of piss sexually stimulating myself, but to each his own. Adjacent to the road and toilet was an area of waste ground, the buildings having been demolished and cleared, but leaving many bricks scattered amongst the clay and weeds. The bashed queer was found rigid in the centre of this site. He had clearly suffered several blows to the head. A murder investigation was started. From the outset the importance of such an incident is assessed with the probability of a detection.

During those days the murder detection rate for Manchester City Police was at 100% and nothing was allowed to spoil this enviable statistic. The general murder investigation lasted for about two days when it was determined that there were no leads and the probable cause was murder, an undetected murder, which was unthinkable. The learned coroner was impressed with the detailed investigation into this "accidental death." It was proven that the unfortunate victim was walking across the brick strewn site. He tripped, banged his head on the jagged bricks, which caused the cuts and bruises, rendering him unconscious. He was found lying next to a faulty sealed gas pipe. He was recorded as dying of gas poisoning. They may as well have stated he had beaten himself to death with a banana. The coroner would accept it and the detection rate remained intact. Fabrication of such evidence was the order of the day. Even today men are being released from prison on dodgy evidence of 30 years ago but of course the executed few have no recourse.

In my day it was common and wouldn't the public confidence in the police be higher than the rock bottom of today if senior detectives had the same values in their fight against crime? It will be difficult for the layman to comprehend such evidence gathering, especially when the end result was the death sentence in some cases. Having been the victim of several mild cock-ups, I am against the reintroduction of the death penalty. Considering the many releases today for unsafe evidence, the posthumous pardons would outnumber any genuine detections.

One night, at about 2am on Princess Street in the centre of Manchester, I saw a silver Mercedes driving toward me against the flow of the one way system. I signalled the car to stop, which it did, perhaps a few yards further on than I had anticipated, causing me to jump nimbly out of its path. I went to the open window, and there he was, the actor Leslie Phillips, looking as if he had stepped straight out of a Carry On film - blazer, military tie, white shirt, and beaming smile. Pissed, but nobody's perfect.

"Good evening officer, how wonderful to see you, got myself lost; these infernal streets all run in the wrong direction, I am trying to get to the Midland Hotel. Could you be so kind as to direct me, old boy?" Directions were not an option. He was too pissed and I told him so. "Oh come on old boy, only had a couple," he slurred with his wonderful RAF Flying Officer voice. The Midland Hotel was only a few hundred yards as the crow flies, but the route included at least three changes of direction and six sets of lights. Being the ultimate protector of the public at large, I told him to get in the passenger seat and I would drive him to the Midland. The night staff were over the moon to see him, and everyone was ecstatic with his final exclamation as he attempted to buy me and the hotel staff a drink. I just couldn't leave, so I had a coffee. "Ding, Dong. It's like a party."

Plain Clothes: It's Much Easier Being Bent When Dressed Correctly

If you were a uniformed officer, you were controlled by the uniformed senior officers. The official view, developed by the self-appointed CID elite was that because you were a uniformed officer, you didn't deal with real crime, unless, that is, by accident and, despite the fact that you wore civilian clothes whilst on duty, you could not claim to be a detective. We still had the old school in those days, the smart suits, raincoats and even trilby hats. In their minds they were the elite and I suppose they were so in our minds also, not knowing any different. The fact was that I was more of a detective, in full uniform than some of the excuses for CID officers in their natty suits. The department was, therefore called The Plain Clothes, strange but there it was and referred to in such a manner in all official edits.

We operated from an office at the rear of the station's public counter and could, as a result, sneak in and out of the building as desired. The art was to grab a charge sheet or a crime report on arriving at the office and then walk about the station and the corridors to bump into all and sundry, especially the supervisory ranks who took pride in seeing one of their hardworkers, having yet another arrest or detecting a crime, which wasn't our job, but if the form was about then use it. In reality most of the bosses didn't know and probably didn't care in any case. Everywhere it was jobs for the boys, boys who didn't know what they were doing, had probably never arrested an angry man but were pleased that some mug was filling the void they left.

There were about 10 of us: assorted constables, a sergeant, an inspector, and later a chief inspector, who all had considerable experience in this department. The Plain Clothes had an existing reputation as resident pissheads, who also drew 'rent' from club owners, bungs from elsewhere and an unlimited supply of booze from the many licensed premises in the city. Such a regime was allowed to flourish because the spoils were shared with the supervisory ranks to a degree, or at least with the ones who had some idea at the actual volume involved. While it took me no time at all to identify the amazing potential for pillaging and shagging the subject of rent paid by club owners in a ranking system from the boss with a big bung to a few quid for the sprogs and of course all they could drink when in the premises was never broached and addressed, especially during one's early weeks. I wasn't spending any money as it was on either food or the masses of drink so an extra bung of a few quid was not a concern.

Initiative was the order of the day. It was a proper word - an action word, aggressive, ambitious. It was not a problem. It just meant a wasted couple of weeks to suss out the rules. And rules there were, with a command structure which had to be respected. This office was like the Mexican Army - all generals, but the last thing on their minds was unnecessary supervision. All the 'supervising' officers wanted was a quiet 'rent drawing' life where they were left alone to pillage the many nightclubs for cash and booze when on duty and when off on holiday have the various villas in Cyprus belonging to the club owners, available to them at a moment's notice. Should the wheel come off, they put it back on with a carefully worded write off to please the boss who was also pillaging, all the usual perks but also some of the finest hand tailored suits from the few Greek tailors in addition to the inevitable holidays.

The perks were an acceptable overhead to the club owners, all of whom were called Chris, or George, which made it simpler when pissed and being grateful. The club owners in return were allowed to open, through the night, until the morning rush hour. As will happen in licensed premises, frequented by all the scrotes and tricky conmen in equal numbers, fights would break out, often resulting in quite serious injuries, which had to be accounted for. There was no such thing as a really upset complainant, even if an ear was hanging off. They had usually picked a fight with the doorman, having been told to behave, only in the main to come off second best with blood and snot everywhere, clothing ruined, ears and noses relocated and just generally beaten up. Today a doorman would be charged with such damage, however drunk the complainant was. During these halcyon days, of beautiful sunrises such matters were treated with the flourish of the Hillsborough Conspiracy and we didn't see the crime in it.

The Chief Inspector would write it up as he felt it should be to pass to the Chief Super who in turn took copies of the report on his next forage about the division, in one of his 'George the Tailor' suits. All the tailors were also called George or Chris for ease of recollection. The 'concerned'

Chief Super would visit the club which the previous night was a battlefield and which showed no traces 24 hours later and met with the owner. With much wringing of hands by the boss and begging for mercy from the club owner the carefully adapted report was produced and the difficulties in preparing such a document which would not be put to the licensing magistrates was produced. Of course next Christmas was covered with a 'few' bottles, a fortnight in Cyprus and spends together with a new suit, sponsored by the club owner as the tailor was by now becoming just a little disillusioned as of course he never had fights in his workshop and no real need for the police in any case. His only fault was that he was fair game as a Greek Cypriot.

Such matters of club violence and late drinking were kept in house, written around and eventually discarded as a statistic once the dust had settled. At this stage in my career I realised I had a God given ability to write off such incidents and as they grew in seriousness I too grew in ability. Whilst at school I had never understood the need for nouns, adjectives, or verbs and therefore never answered any of those questions, preferring to spend all the allotted time writing the essay. It was easy, it was natural and I was always first. The law of the land was different in clubland, however serious the offence, the charge if not totally avoidable had to be diluted. I witnessed the aftermath of terrible wanton assaults by club doormen and warring customers alike. It was impossible to report such an offence in a club at 4.30am when the licence finished at 2am. Of course a report would have to go to the Licensing Magistrates who in turn were also having a pissed up, frivolous existence on the Manchester club scene.

Our perfect existence must not be affected as nobody from the Constables up through the ranks to Chief Superintendent and then onto the Licensing Bench wanted any ripples in their perfect 'bent' world and so it was. The report writing at Hillsborough was born during this period of policing and whilst it was much bigger than anything ever written around before, it attracted the same principles of 'The Police are never Wrong and Must be Believed.' Basically everyone was in it together and we were deemed fireproof and would be believed.

It was easy for me to fit in, I already had a worthy reputation for psychopathic lunacy shown whilst actually making arrests. Despite the drunks' playground which was Manchester we could not only 'holiday' and also had to show arrests and figures in an attempt to convince all the casual observers that the department was actually serving a purpose and doing its bit in the fight on crime, protecting and serving the public as we went along our merry way. Shifts were basically minimum day cover by two men, with everyone else working the evenings which inevitably led to nights and often arriving home with the milkman. We always worked in pairs. I had several partners in my 12 months, but I remember my time with Tony Scanlon fondly. We worked hard and played hard. He is now at some dizzy height in the ranking structure of the police around Oldham.

Our time together involved the work. I was happy to do it, but not totally at the expense of a social life. I would drift off to enhance my sex life and he would have a pint or catch up on his reports. On several occasions, both of us would be strolling alone somewhere in the city, walking to one of our individual rendezvous, when we would stumble over a thief breaking into a car or something similar. These were, of course, arrested and we used each other as a witness. The figures showed we were a hard working pair and nobody suffered or became any the wiser. Work, using the widest definition, in the Plain Clothes Department consisted of four defined areas all of which sometimes blended into each other as we trekked through town, pillaging and arresting as we went.

1. The homosexual act of Importuning for an Immoral Purpose, then an arrestable offence.
2. The loosely termed and enforced licencing laws.
3. Prostitution
4. Street thefts and crime

During these wonderful, formative years it was an offence for a male person to importune another for what was then regarded as an immoral purpose. The law in its wisdom felt that if a man was prepared to enter a gents toilet urinal and wave his dick about in a display of arousal then he was more than likely to engage in an immoral act. Such acts were not only the actual act of copulation and in this case, man on man which still defies my imagination, despite my years of warped heterosexual practices. It's just not the same without the kissing and how on earth can they keep it up looking at a bald head and surely stinking of shit and Vaseline. Homosexuals met in 'cottages,' which I have already explained as actually being gent's urinals. The participants having identified a potential 'lover' probably from the waving erection, would reach into the adjacent stall and masturbate each other whilst stood at the urinal in case an occasional straight guy in need of a piss walked in. 'Daisy Chains' were the end product of them all joining in, where they all had hold of the 'member' each side. Who said romance was dead? Getting carried away, due I am reliably informed to the drifting aromas of urine and cig ends often resulted in actual oral sex. However, they might simply meet and when all the Old Spice, stale urine blended with soaked tobacco bringing all the chemistries and temperature to an agreed conclusion, they would simply leave the urinal together and depart in a car, to perform elsewhere in a little more privacy.

Many were arrested and taken to Court and in my early days, the CPS solicitors were not there in force and evidence was given by the arresting officer. Great delight was taken in relating the sordid details of the offence to the Magistrates, particularly if we had a tweed-suited ex-headmaster who had never experienced any real sexual encounter involving anything other than missionaries. In true Albert Steptoe grimace we would relate all the finer details, often to the amusement of the clerk sat in front of them. Every sentence was splattered with the terms penis, erect, masturbating etc but in such lurid detail that a hush fell over the courtroom. They usually pleaded guilty and often offered a charitable donation to keep it out of the Evening News. Stan the honest reporter of the day was never approached and printed whatever he liked without any such interruptions.

Locking up 'wankers' as 'male importuners, as they were fondly referred to, was the only thing to do on some days. It wasn't that we were homophobic in any real way, it was just that they were there for the locking up. Something I learnt very early in my police service was the fact that, whatever the offence, the arrest and the conclusion, however damaging was of no real concern. It was just a figure and a means to the end of going on the piss. It became a sort of competition amongst us all. To arrest a wanker granted an award of one point, whereas a street theft brought you three. We would stroll the parked car areas in the hope of an early thief, who had probably wet the bed, having had a deprived violent childhood as they so often claimed through their legal aid solicitor at court. In the absence of a bit of luck in the real arrest department, we went for the 'cottages' where success was guaranteed. These guys couldn't help themselves. It was as much an addiction as it was desire, or some combination of the two. The thought of the damage such an arrest would do to the prisoner's family, work, and the rest and for something so minor, was never a consideration. Police work was never confused with horrendous family consequences for the 'victim.' It was just a joke and basically a game.

The wankers were often out and about the cottages from as early as 11.30am. They were usually reps with their own cars and often used them with their newly found pals. Daylight prevented the daisy chains of the dark hours because toilets in the daytime were also used by straights, innocently coming in for a pee. Limited observations had to be taken to differentiate the wankers from the straight members. Knott Mill cottage was a favourite daytime haunt and still is today. Cars remained outside for much longer than is usual to relieve oneself. Inside the importuners were standing in a stall, getting a buzz from the smell and showing all and sundry their raging hard. When anybody entered they turned into the stall until the leanings of the new boy had been assessed.

The only way to establish what was really happening, was to occupy a stall and pretend to be one of the boys and being a proven heterosexual with a well earned pedigree I did not have the necessary hard to wave about. I pretended to be shy and covered it with my hands. (Forgive my referring to that in the immodest plural). Anyway, the act served its purpose. 'Members' were waving in the breeze, and one or even two culprits were grabbed as the others ran hysterically screaming from the entrances at each end. We tended to choose the ones who appeared to have the most to lose. An expensive suit, a wedding ring, a concealed dog collar of a vicar, or even a well-known face off Coronation Street and a couple of those were captured both in my day and after. This usually assured us of a guilty plea, without any publicity, or an instant fine in some cases. As with the parking and instant fines of the uniform days, they had to know a mutual friend, the name was dropped and the settlement agreed, ensuring no comeback or being set up in a sting operation by the Y department.

One extremely hard fought Not Guilty plea came toward the end of my tour of duty in the Plain Clothes. It stays in my mind only because of the inability to rid myself of it. Corruption can do that. Leave little stains on the memory, whether the actual corruption touched you or not and it usually did. We were close to it all the time. But it wears such an acceptable face, such an approved face, a face of entitlement and privilege, it is clothed with such care and diligence, so thoroughly camouflaged, it is difficult to see it clearly. We called certain individuals, 'the untouchables' and they were friends of senior officers, magistrates and the like. Some were friends of ours, being club owners and licensees and actually were easy to deal with.

The place on this occasion was High Street cottage. This cottage had an entrance from High Street and also to Marsden Square at the rear. Three of us were working together. We had no luck in the street thefts department and decided to pull a wanker, so to speak, on the way to Bootle Street for our break. One of us initially walked in, had a pee, established we had some activity and picked the target wearing the expensive pinstriped suit. I walked in, had a pretend pee, and stood there to be given some timely flash of erect maleness. The other two also got the view at differing visits. Sometimes two of us were there, sometimes one.

The victim, we discovered, was a solicitor from Bolton in his 40s. And to say he was not impressed at being arrested was an understatement. He begged for mercy, he threatened us with our careers and then named names in the judiciary. This was instantly, like a 'red rag to a bull.' If we were to let anyone off it had to be due to money changing hands, or a mutual friendship when the payment changed from being a bribe to a gift. Threats were not a consideration. We took him into custody. On arrival at Bootle Street, he was marched to the counter in the usual disrespectful manner. The man addressed the duty inspector, but the inspector wasn't falling for the raging: "Do you know who I am? You will all be dismissed! I know your Chief Constable!"

The outburst brought several laughs and "Oh, sweetie!" from the assembled ranks, who seemed to appear from the woodwork when a colleague's career was in the balance and wild threats were being directed at anyone stupid enough to be involved. It turned out that he actually did know Deputy Chief Constable Hood. Now Hood was old school and, while he never seemed to leave his office for anything resembling police work, he always managed the many town hall receptions. He did, however, know he had to be politically correct. No longer could he say, "No more action" in this matter. He could, however, question the safety of the evidence; promise no disciplinary action or investigation and as a result he would ensure that the complaint from the accused would be quashed.

This was put to the three of us by Chief Superintendent Alec Dingwall, who by now knew me well for all my work. Whenever an arrest was made it was the custom to parade in his office before attending court and relate the details of any arrests. This was known as Court Parade and it kept the boss in touch with any activity on his division. Such a parade proved helpful, in case friends of Mr Dingwall from the nightclub fraternity and of Greek origin had been involved in anything of concern. I was there every day when on street thefts, and received a commendation for 29 real arrests involving dishonesty in one month.

Dingwall clearly took some amusement from Hood's predicament and the requirement for political correctness. He gave us the choice with no pressure at all. I think to the delight of Mr Dingwall we chose to proceed. Perhaps not a great career move, but it was the morally correct decision, the one I preferred over the political one. We had never been offered a bung, we had been threatened and now we were being mildly pressured. We attended the courts where the prisoner was not known by the magistrates and without doubt would find him guilty. He elected the unthinkable of going to trial at the Crown Court to be in front of a jury.

Though it was not so well known, during those days great numbers within the legal profession were sexual deviants, at all levels and often the judges themselves. It is easily forgotten that a barrister is little more than an actor with a law degree. His presence and presentation are vitally important. Paedophiles, rapists, and the like get fairly light sentences from certain judges, but certainly not all, as a by-product. I don't recall the identity of the learned judge in this trial, but the description of fair and impartial could hardly be a feature of his conduct. Throughout the proceedings he unnecessarily criticised the three of us. He agreed with so many misleading questions by the defence barrister, that there was actual unrest in the jury box where the members were openly mumbling at some of the very biased questions. Our complicated coming and goings from the cottage were given in evidence with precision and reputable execution. And whatever the judge and the defence barrister tried we could not be shaken. The evidence remained firm. His Honour was becoming disturbed at the prospect of the restless jury bringing in a Guilty verdict despite the biased summing up he was later bound to give and the earlier explanation from the accused if he was called to the witness box to give his version.

The learned judge, made the extraordinary decision to stop the trial after our evidence and accept a weak submission by the defence council that the evidence was unsafe. It was all he had to prevent the evidence going to the mutinous jury. The evidence was not unsafe as he said, it was faultless – yet the case was dismissed. We were all amazed, but I had a lingering admiration for the strings this chap could pull with his friends in high places. You've got to give him that. Cultivation that thorough takes time and planning and do not be in any doubt that such evolved corruption exists today. And that same corruption operates at all levels of the legal system.

But most importuners went with the flow and, like shoplifters, I had little sympathy for their predicament. Sometimes I felt disgust, but whatever I felt didn't stop me boosting the figures and my reputation. Once again in the High Street toilets I was in the line, playing hard to get as usual, concealing my true lack of interest with both hands. Eventually after a few minutes of amorous glances and when I had done such a good job of driving my new pal wild with desire he suddenly tried to pull my hands away. His head was bent in the area of my tackle, perhaps for a look or even a blow. The heavy slap on the head that I gave him instead, knocking him into the 'piss and cig' ends, prevented whatever amorous conclusion he had in mind. There was no way we were going to have him in our little plain clothes van, dripping and wreaking of piss, so we left him there in tears, shrieking uncontrollably on his hands and knees in the filth of a city centre gents toilet.

What is now the Gay Village was then only The Rembrandt Pub, and further along Canal Street, was The Union Pub which tended to attract the lower end of the gay market, if that, indeed, is possible. Reg Kilduff, the landlord, of the Rembrandt was gay and even he regarded the 'cottage crew' as lowlifes. He had a cottage right outside his window and, as a result, the users would also use his pub. His clientele consisted mainly of unabashed 'queens' and transvestites who frequented the upstairs bar, keeping away from the cottage crowd on the ground floor. All the upstairs clientele had come out and didn't care who knew. The upstairs bar was managed by Reg's live-in queen who was the same 50 years plus as him. Not a man I liked, he was so up his own arse he couldn't use his sphincter plug. Knowing we were straight did nothing for him as he minced the length of the bar, holding his arse together in taking little steps. His lips pouting and eyelids fluttering he would eye up any new gay talent, just to make Reg jealous and we were often called later on a 999 to drag them apart before they eventually kissed and made up. The regular upstairs clientele didn't mix well with the married wankers who didn't know which way to turn. Reg got so pissed off with them, he adopted his straight, God-fearing citizen mode and continually complained that Joe public couldn't get near the cottage and accordingly the council eventually bricked it up.

I will avoid relating any other stories in this vein. There are many of them, it was a culture and not merely a couple of rogue officers, but however pitiful and amusing at the time, they seem to lose something in black and white. I spent a career's worth of time in the police force. I invested my youth in it. Whilst I don't regret the start it gave me and, though the lessons learned were worth the investment of time it took to learn them. I eventually had to weigh all things together; the good, of which there is ample supply, good men and women with good hearts working for sacrificial pay but in the firm belief that they are untouchable, above the public and can do and write anything they wish in the interests of an easy time or even justice on occasions. And there are the imperfections, in the main, the university graduates, career minded, with no concern for reality, which were just too much work in the end. The reckoning was painful. Still is, at times. It tears at the foundation of all you have worked for, gnawing at the root of all you believed. The fact that I left the police is evidential. You can read quite a bit into such a decision, a decision that wasn't easy.

Open to Interpretation: Moses and the Ten Suggestions

Licensing hours were, and still are, a very confused entity and realistically were paid no real heed by the club owners and the plain clothes department alike, provided certain rules and monetary guidelines were followed. You can now drink in Manchester legally for 24 hours, that is, if you are a market porter or a casino croupier, who are allowed special hours. Funny, I never realised there were so many market porters and croupiers in the city. But the actual customers of the club also consisted of journalists, printers, gamblers, ladies of the night, plenty of villains and police – some on duty, some off duty and some on their holidays.

Generally, by some rule, which must have been legislated at some point in time, pubs opened at 11am and closed at 3pm. Pubs were generally managed with little spare cash to pay rent for extensions to the hours of opening. There was no point in staying open because there were so many clubs. The pub reopened at 5.30pm and closed again at 10.30pm, but especially at weekends they often had lock-ins – a quaint custom of locking the door, pulling the curtains and basically pretending everyone had gone home while continuing to serve just as before. This little extended opening venture allowed the landlord the liberty to sell his own spirits and not those from the brewery – hence make a nice tickle by charging brewery rates for wholesale nips

There was supposed to be no flexibility to these opening hours, unless a special extension had been granted by licensing magistrates - for example, a wedding or New Year's Eve. Even if you were not busy at lunchtime you still had to open. If you did not, anyone, including the police and the public, could attend at the Brewster Sessions where licences were renewed annually. All comers could object that the premises concerned were not providing a service. Equally, objections could be made on the basis of numerous police attendances for violent conduct, drinking after time, and many other petty things that are pursued today with vigour.

Nightclubs opened at 9pm and closed at 2am. They could only do so if they provided live music and dancing and, also, a meal - one consumed with a knife and fork. This, in reality, meant a DJ and a hamburger and chips, sausage and chips, etc. Membership was also a must and a membership and admittance book had to be available for inspection.

The reality of the licensing laws was that the 'dual' drinking hours meant none of us really knew the full law because such knowledge wasn't really necessary. The confusion was part of the charm. It worked for everybody. The law was elastic at best. And we gave it a lot of stretch.

Chief Superintendent Dingwall had his own interpretation of the licensing laws and his friendships with Greek Cypriot club owners flourished along with the late night drinking scene. The clubs were everywhere. Each had their own particular clientele, some of which required more supervision than others. Many hard men of Manchester, all very capable but with excellent manners ran the many clubs to perfection. This was Dingwall's main criteria, and the owners were very conscious of this. It is fair to say, there were more than 70 clubs operating in the city in the Sixties. And many became well known habitats of the celebrities of the day with lots frequenting Annabels, Slack Alice, Foo Foo's Palace, Portland Lodge, Cabaret and the Cromford Club. The latter was situated in Cromford Square and operated by Owen Ratcliffe and Paddy McGrath. They were friends and Paddy later sold the licence from the Cromford which permitted gambling to the Playboy Club which opened on Canal Street. On transfer of the licence the Playboy Club recruited Paddy as a consultant – a shrewd move as he'd pulled off the rare gambling deal by having some of the licensing magistrates as regular customers.

There were lots more highlighting the extent of the club culture which operated at this time. It makes one wonder how so many could survive? The flexible licensing hours were obviously a major contributory factor. And the various rents paid were an economic necessity to exist. The wheel came off one memorable time when Bernard O'Sullivan – a 6ft 8ins tall doorman – attended Sid Ottie's club which also had a casino licence. It actually traded as a private members club which encouraged gambling for small sums when actually sums in excess of thousands of pounds changed hands during card games and private bets on the horses. The actual moniker of the boss was Sadotti – an Italian name, but most customers genuinely thought it was Sid.

Anyway, on this particular evening Bernard was refused entry by one of the 'Fighting' Camalleris, of Manchester, who met him later along with another member of the fearsome scrapping family. The result was a dead Bernard.

He already had a steel plate in his skull, and having his head kicked in this latest brawl, pushed medical science a little too much. He was driven to the hospital in a taxi by a driver with a prepared script for the medics. When he was found to be dead on arrival the script had to be amended to Bernard butting the dashboard in an emergency stop situation having refused to wear a seatbelt. This was even before the Jimmy Savile Clunk Click every trip TV advert campaign – but more about that filthy pervert later.

The stories scripted for the dumb driver were a little flimsy and were not in anyway assisted with the discovery of footprints on Bernard's head. A murder charge followed for one of the Camalleris – which was eventually thrown out by a jury, possibly selected from the local populace with some knowledge of big Bernard and his shovel-sized hands. The 12 men, good and true sitting in judgement on Bernard's untimely demise dismissed the murder charge. Dingwall was not impressed at all by this episode of lawlessness in his city and did not wish such a misdemeanor to cloud the oiled workings of clubland or his peaceful existence. In his eyes he feared the Greeks and Cypriots would suspect he'd begun to lose control allowing for more criminality to follow along with the inevitable raids, then tighter licensing laws that would eventually affect the income of all concerned.

The Plain Clothes posse was immediately mobilised to visit all the dubiously licensed establishments – no matter where they stood on the rental ladder. The police had to be seen to be still in control and to give the fresh invasion some credibility a few of the really shitty joints not serving hot food in the statutory seated position and with guests not signing the membership book were closed. Our Cypriot chums had an instant lesson in the licensing commandments as in place before the unfortunate Bernard departed his mortal coil.

The odd stabbing in any club would also cause police concern in the guise of outrage and instant fines, as it drew attention to the loose interpretation of the licensing legislation we were enforcing. There were many stories of violence in the name of in-house security at untold clubs, and while the severely bruised member complained, the complaint was written around and no action taken. Even so many decades ago and in the style of the Hillsborough Conspiracy such report writing thrived and with the untouchable philosophy firmly in place it blossomed into so many much smaller conspiracies. Such Enid Blyton endeavours did not come cheap and most of the senior club owners were summoned to await an audience with the 'Boss' for a public relations dressing down and all that came with it....basically nothing. It was simple PR as long as the correct palms were greased all continued running smoothly.

The sergeant, sometimes the inspector and, of course, all of us minions of the Plain Clothes Department were seen as Dingwall's 'eyes.' We were treated with the necessary respect. The bungs didn't meet a holiday, but we got fed and we got booze, lots of booze, especially at Christmas. In addition, we drank for free in the clubs and even this had a pecking order. We didn't go in the Cabaret, Dinos, The Garden of Eden or the Cromford Club except on rare occasions, usually only to up the ante for the inspector who would then tell the club owner that he would never see us again. We still had plenty to visit.

Later, in my service at Bootle Street and beyond, the university graduates were still creeping into our perfect world like a dose of crabs on one of Liston's

Music Hall girls. They were showing too much interest in the licensed premises and their hours of opening. We were instructed to raid a few as an example of our 'finger on the button' approach, but only after they were tipped off so that the names would be in the member's book; nobody would be very drunk, the kitchen would be staffed, and they would all be eating when we arrived. The club owner would appear at court and, because of the circumstances of a few friends drinking after time, he would suffer hardly any fine at all. Well, that was from the court. Their local intelligence service needed a little more priming for future incidents.

Of course, even Chief Constable James Anderton would not be fooled by such immaculately run premises and further raids would prove the point. After only a few months we were once again working in conjunction with the club owners. We would plan the raids and then pass over the details. It all grew to a point of principle around the raids with trust at a minimum between all the police departments and the club owners. Later, the powers-that-be – recognising the cracks in the ranks were the club frequenting officers - formed a separate licensing supervision department. They trawled their partially lawless force for a variety of officers who resembled non-drinking Methodists in as many ways as possible.

Years down the line when I started in business I had a wall plaque extolling the virtues of drink with the slogan: 'NEVER TRUST A MAN WHO DOESN'T DRINK'. It stood me in good stead, but on occasions I made a mistake and our non-drinking brethren had me over on at least one occasion.

This newly assembled gaggle of humourless shithouses- dubbed the Hush Puppies - was every inch the proof of this interesting little message. They were spoilt for choice on premises to raid and rumour had it that they worked unpaid hours of overtime – even working weekends off – if a raid on an unsuspecting little 'drinker' was imminent. They chose such ridiculous hours because they were swamped with licensed premises operating out of the rather restrictive licensing hours.

They had the entirety of Greater Manchester to go at, as if the 70-plus premises in the centre wasn't enough. What a dream. All they wanted to do, as with John Cooper, was the work of the Lord, but with the virtues of non-drinking aimed deliberately at the club owners, rather than the unfortunates who consumed untold amounts to the point of arrest for a variety of offences.

They raided many and, on some occasions, serving police officers were found drinking, sometimes with an unsigned police car outside. They were reported along with everyone else, often resulting in unemployment. In the early days the Hush Puppies had a few real policemen, who, for part of the proceeds, would tip us off and we, in turn, could tip the club. They would then take part in the share out. The owner wasn't prepared to risk a court appearance and closed the club on time. It took only a few amazingly straight clubs when raided to provide suspicion of a leak.

The cat and mouse game continued. Sometimes we were able to establish where the raid was to be and sometimes we were not. This did not do well for our long-term financial relationship with the club owners. The chinks in our pardoning armour were showing and consequently the 'gifts' were drying up - which in the fuller picture was a cause for real concern in our 'camp.' There was not a great deal we could do and the club owners were becoming aware of this.

As if they couldn't make matters worse, they did with alacrity and recruited Inspector Peter Jackson. In the belief that his control of the Hush Puppies would improve his promotion chances he became absolutely fanatical with his raids and even had a 'fifth column' to feed us false information. We would then tip off the wrong club and the club raided would be caught bang to rights with all offences you could name – from non-members, late drinking, no food service and any number of what to him where heinous offences. Yet in the cold light of day, so many years later they appear to be unbelievably childish and pointless in the fuller picture of law enforcement. Later in his less than illustrious attempts to rise through the ranks he was to fall foul of the very bosses he crept up to and was subsequently dumped on from a great height. It was the old story of someone protecting themselves and it really couldn't have happened to a nicer chap. Sadly, by then it was too late to celebrate as all the damage had been done with his over-zealous policing of liqueur licenses.

His obsession for secrecy and misinformation had yielded results. We were embarrassed to the point that we even showed leniency in the area of our gifts as he'd had such success. In the time honoured fashion of Enid Blyton and the early report writing epidemic – which was clearly witnessed by the Hillsborough mob on other Forces – we resorted to blatant fiction. We told the club owners that we were having trouble identifying the people coming into the clubs as they were being brought in from other Forces to get the evidence of late drinking and all the other 'crimes' earlier revealed.

Thus we told them to treat all strangers with suspicion and to just serve their previous customers who they knew. If they had already allowed strangers in the premises then they would have to serve them and close at the appointed time according to their license. We had some initial success with this scam for a while and it probably helped police the clubs better than all the raids ever did. In those distant days policemen looked like policemen and were often quickly sussed. The counter measure to this when the Puppies realised they were being rumbled was to observe the clubs from outside. This made our job much easier as we could identify their observation points and then telephone the club owner with the heads up.

The clubs in recognising the potential loss of readies would then get the doormen to pop over and offer them a cup of tea – to let the Puppies know they knew of their presence and that was generally enough for them to go away and pick on someone else.

Of course, this had a poor effect on their overall thinking and in fact it really pissed them off as their successes dwindled, but even so they still managed to maintain a certain level of success. The fact remained that too many licenses had been granted in the interests of a very wet Christmas – while some in authority were looking forward to a new suit, or a lengthy sojourn in Cyprus courtesy of a club owning chum. Ultimately, too many difficult and pointed questions were being asked and as a result Dingwall couldn't stand the strain and retired with an unblemished record, an overflowing cocktail cabinet and a wonderful tan.

As the Hush Puppies grew stronger, they imposed a directive that police were not to use the clubs for any reason on duty and be aware of the closing time if off duty, as serious disciplinary proceedings would follow. This short-sighted directive had an adverse effect on real policing which was continuing in the likes of the Serious Crime Squad as these venues were used for a considerable amount of business with informants. It was a regular occurrence to get an informant pissed and have him then part with some very interesting information which often resulted in arrests for real crimes. Now such meetings had to be planned to fit in with the licensing laws and villains by their nature operated largely outside the law – if only the Puppies understood policing they could safely have been let off the leash. Those important informant meetings now had to be planned and this alone created a level of mistrust as both parties believed they may be the victim of a set-up. The gratitude from the club owners was becoming more begrudging and they even turned turtle and ran their clubs to the rule and in doing so informed on 'friends' who were continuing with the old ways of flexible licensing laws.

Informants were everywhere. Club owners were informing on club owners – with the Cypriots informing on the English and vice versa. Ernie Derbyshire, who ran The Russell Club, informed on everyone as often as possible and in all directions. All hell broke loose and questions were being asked from a great height. The objective of our office was to keep friends with the heavy tippers, who of course were the Cypriots. The English club owners had their own friends in 'the job' and consequently were not tipping us at all.

Club owner Les Sim was number one man in the city and got more than his fair share of assistance from all and sundry. He had some nice clubs, where wives would be welcome and officers and officials could relax and as a result he attracted licensing magistrates and several higher ranks within the Force – who wouldn't be aware at all of our little war with the Hush Puppies. Les had a club on Wood Street called Annabelles and one on the upper floors of an office building in Brazenose Street both off Deansgate, the nicer side of town. Once I had left 'the Job' and became a spender Les became a good friend – sadly he's now passed away, but the legend lives on.

He had absolutely no time for the Hush Puppies and little for the Plain Clothes, but tolerated the system by giving out a few drinks. One night the Wood Street premises were raided after 2am and the very secure and heavy front door was locked. We rang the bell. No reply. We rang it again and once again, no reply. We rang it insistently, ad nausea. We irritated ourselves almost. Then we heard the pleasing voice of Les Sim: "We are closed. Fuck off!"

"This is the police. Open up!" we bellowed back. The retort from Les came with pure comic timing: "I don't care who you are. The licensing hours apply to everyone!" This little comment echoed with the ring of a piss-take rather than Les upholding the law. He was told there was information that he was serving after hours and we would obligingly break the door down. He replied cheerily: "It will cost you a fucking door! Now piss off, and leave me alone!"

He was a man of few words. The door took a lot from the sledge hammer; it had about three five lever Chubb locks, bolts, and a metal frame. As he said, it did cost a new door, locks, and bolts - all that and an apology on top. Once inside, there wasn't a real drink to be seen. All 20 were drinking tea from nice little teapots, served by a big, but extremely nice doorman. Les had been tipped off and we loved it. The boss wasn't so wild.

Les was a true legend. The raid at his third storey club didn't fare any better. It was another nice club, where you could take your wife, a friendly magistrate, and even the Stipendiary Magistrate John Bamber, if he was still standing so late in the day. This club was doubly secure. It had an electric lock door at street level, which admitted the customer to the stairway. This was covered by a camera, so the bouncer could see the quality of the incoming person. The door was at the top of the stairs, leading onto a small landing, and it opened outwards. It was metal-lined, metal-framed, and very thick. In short, it could not be broken into. In the door was a small opening window. With strangers, the doorman could ask for membership proof, even though cards were never printed. Should the prospective punter claim they had forgotten their membership card, the alarm bells rang and they were refused entry. This card trick was the perfect ruse to deny entry without any trouble and they could kick at the door all they wanted.

The entry system was, on the other hand, not perfect for a raid scenario. One raid went so badly that the raiding party was locked in between the two doors with the lights out. During that time the clientele escaped through a prepared exit into the next building and out onto Queen's Street, right next to the Queen's Club operated by Dougie Wellsby. Doug was another of the city's legends - a very hard man, of the old school. On entry, profuse apologies for the power failure were issued, drinks were offered, but refused, and off we went with our tails somewhere up our arses.

The club scene was going wrong in so many directions and we would have to find new pastures to engage ourselves. We would find uniform officers waiting outside one of the better clubs, hidden in the shadows, waiting to swoop on an unsuspecting drunk driver. The initial motive was not always clear. It could be an instant fine but, on occasions, the subject was a magistrate or a senior officer. The magistrate was given a difficult few minutes so they would remember the face, before they were allowed to continue. The production of a warrant card meant only a wave goodbye. Such action could later lead to prosecution for such a charitable act and the usual confidence we all had in each other was rapidly draining. The rest of the public were fair game and had to be treated on their merits. If they didn't seem genuine, they were arrested for drink driving. It was all becoming too dangerous and, even less, a career move. To be honest, I never put myself in such a position because I felt the breathalyser was below any of us in any case and hypocritical, to say the least.

In Plain Clothes we were trying to look after the interests of our 'clients,' the club owners. If drivers were stopped more than the average outside a club, they would cease attending, and our "retainer" would stop. In some cases the uniform was as aware as we were of the situation and looked for a cut. The club owner would be told of the pressure and he would give the bung to be passed on to the uniform, which was halved, without anyone knowing, before being paid.

The same law of the jungle applied to prostitutes and we were forced to concentrate in that area. They frequented the same clubs and had 'regulars,' though being constantly interrupted in a nearby deep doorway, or back entry didn't help the repeat business. Part of our duties was the arrest of prostitutes, and through taking an 'on-the-spot fine,' in the manner of the punters, we got to know them well. They were never happy parting with their well earned cash, and so everything else was on offer. The uniform either accepted or moved to another area. The club owner was again grateful to the police in whatever form, for ensuring that he remained busy. They had to take all sorts of assistance if they were to continue with late opening. Despite Anderton's later attempts at cleaning up the city, late drinking and prostitution still thrives. There is now a culture of "shop everyone in the police." Care has to be taken.

Girls for Sale

The oldest profession will never be stopped. It can't be stopped. As long as a man can pay for it, he'll pay for it. As long as it can be sold it will be sold and in any form that pleases. It has an old presence in the world. It also takes many forms...especially today. It wears many disguises. The higher you ascend up the food chain, the more cunning the counterfeit, the more ornate the disguise. Though sex is the issue I'm writing about, prostitution is not just sexual. I think I've done a decent job so far in exposing some of the whores I have worked with over the years, those who sell their otherwise noble services for a bung. I guess if I'm truthful, we were all pretty much whores. It's an old infection, like herpes, that you just can't rid the body of. But that's a philosophical consideration, a semantic debate. The kind of prostitution I'm talking about now doesn't take that much to understand; it's the sale of sex – simple as that. Pay and somebody gets laid, or some variation on a theme. No lofty metaphors here to dazzle or perplex. No writer's tricks to misdirect. Just old fashioned sex and that's plain and simple.

The entire city centre area oozed and festered with prostitutes, but particularly around Liston's Music Hall down an entry off Market Street. Unescorted girls for sale were often 'fined' in doorways. The fines were usually immediate, collected in the form of a good wank or an enthusiastic blow job. This example of a fine, quick thinking juris pudenda gives a new meaning to the term 'hard' working or maybe even 'unlawful entry'. The beat cop, in his relaxed state of smiling sexual convalescence, would sort of stagger happily from one doorway to the next.

Liston's was the grand central station of this type of activity, before the privacy of the doorways became popular. It was really a terrible place. A neon illuminated room with a long bar, a piano at one end, which was one of the only reasons it could be called a music hall. The name helped the image. In such a place, all meanings were fairly loose anyway, along with the women and virtually all the females were prostitutes. Some were well past their prime, though by the looks of them you might wonder if there ever was a prime. The darkness helped. And then, alcohol helped even more. The men were all clients or drunks, usually both and perhaps the odd off duty officer, mingling with the Listons regulars as was their whim as they wended their way home to their loved one.

During these early days the prostitutes used to parade outside, and indeed, inside the Long Bar, which was beneath the Gaumont Cinema. Outside the Long Bar was a gent's urinal (a cottage), so we had the best of both worlds. We even got a free drink in the Long Bar. We used to arrest the new girls, fine the existing faces in the back entry, and also 'pull' a quick importuner, so to speak. It is strange today to see the toilet which has now become a bar. It is even stranger to have a drink there.

Prostitutes are an odd race. They cannot be trusted at all. They generally hate men. They are often badly treated, so why should they like the male of the species? They were clever at saying how different each punter was and how much they would like to see them again. In conversation they would determine if the punter was married and, if so, usually felt safe picking his pocket whilst he was trying to navigate his dick through the pants with the loose legs, amidst the deliberate squirming and general business of feigned passion. Anyone so desperate to pay for a trembler usually had a bad attack of premature ejaculation anyway. To have had such a bad time and then find the wallet missing was the last straw and they usually went home without reporting the incident.

Lewis's store now Primark, is still on the corner of Market Street and Piccadilly. Apart from being a shoplifting haven, it had Lewis's Arcade. Today the store is a mishmash of several suppliers who appear to be renting space to sell furniture, clothing, perfume, and sundry other items. It is not the store it once was. I remember all the windows being dressed and illuminated to give the window contents a 3D appearance. At Christmas, the windows were magical and the Father Christmas grotto was the best in town. In the arcade, the girls of sale used to stand. They were tutted at by the old shoppers, who appeared to go out of their way to do so. Woe to one of the girls scoring and walking off with a man if the local Mary Whitehouse was passing. As everywhere else, we made a show of arresting the odd one. Sometimes there was a deviation from the route to Bootle Street nick. And sometimes they were charged.

Today, the girls parade in the area near Piccadilly railway station. I don't think any of them would be taken up on an offer. They are all on drugs, riddled with some sexual disease or other. The Plain Clothes arrests have been taken over by the uniform in a large police van, marked with Vice Squad to put off the miserable bastards who pick these girls up in their cars, whilst the wife is at bingo. As I proceeded through my various police departments, the girls left the streets and went into the clubs and bars of the many city centre hotels. Only the smarter ones were permitted indoors and the differential between the types became very obvious. The basement of the Britannia Hotel, Portland Street, where in my early years I had given an unsuccessful 'kiss of life' when it was the Watts Building, was a major meeting place for the reps, businessmen, and the girls. The clubs that existed still had a few and the Cabaret Club, still protected by Albert, had many. He did quite well from the tips here and always laughed when I accused him of doing better than we were. But he never parted with any and realistically wasn't expected to.

Nothing particularly earth shattering happened worth relating except a few of each shift always had crabs and the odd member had a dose, from riding bareback in a period when condoms weren't so vital. Then, syphilis was a disaster. Today it is looked on as a bonus in taking the place of its feared cousin AIDS. With the absence of the clubs to 'monitor' we put more effort into street thefts. We always did a considerable amount, but I may have given the impression that all we ever did was totally bent. There are only so many hours you can spend in clubs, prostitutes or generally socialising.

Thefts from cars were rampant. We hadn't the luxury of the sophisticated anti-theft devices of today. Fords, in particular, could be entered with a number of childish methods. The easiest one was to purchase an FT 200 key which opened most Mark II Cortinas, of which there were many. Some beat men also had a bunch of keys and I often wondered why?

On occasions we had seen the same officer 'loitering' in the same area and ultimately we told him to desist in a none too fraternal tone. Reporting them to the higher command was an unthinkable option. If they were seen again they were taken somewhere quiet and given some instant justice. One officer had the sand to fight back and was so badly marked he had to report sick, saying he had been assaulted while trying to arrest a car thief. Instant justice such as this was regularly doled out to shitheads whose typical arrest would take more time than it was worth. They knew the score. No complaint was ever made and the equilibrium stabilised.

The rate of arrests was impressive, even through the good days of the drinking and shagging era. It even improved during the latter months of my Plain Clothes term. It became a competition between each set of pairs and with Tony Scanlon, I had many successes. A great deal of property was recovered from the prisoners' houses, all turned into TICs which then affected the divisional detection rate, but not as much as the fabricated figures of the CID which were based more on shoplifted items than actual criminal offences and burglary.

The CID Hierarchy: Still Learning

The CID office was situated on the second floor of Bootle Street Police Station, immediately above the canteen. In its large general office we each had a desk or some form of writing surface. A constable - not a detective, but often so tricky he should have been - answered the phone as admin clerk and dealt with all the incoming correspondence and internal paperwork. There were two separate offices, one for the detective inspector and one for the boss, the chief inspector.

It is not necessary to name names here and indeed if I did there could be 'fallout' from some of these disclosures. Such a department is the breeding ground for bent file preparation, the scripts for perjury later in court. The Hillsborough Conspiracy would have had its humble beginnings in such an office. Such exotic file preparation as Hillsborough was a daily occurrence, but certainly not on such a grand scale and generally for the good of the general public. The 'Enid Blytons' of the CID blossomed in such a 'greenhouse' of innocent little shoots, growing quickly as they were chosen for the promotion trail, through the Force of choice initially, along the winding promotion trail and then onto other Forces to the eye watering ranks of Chief Constable etc. As I have stated previously this behaviour was not the action of a 'rotten apple' or a 'rogue unit' of a select few....it was a way of life.

The Hillsborough Conspiracy will come as no surprise to any CID officer serving or retired. What does shock is the enormity of the venture and the fact that the officers concerned were so embedded in the historical beginnings of such file preparation. They were arrogant enough and stupid enough to believe that they could remain so fireproof that they could write away 96 deaths and fabricate many elements of the behaviour leading to the deaths and then corroborate the lies with edited statements.

Having said all that I certainly enjoyed working in this office, I enjoyed the company and camaraderie it brought and the education was invaluable and has lasted until the present day. The two offices occupied by the venerable bosses had wallpaper whilst the general office was painted in glossy shades of whatever was tasteless and left over from previous painting exercises in police stations throughout the city. I can only compare the set up to that seen in the television programmes NYPD and Hill Street Blues; which generally was gross overcrowding, poor dated furniture and a strange smell synonymous with men who tended to consume vast amounts of curry and bitter beer.

There was no vacancy for a full detective, but in any case whilst I was regarded as good for the figures, due to my many arrests and commendations, I was already considered a "loose cannon". Remember I was previously exiled to Newton Street Station, thought of as Siberia in the CID where uniformed men were deposited and never seen again. I was given the rank of CID aide, which was a six month posting, with the intention of being assessed for the real thing. With a few exceptions, the assessment was judged on my being able to do the minimum and appear busy. I would not attempt to blend in too soon. I would not wear a creased suit a size too small, or squeeze a gut too large into a shirt too short and become "a man with a belly," as some might call it with an odd tribal kind of pride.

CID work in the city centre was a sham because the detection rate was always present, in the form of simple offenders such as shoplifters and car thieves, which invariably dropped in the lap of any officer lingering in the office. I thought the life on earners in the Plain Clothes was easy, but this was amazing.

I was surprised, and then maybe I wasn't so surprised, to observe the cozy working relationship between several store detectives and the old hands in the CID office. These were the veterans of a Life On Mars style of working – experts all at the good cop, bad cop. While shoplifting is now a real business to the perpetrators of today, back then it was generally a day out for the many unfortunate women suffering the menopause, a bizarre side effect of which was often petty pilfering.

A shoplifter was arrested and transported to Bootle Street where various CID officers jostled for the privilege of dealing with the prisoner, especially if he or she looked like a professional: smart clothes, middle-aged, educated accent etc. The prisoner would be interviewed by the CID officer, who, with little difficulty, would persuade an admission of the theft for which they were arrested. They were then informed that it was clear this was not the first time they had committed the offence. Information would then be gathered as to former offences; when, how, what, and where? Initially all prisoners denied other offences until it was explained to them how their home would be searched and they would then risk additional charges. However, if they cooperated and admitted to their history before too much time was wasted, all other offences would be considered TICs. These were explained as offences admitted which would be listed, 'taken into consideration' but not used by the courts to impose a greater sentence. Many offenders were very disappointed at the result of having TICs, but by then it was too late and sometimes they were even imprisoned as a result of their frank admissions. Before an agreement regarding TICs was reached prisoners were often told that if they continued to be difficult, their spouse, or their mother (if they lived at home) would also be arrested and charged with handling stolen property.

Of course, they soon became cooperative. The prisoner, the store detective, and the officer all went to the home and removed everything, many items often still boxed. Then they returned to Bootle Street where the interview continued, an admission statement was taken, the prisoner charged and released on bail to appear at court at a later date. All the additional offences would be typed onto a TIC form to be signed at the court hearing. A realistic number of offences, admitted and taken into consideration made a tremendous difference to the divisional detection rate. Each offence admitted was treated as a detected crime. But if, by the time the prisoner appeared at court he changed his mind - he would then be threatened that the case would be adjourned for further inquiries and charges, based on the statement he was stupid enough to make in the first place, would be laid. The prisoner, with little option, then usually changed his mind back and cooperated. The entire matter was then dealt with, often with a minor sentence, however many TICs he had admitted to, but of course there was always the unfortunate who suffered the wrath of a 'bitter' magistrate and was sentenced to prison.

In such a situation where prisoners were bailed to appear at court at a later date, they always had the opportunity to discuss their plight with an associate who had fallen foul of the TIC system or indeed remained uncooperative during the initial interview. There was always going to be the odd one who would remain confident that if he admitted nothing then what could we do? We could do quite a lot, actually. And did.

The same posse would go to the house and search. Anything still in a box would be seized 'for inquiries' and indeed any ornaments that didn't appear to blend in with the décor of a typical Salford council house. The key and general rule of thumb was that if Coronation Street's Stan and Hilda Ogden didn't have it, then it must be stolen. Stan and Hilda had flying plaster ducks on the wall, a plastic tablecloth and milk in bottles on the table. Crystal decanters and bronze figurines just tended to clash with their 'seconds' flock wallpaper and utility furniture. Kenwood Chefs, sandwich makers, kettles, and other luxury items in the kitchen were also seized. The prisoner, obviously going ballistic, was again given the opportunity to cooperate at which time they either admitted to the stolen items or produced receipts. Often he did neither. The goods were never returned and it all went quiet as the prisoner clearly thought he was testing his luck. As a result the arresting officer would treat such goods as lost property and after the passage of say two months it was regarded as that of the finder with the arresting officer regarding it as his.

Any property recovered either by admission or seizure was held in the Station Property Store. Once the case had been dealt with, the property was signed for by the store detective. Half of the property was returned to the shop by the store detective, usually the cheaper items, whilst the rest was shared between the store detective and the arresting officer.

The TICs were shown as separate offences, even if 10 items were stolen during the same pillaging run. The matter could easily involve 30 detections. The statistics department that prepared detection rates for publication made a half-hearted attempt to make the detections look genuine. The detective inspector on each division made an art form of submitting a few connected to the same offence over a period of time. In doing so, it kept the detection rate at a figure similar to the previous month. Today, the Statistics Department tries a little harder, but so do the arresting officers. It wouldn't be appropriate to have such a wonderful chain of detections put down to the level of reality.

In the days when Stockport was a borough force, the town's CID was always a prime area for ridicule and the term 'Stockport Detective' meant a real 'wooden top.' In the not too distant, they yet again proved they shouldn't be allowed in the real world. They were so amateurish that even the Statistics Department noticed and held a major investigation into their TIC conduct.

If a cheque book was stolen, this would be recorded as one crime of theft. It would remain so until the culprit was apprehended. Each stolen cheque that had been used was magically turned into a separate offence of 'obtaining by deception' or 'using a forged instrument, etc., depending upon the actual circumstances. This became such a lucrative source of TICs that Bootle Street formed a cheque squad, so numerous offences could be squeezed out of each single book theft.

As if all this existing fabrication wasn't enough, the CID inspectors throughout the city and even other forces up and down the country appointed a man to visit convicted individuals in prison. He was to go as the prisoner's pal and yet inform him that he knew there were still some outstanding offences against him and that he could be rearrested on his release at the prison gates. Shock. Horror. "What can I do?" The friendly CID person would then come up with the TIC option. He would inform the desperate prisoner he could have them all on a form, they would be written off to him while he was in prison and he could leave with a clear conscience. As the crooked individual had nothing to lose, he would admit to let's say 20 offences whether he had done them or not and so on and so forth. Certain professional criminals would commit offences throughout a county and even adjoining counties. In such a large area there were likely to be several police forces, which would then be split into various divisions. Wherever the prisoner said he had committed the other crimes, they would be put against unsolved matters on the division of the detective officer actually interviewing the prisoner.

This was of course another popular method of bumping up the divisional detection figures and with the added bonus of involving more serious crimes, such as burglary. Prisoners who were arrested for a burglary would again go through all the TIC script with the arresting officer and all the potential consequences if they were not admitted. There was often a 'one born every minute' scenario and because he admitted to so many offences he was not dealt with at the magistrates courts with a minimal sentence but sent to Crown Court for sentence as the magistrates felt that as they could only impose a maximum six months imprisonment, it was insufficient. This obviously caused some considerable and inconvenient alarm as there was always the danger that the prisoner would blurt out the details of the travesty of justice he was party to.

Again, he was talked down to calmness and it was explained to him that he would have to shop someone else, a friend, or even a relative, for something serious and we could then quietly inform the judge of the cooperation. The judge would then remark that in taking all the matters into consideration he would be lenient. Today, imprisonment tends to be avoided, but in my day, as a matter of course and without hesitation, they were given prison and could be heard hurling abuse at us all the way down to the cells, under the dock, before being given their first good hiding by the stalwarts of the prison service to shut them up.

The statement made by the prisoner during his period of openness, related to many offences all over Manchester, Oldham, Rochdale, and even Blackpool. Had we worked so hard to clear up the crimes of other divisions? No. We had drawers full of undetected crimes and there were not enough hours in the day to deal with TICs, let alone real police work. It was a simple matter to substitute one of Oldham's with one of ours, in a rewritten statement and again, enhance our already wonderful detection rate. And also illustrate we were detecting the serious burglaries in the centre. We often had a store of many more admitted burglaries than actually existed.

Interviewing a prisoner was an art, and several of the stalwarts were very experienced. It was common practice to beat confessions out of a prisoner but not all of the detectives resorted to pain, especially if mental cruelty and game play was an option. Here again I can make comparisons between the way it was then and the way it is today. There were no taped interviews. Prisoners were not told they could have a solicitor, so if they didn't ask, they didn't get. It was a simple matter to casually engage them in conversation and explain how difficult it could all get if they didn't tell their story. This scenario worked much better if two or more people had been arrested together. One could be played against the other. It was a sport, only better, because we could not lose. We casually put confusion where trust might have been. We saw friendships splinter. We watched commitment fail, with the drainage of colour from their faces, or seething rage. At times it beat the movies. The criminal sense of devotion, even the petty criminals, has its breaking point.

Each of them would be put into separate rooms, then interviewed, and their version written down. They would then be left alone for a time, and when we returned, each would be led to believe all sorts of fabricated things. We were looking for one thing, and usually got it. The interviewing officer would, by intimation, allow the other to believe he had been blamed for everything. He did this without really saying anything, because it would have to be adapted. After reading a lot of unconnected notes and plenty of 'plumber's-style' intakes of breath, the officer was usually able to get all the prisoners sufficiently concerned to make a statement against each other. If only one cracked, that statement was shown to the others. Then more statements would follow, especially if they were told the one who had made the statement was likely to go free, giving evidence against them.

The good cop, bad cop scenario is not something taken from TV shows, it actually happened. You have to remember that most villains were petty criminals, not really hard cases they just thought they were as they strutted about their own localities bullying the school kids and pensioners. Once in a police station with real nutters and hard men they changed quite dramatically as the 'interview' wore on. Between the men working together, it really didn't need rehearsing or discussing.

Both the prisoners were sat in separate rooms. The one who appeared to be more experienced, would be left alone with a none speaking guard. In the other, the first officer would burst into the interview room, no tape recorders remember, and aggressively shout at the prisoner in a loud but controlled manner with the projected expectation of an immediate admission to all. It never happened that early. He would leave the room and could be heard shouting and knocking furniture about in the next room, so that the prisoner could hear but not understand. In walks the nice guy with two cups of tea and sits down in a friendly fashion, relaxed, lolling over the chair and even scribbling on the paper left for the prisoner to write his admission on.

The tense little hero opposite, relaxed with a quizzical look on his face clearly believing he had got away with the denial and it wouldn't be long before he is again strutting pensioners out of the way in his Wythenshawe local. A slight error of judgement and as we sipped our teas, casually mentioning the reason for his arrest in equal parts to the health of his mother and dog. His cocky little shithead face, pursed lips of his permanently sneering scrote's mouth illustrated his total belief that he was on top. Well that was until 'the raging bull' stormed in the room, shouted at me for being so soft with him and knocked him straight off the chair, onto the floor where he immediately picked him up off his feet and held him against the wall. It was difficult to tell at this stage, who was making the most noise. The arresting officer with his pantomime baddy act or the terrified scrote screaming in fear and searching with his wide open eyes around the room for a friend.

There was his friend looking equally concerned and asking the mad man to put him down as he was sure he wanted to help. With this he was thrown to the floor yet again, his fingers stood on with yet another loud verbal warning of last chance as he blundered from the room yet again, slamming doors and shouting. Not quite the way he thought the morning was going and the need for some hasty admissions to the good guy. The resulting statement always tended to be biased against the accomplice who in this case was in a nearby room.

The entire scenario started again with his pal in the next room who had heard the louder elements of the 'interview' and immediately came out with the usual bullshit, of I know my rights, you can't beat me up, I want a solicitor, I'm saying nothing. Clearly, an expert who warranted the need for more diplomacy. 'Well Sir, what have you got to say?" I'd ask in such a charming manner, but before he could repeat the I know my rights act, he too was knocked off his chair and stamped upon. He was dragged to his feet, punched a couple of times and sat down. No more messing, he was shown the other's statement, which implicated him in all as the ring leader.

It was then a simple matter to get the full statement from him along with stolen articles from both their homes. British Justice at its best with yet more to come from the Stipendiary Magistrate John Bamber who refused to hear of any solicitor criticising 'his' officers and making any suggestion of such violence.

A similar interview took place at Platt Lane Police Station where the investigating officer, being the bad guy had the prisoner pinned to the floor whilst he jumped from a table aiming his feet at the prone face intending to part his legs at the last second. All went well. Really, the screaming victim played his part, the officer jumped, legs parted but oops, he had miscalculated the depth of the jump and landed on his collar bones breaking both of them, leaving all of the officers in a stunned silence already typing up a charge of police assault and the rest. Again Uncle John Bamber would not hear of such an accusation and even admonished the solicitor for making up such a fanciful story. The officer in question went onto the dizzy heights of her Majesty's Police Inspectorate and then to be the commissioner on some Caribbean island, clearly recognised for his devotion for police work.

There were many detectives who were excellent at this type of interview. It's like sitting at a poker table with a great hand, I suppose. You still have to play the game, weigh the bluff, even if it's your own, watch the tell tale signs and so on. Equally so, there were others, better at writing verbals, the Enid Blyton version of an admission. The great prevarication and the old equivocation - that is the beauty of language. It is so pliable. The art in writing these admissions was to sit with an arrested person, never mention the offence, and ask questions about his family life, his girlfriend, his kids if any, his mother, whether he plays football or supports a team, the car he drives, the colour, and so on. Verbals were used in quite minor situations, but the five star scripts were saved for the real professionals who thought the caution, "You are not obliged to say anything . . ." actually meant that you didn't have to say anything.

In the statement written by the officer you would blend the circumstances of the offence with real detail from his personal situation which had been noted in the casual friendly conversations which had taken place, whilst tea was being served by the 'nice cop'. For example, if the offence was a burglary, the verbal might read: "I climbed through the first floor window. As I was doing so, I slipped on the window sill and thought I had ruined the next night with Denise (the prisoner's wife). We climbed out with the gear and I tried to get into a blue Cortina but it wasn't mine (prisoner had used his own car to drive to scene and how would we know this was a blue Cortina - what are the chances of that?)" And so it went on into a full statement, blending in fact from the casual conversations with the fiction of actually admitting the offence, which in truth had been denied throughout the interview.

At the Crown Court, the prisoner gives his version and still protests his innocence, saying it is all lies. "Well then, Mr. Smith," pontificates the prosecution barrister, "Are you saying that you did not commit this offence? That you did not sell the property? And, in fact, that you are totally innocent?" Then in a totally sarcastic tone of voice adds: "Why is it then, that you mention your wife, that you admitted her name is Denise and, 10 minutes ago, admitted supporting Manchester United and that you were driving a Blue Ford Cortina? Are the officers psychic? I put it to you that you are admitting half of the facts in your interview but not the parts that incriminate you and you actually expect the jury to believe that version?" They usually didn't and another professional criminal was off the streets.

It must be remembered that police officers, in committing acts of perjury, as this was, were doing so to keep the equilibrium. There were no extra wages, commendations or anything and in fact nothing but aggro if the wheel came off. This was a public duty and the public got the benefit.

Today, verbals still take place, but usually before they arrive at the station for interview. When on the premises they are told their rights, fed and watered, offered a doctor, and lots more, except the opportunity to admit the offence. When interviewed, the conversation is recorded and usually in front of a solicitor. The interview is often so poorly conducted that the prisoner is not charged, but released on police bail to a later date. That way, he is free to carry on with his labours, committing more offences until, by some chance, there is enough evidence to get to court - usually, with the aid of an informant.

If it was not for TICs on every division, the true detection rate would be highlighted and it could be easily seen how little actual police work the CID complete. Crime reports take so long to update, the slower members can hide behind this duty. CID officers are not allowed to mix with the criminal populace in licensed premises and, as a result, they are not able to recruit informants. The only way was to offer leniency to a prisoner was on the understanding he would "shop" someone else for something more serious.

Part of the CID social life was nurses' nights at clubs or even their flats, both of which tended to lead to a sexual encounter. I was put off by nurses, at least for a few days when I was engaging in my fabulous chat up lines with an attractive little number who was clearly wearing perfume, but despite the generous use was failing to conceal a hospital type cleansing smell. I remarked on the fact and she explained that she had just been laying out a body and had not had time to shower! A lot of policemen married nurses and a few married policewomen, which I did back in my uniform days. Policewomen tended to be divided into two defined camps, namely clear lesbians, fat arses, short hair, cocky walk and the like or absolute ravers most of whom frequented the beats of Bob Davenport or Barry Good. I was fortunate in preventing my young lady from falling into their clutches.

We were having a healthy sex life without marriage. I recall how on one occasion whilst at it like rabbits we broke the settee arm in her cousin's lounge where she lived in Gatley, Cheshire. I wasn't proposing marriage as expected at the time. I was happy with a few pints in Sefton's Pub, Alec Dingwall's local, and a legover on the cousin's settee later. I'd arrive at Cannon Street Bus Station where the number 26 terminated from sunny Cheetham where I lived with my landlady and her prison officer husband and go to Piccadilly where I caught a further bus to Gatley in the south of the city and at this time still in Cheshire. It is now in Greater Manchester but, of course the pretend 'Cheshireites' continue to show their address as in Cheshire. At his local Dingwall always offered me a drink which I accepted. The landlord brought it down the bar and of course paid for the boss' generosity. I suppose it's the thought that counts.

My wonderful existence wasn't to continue. She told me she was pregnant. I was only 21, but marriage seemed all right. I wasn't enjoying living in digs and in any case in those days young men did the honourable thing. The wedding was arranged. She probably wasn't pregnant and said she had suffered a miscarriage which in retrospect I doubt, but we went through with it. We had two great kids and we were together for 24 years, so no real complaints there.

CID duties consisted of a parade meeting in the morning when all the crimes of the preceding day and night were discussed. The crime reports were allocated by the chief inspector and everyone went out to visit the complainants at the various shops and offices, if burglaries had taken place. In my case, I only got thefts from cars and thefts of cars. A simple phone call was all that was needed and an explanation of how cars are usually recovered and returned in 48 hours. I would then go visiting with an old hand, an experienced CID officer who was basically passing time before the army of shoplifters appeared. The professionals from Heywood and Liverpool and the menopausal crew from Cheadle - a nice little village in Cheshire - which for some strange reason had well above the national average of shoplifters of the middle-aged commuter belt persuasion. The supposed purpose was to see how 'real crime' was dealt with.

Forensic officers were called, to scatter fingerprint powder about the scene, more as a public relations exercise to look like we were trying, rather than any real attempt to catch a culprit. Sometimes mug shots were shown if a suspected offender had been seen. The unfortunate and trusting complainants, trudged to Bootle Street station to examine the photo albums, again purely as a PR exercise to make them think they were helping and more importantly, that we were trying. The real reason was to find ways to show, how the dismal investigation could be written around, without any real police work, in the knowledge that we were always able to fall back on the many stored TICs.

Writing up a crime report was a form of creative writing. Everyone knew this from the bosses down, but it was as important as the Ten Commandments as it had to be correct in every detail. The initial visit was reported and all the services, such as fingerprints and photos were listed. The report would go to the inspector to write back with questions on procedure for you to reply with the answers, not necessarily true, but what he expected. This 'clerical badminton' would continue for about a month until the crime was filed as undetected or until a TIC fell into the picture. The type or location of the offence didn't matter. The complainant would be over the moon at the success, and the image of the police would be preserved for yet another day. It was all a public relations joke.

It is clear from the numerous media reports that nowadays a great deal of public confidence has gone in the police. The feigned interest we showed is not even visible. As we proved, it took little effort and meant so much. For us in taking part in each PR exercise, we often met the means for a little earner in the form of a present, having established the name of a registered owner of a car or even a casual sexual liaison with a grateful complainant.

A lesson in recycling: The Drug Squad

Drugs during the late Sixties were not the real problem they are today. They were just a joke in the news media – used by those on Top Of The Pops and on TV generally. Remembering the cultural upheaval of the Sixties - the psychedelia, the music, the hair, the attitude - these are the things we associated with drugs. Not the dealers, the guns, the armies of youths on mountain bikes, young but armed, or the massive amounts of it with street values of £1M plus, so common in today's narcotics marketplace. It's especially evident in areas of reputation in Manchester such as Moss Side and Cheetham Hill, but the real rot and expansion has emerged from the leafy suburbs of all our cities.

On the outskirts of Manchester places like Alderley Edge, Wilmslow, Hale Barns and even Didsbury have seen phenomenal drug abuse among the well-heeled. The all fur coat and no knickers brigade that hang around following the many professional footballers about the scene – like lap dogs spending their last few quid on over-priced champagne and cocaine – which has often been dealt from only the next street, saving the risk of being mugged in the more notorious areas.

Today the drugs scene is a real problem, but the drug we saw mostly was cannabis. And it came in different forms - resin, bush and Lebanese gold, which is a dry powdered version of the resin blocks, which was also then pressed into blocks. The blocks weighed about two pounds and were often stamped with a gold seal as a sign of quality - an Afghanistani or Jamaican kitemark so to speak. This was smoked by all quarters of society, from young businessmen and women, the student population, hippies, and, of course, the blacks, hailing from Jamaica and other picturesque Caribbean islands – though often with slightly sinister under bellies away from the well trodden tourist beat.

I would like to make it clear that I am not prejudiced. I have many black friends. I am white and proud of it; they are black and equally proud. I don't mind a black calling me a white bastard, honkey, etc. I objected to it in the police because it was a statement of disrespect. I still have absolutely no regard for the present day young black and white scrotes - who beat up old ladies, snatch their bags, and, generally put fear into the law-abiding populace.

Besides marijuana, 'Speed' was also in wide use. This consisted of 'purple hearts' (5mg of dexamphetamine sulphate). These were a lavender coloured tablet, the same strength as Dexis, the yellow version, also of a 5mg strength, and apparently more accessible and popular, giving rise to several fashion terms, relating to Speed as it was known. Dexy's Midnight Runners, a popular group in the early 80s, was a typical example and they named the band after Dexedrine, a brand of dexamphetamine popularly used as a recreational drug among Northern Soul fans. The 'midnight runners' referred to the energy the Dexedrine gave enabling them to dance through the night.

Also in wide circulation were 'Bombers,' a coloured capsule ranging from 10mg to 25mg of Speed which were also called 'Black Bombers.' All were amphetamine-based drugs, legally available on prescription as a slimming aid that became available to the dancers as proceeds of chemist shop burglaries, which were becoming a problem.

The black variety was the most popular, it was the strongest at 25mg and therefore, the consumer could stay awake much longer, dancing the night away in darkened black painted cellars, swimming in condensation and sweat at clubs such as the Twisted Wheel and, of course the all nighters at Wigan. They had to stay awake to dance. They did just that, and with an amazing dexterity. Few had any regard for the 'come down' as the effect wore off. The lack of attention to detail could be fatal. Sleep was vital. In my uniform days, I found 'Wheelers' (Twisted Wheel customers) asleep on benches and in railway stations, even in the middle of winter. Suffering from the next best thing to hypothermia and the wildest hangover ever, they were sent off to hospital, as they had often suffered side effects, burnt themselves out with all the accompanying heart dangers, or perhaps they could not wake up. At this time I found it very surprising that these youngsters did not drink as today. They popped pills and drank gallons of water – which came full circle when the warehouse Rave scene hit Britain in the 90s. Back in my day such abusers were in danger of becoming unconscious and, perhaps, choking on vomit, or even succumbing to the rigours of a typical UK winter, wearing just a smart shirt and trousers.

Sleepers was the title attributed to the users of strong sleeping tablets such as Mandrax, which was eventually withdrawn. The hippie dropouts and registered drug addicts took Mandrax and then staggered about all day, fighting off sleep which was the 'kick' they got from this drug. This strange phenomenon was difficult to understand and I had little patience with the users. I would often wake them up in my own charming manner by perhaps pouring water over them in the crappy little cafes they often frequented.

There was a comparatively small amount of registered drug addicts who had found a supply of a Class One controlled substance, such as heroin. Addiction was inevitable and common. They had to be registered with a doctor and were prescribed with Methadone, a heroin substitute, in the belief they were taking steps to cure themselves, but without the doctors' knowledge they were taking cannabis and sleepers. Even then there were numerous do-gooders who were taken advantage of by these people. These unofficial support bodies thrived and, eventually, gained some financial support from charities and, I believe, even Manchester City Council at one stage. They tended to be staffed by what I saw as middle-aged hippies, all flowing skirts, flowery shawls and they had often endured an arduous morning jam-making or plaiting beaded hair. They had themselves suffered from the effects of drugs, had beaten addictions and felt they could lead the rest to being saved in their wonderful little world of incense, flowers and Bob Dylan.

It is true to say, the hairy-arsed brigade of psychopaths, collectively called the Drug Squad had little faith in such a rose-tinted outlook and we made every effort to prove them wrong in whatever manner we found appropriate for the set of circumstances we were in at the time. The truth is that these misguided souls were even hiding drugs for the users in the mistaken belief that they were weaning them off the drugs. In such proven cases they were also arrested and charged with possession of drugs. This had a significant effect in two important areas, the drugs were removed from the streets and the shocked 'carers' would return to full-time jam making. However, caring they once were, they now had a criminal record and were immediately unsuitable for such work, especially if completed under the auspices of a church or a charity.

LSD is a hallucinatory manufactured drug and the quality of such a drug played a great part in the after effects. The taker either had a 'Barbie pink' nice hallucinatory moment, or with the cheaper versions they often experienced horrible hallucinations. Sometimes to the point that they believed they could fly, often jumping from a window to prove the point. The occasional fatal consequences were often enough to dissuade great cross-sections of society from experimenting.

The Drug Squad office appeared to be an afterthought by the police hierarchy, which didn't really understand the drugs issue. They treated it like 'a phase' kids were going through, ideally they wanted to ignore it as there was no immediate 'rent' opportunity. Yet as it grew they decided to jump on the USA bandwagon – our cousins across the Atlantic were dealing with it seriously so we followed suit here. We almost always ended up following the American lead – years later when George Bush went into Iraq his puppy Tony Blair took us into an unjust war to ride the coat-tails of the Yanks.

Back in the late 60s, having seen various media and US television reports, the powers that be thought it would come across as forward thinking, clever, and even trendy, to show they were addressing the issue. As a result a couple of what must have been over-sized store cupboards were changed to the Drug Squad office with a few very aged chairs and tables chucked in, a sign on the door and a few filing cabinets. The newly formed Drug Squad hub of operations was situated in Whitworth Street Police Station, on the eastern boundary of the city centre in the same building as the fire brigade which serviced the central area. The location was 'the pits' it was just a gesture to be bragged and boasted about, but never visited by the media or anyone as it was regarded as top secret and completely confidential. The over sized cupboard could barely accommodate the Drug Squad – a TV crew would have had to shoot footage from the corridor.

The constant alarm bells, claxons and sirens which resulted from the many turnouts of the Fire Brigade would have given Health and Safety of today a nightmare due to the excessive noise we suffered. Today, we could have applied for ear plugs and we'd probably have had to hit the suspects harder as we'd forget we were wearing them during the old fashioned wet towel interviews when not being able to hear the confessions clearly.

During these times we were satisfied with our lot in a department, which was doing what could only be loosely described as police work. For in reality, absolutely none of us knew what we were doing and perhaps, this period could better be described as an elongated method of suicide. As we ate rubbish often in the form of goat curry in every shebeen (unlicensed drinking dens in the cellars of generally Jamaican owned houses), we drank at literally no charge to the verge of alcohol poisoning. For in addition to being unlicensed our Reggae rooted hosts often brewed their very own strong alcohol usually from potatoes to a traditional recipe possibly based on Ireland's Pochin – another home brewed spirit that could provide a near death experience. The 'Pochin' recipes in Moss Side dated back to the days of slavery and the free time on the plantations. The slaves grew potatoes for sustenance and whipped the course sugar cane from the plantation owners. The latter was quite tough to come by in Moss Side in later years, but Tate and Lyle refined it and sold two pound bags in the supermarkets.

Whitworth Street police station was actually situated on the A Division, but serviced the C Division, which was basically across the road and just opposite two of my beloved point duty stations at Piccadilly and Store Street and Piccadilly and Whitworth Street - a very technical point duty operation which sparked considerable difficulty to the uninitiated and much mirth to everyone else. In the opposite direction and completing my point duty Mecca was Whitworth Street and Sackville Street, a cross roads, which is now on the edge of the Manchester University complex, once the Polytechnic and bordering what is fancifully referred to as The Gay Village, frequented by homosexuals of both sexes and served by a multitude of excellent bars and dining establishments. Inside waiters can be men dressed as women and bouncers can be shaven-headed women who think they are men. It's a multi-cultural 'cess pit' as former Chief Constable James Anderton might say. But virtually everybody there is having a good time, straight gay or Tranny and I don't mean the dog patrol van. En masse they hold their mini-skirted or tight trousered legs together and the place is packed with plastic lovey greetings and more air kissing than at an air kissing convention. Suffice to say it is an entire quagmire of what might be deemed to be morally wrong according to the book of Genesis. We barely walked through this area for fear of a bolt of lightning from God and there were often enough helmets on display without us bringing our big ones along Canal

Street. Anyway, such is the Gay Village area, where condoms are placed on the bars as free promotional gifts, just like the boxes of matches you find in certain straight establishments. I know of many straight people who frequent this area for entertainment, but for me the constant shrieking and masculine/effeminate laughter does become irritating.

In relation to point duty and my exalted rise to the drug squad I couldn't help looking back and recalling the amusing memories. I really don't want to appear addicted to point duty and perhaps become boring in extolling its virtues, but it really was an amusing duty though only if treated as such. In every case it was not and the sadness creeps in when the individuals treated it as a chore – you should always try and be happy in your work. Be it beating a confession out of a bad 'un, fabricating a crime form, or doing a bit of point duty – it all goes so much quicker if you retain a sense of humour. Some humourless tossers, sorry officers, could study for promotion, climb the greasy pole (not the Gay Village variety) and perhaps finish in the Y Department or even end up as Chief Constable of South Yorkshire with a knighthood to boot.

It was vital to be noticed and therefore point duty entailed wearing a long white, heavy, dimpled plastic raincoat – which was worn in true Uncle Fester style down to the ankles as protection from all weathers, dirty water, oil, urine – the latter as people often took the piss out of the wearer. Yet to further the appearance as that of a total tosser the officer then had to stand in the middle of the road, waving at passing traffic.

The wearer would often hurl abuse at drivers for the crime of driving too slowly, or simply show off to passing females by halting the traffic in an instant to wave a stunner across the road. Authoritative hands were raised in a training school stop signal, to allow the girls to cross, sometimes suddenly and, sometimes, with the end result of a collision caused by hasty braking. I remember vigorously waving traffic on along Whitworth Street in both directions only to realize too late that there was little room between two buses travelling in opposite directions. The spinning top effect which followed as I reappeared from the moving buses was, as an afterthought, amusing but at the time could even have proved fatal. My gleaming white Fester coat was covered in grime from the sides of both buses as I was spun out of the rear.

Collecting my shiny raincoat from the charge office cloakroom one day, I passed the main desk, just as a female army officer, in full uniform was claiming her lost suitcase and, for the report, was checking the contents in front of about six officers which, in any situation was a lot for the task at hand. Of course, the station clerk had already searched the case and was aware of the contents. At breakfast he had related the tale in the canteen to all the other time wasters with office jobs. When told it was being claimed they all flooded the lost and found area clutching bits of paper as an excuse for being there. I joined the throng, purely as research, as the scene was now better staffed than some murder investigations.

By now I could see the contents consisted mainly of kinky leather underwear, a strap on dildo and several other hand held vibrators. All of us in our childish schoolboy manner hung on every word, sniggering and having fantasies about the 'gear' and the action it had seen as the user, who was certainly a big girl, with an upright stance and general military bearing retrieved her possessions. The army officer, in typical stiff upper lip fashion expected of the British Army, never showed any embarrassment, perhaps there was some pride. And she exhibited a demeanour and expression which clearly screamed 'You fucking wankers' as the surrounding horde tittered and giggled like a group of schoolboys.

I was moving onward and upward but was certainly surprised at the Drug Squad headquarters. It consisted of two offices - one smaller for the sergeant, and the larger for us, all 10 of us. At the time of joining, the sergeant was Brian Hill, the singer mentioned earlier, who ended his life in an argument with a tree. The tree won. He was a detective of the old school – grey-haired, sly, not necessarily twisted, but effectively bent at times to achieve a result. He had a great personality and was a great cabaret singer. I only went out with him on a couple of occasions, to places like the Albert Pub in the town centre, or a working men's club near Mill Street on the east of the city where he was famous for his 'Mardi Gras' rendition. Some of the older regulars remembered me from my uniformed cycling days from Beswick Street and had a gentle piss take. Some of the younger scrotes were still suffering from an attack of the Enid Blytons resulting in a brief term of imprisonment or hefty fine and, were not so pleased to see me.

We all attended his funeral at his unfortunate passing. I still remember how upset his wife was, and how attractive. I think this was my first experience of a young and violent death of someone I had known and the devastation it caused to loved ones and colleagues alike. Brian's position was filled by Hoagy Carmichael. I still do not know his real name, he was a big bald man who looked less like a Drug Squad officer than you could ever imagine. He was 6ft 2ins tall with a heavy build. He always wore a suit and looked more like a bank manager than yet another psychopath. He soon fitted in and was dishing out confessional assistance to the unfortunate 'clients' like the rest of us. His use of a wet towel to the balls with his own very heavy flick action became well known, especially at court where it started to get attention a little too often. A parade of drug abusers began appearing and explaining the reason for their initial guilty plea - which by now had changed to not guilty once they'd had the free legal advice. It was only the disbelief of the Stipendiary Magistrate John Bamber that gave him the little support needed which allowed him to continue for as long as he could.

A man who never really got involved in dirtying his hands with the crapheads off the streets was a slimy bosses' pal I'll call the Handler. He was the best of friends with the bosses. He was close to Brian Hill and now he was sucking up to Hoagy. Being such an afterthought, the Drug Squad was put under the Special Branch Chief Inspector, who knew nothing about drugs, didn't want to learn, and only wanted to play at James Bond all day. The Special Branch was, of course, designed to infiltrate political activists, agitators, the IRA, then in its infancy and any other wayward group, which could have threatened the Crown. Why such a department headed the drug squad still escapes me.

The Handler also spent a great deal of time with the Special Branch bosses – in part we believed this to be a Masonic connection – certainly with DCI Dougie Heywood, and DI George Dampier, but not so with up and coming Catholic DI John Stalker. Stalker was following Superintendent Stan Shaw's promotion trail, for reasons unknown to him, to keep him at work whilst Stan always appeared to be missing from headquarters during the afternoons, reappearing when the George and Dragon closed. The George and Dragon is no longer and has been demolished to make way for less attractive buildings on Bridge Street in the city centre. It was situated close to the new site of the Crown Court and was where Stan and the rest of the CID hierarchy met with the YES men of the Manchester Evening News and some of the crime reporters of the national dailies, who still had printing presses in Manchester, such as the Daily Mirror and the Daily Express. The Daily Express crime writer Don Blankley was later to be caught importuning in one of the cottages in the city centre. After that episode Dirty Don was no longer welcome in the higher sanctum for cocktails. He had clearly had one 'cock tale' too many. Perhaps if he had been arrested for bank robbery, burglary or caught shagging any underling's wife, he would have been okay, but not importuning. It just wasn't done. And it gave rise to all the furtive imagination which could possibly be brought to play of Blankley actually shagging an arse, or giving a blowjob around his enormous beer inflated nose.

Now the Handler's duties were two or threefold and perhaps even more as it wasn't really clear what he was supposed to do, or where the boundaries between police duties and his other activities began and ended (I suppose, in retrospect, this was just like the rest of us). Despite his imposing height and portly frame he was issued with a mini-van. Not just any mini-van, but one specially adapted for his arduous duties. The van was caged in the rear so that the Force canine drug detector Benji could be transported without slavering affectionately over his lord and master. The dog was a black Labrador, complete with dubious claims of a pedigree. I have had several Labradors and never seen one the size and shape of Benji with his short legs to waddle along on. He was a friendly little dog with the countenance of Royalty as he sat in his little cage, peering out of the window with peculiar interest at any passing hordes, pedestrians and traffic alike. He would ride about all day in the back of the vehicle, get out now and again for the odd pee and also at various premises that were being raided, say hello to everyone, and then fuck off, having done absolutely nothing.

I often imagined him waving a regal paw on route to the next raid. When he arrived for action though excitement just wasn't in it, his tail would go mad at the sight of his colleagues from the Drug Squad, all of whom had worse breath than he did having had yet another night on the piss and goat curry. He loved the interesting smells and would happily wiggle himself about our feet before we entered the premises in question – focused experts we were not. His affectionate greetings were carried on with the unfortunate householder as he was shown the search warrant. I used to be quite adept at finding drug stashes. All the scrotes believed they were being so clever and original by lifting a floor board, hollowing out a book in the bookcase and even wrapping their gear in cling-film before putting it in the bottom of the chest freezer. The search completed the gear found, never by Benji, but off he'd trot wagging that tail of his behind the Handler, who was yet again embarrassed to the max by man's best friend.

Before I forget the main reason for such a disappointing result from our canine drug sniffer was in the main down to one of the lads – Paul Giles and the manner in which he took part in the dog training. Giles had fur-lined gloves, summer or winter. This had something to do with him not catching anything off those, "dirty bastards." I always thought he meant the druggies, but later I wasn't so sure and thought he meant the rest of us.

There was no such thing then as face masks and rubber gloves, and some of the places we had to search should have been condemned. It was a wonder that the Black Death didn't break out again in Didsbury. It was the Handler's practice to hide a piece of cannabis, about two inches square, somewhere in the office for the dog to find. If the Handler hid it, it was always at nose height. If Giles hid it, it was usually on top of a filing cabinet or picture. The Handler would say: "Seek, seek!" The dog would, in turn, say hello to everyone who was sitting around, sneaking bits of food to Benji. He'd basically greet all his pals in the office, tail wagging saying hello to everyone safe in the knowledge we would sneak him crisps, bits of sandwiches and even pizza from the previous night. Funnily enough never the goat curry, but the rest would be carried in the pockets of the troops just in case anyone got over their hangover before lunch. Giving him food was of course totally forbidden by the Handler. His handler was intent on his training and wished to prevent any confusion between food and cannabis, which to be honest happened all the time, even on our searches.

But even worse than the food was Giles and his fur-lined glove – which would be inside out on his right hand with fingers operating like a puppet. They would be wiggling away at Benji from under his left arm and the deluded drug detector was so distracted that finding drugs wasn't ever an option. He would go mad for the Giles' glove trick – even if the dog at some point had wanted to find the drugs it was that engrossed in everything else that a discovery was never going to happen. The Handler wanted to make the find and couldn't believe the dog's numerous failures and loyally always came up with the excuse of: "Well, he's young and needs training."

It was a popular theory that drug dogs were actually given drugs to make them addicted and therefore they'd find the drugs much quicker in the belief they would be given a joint. In Benji's case the theory seemed to work in relation to food rather than cannabis. He could detect a half-eaten butty from the corridor outside the office and go straight to the culprit with the best bacon barm from among the crowd of the 10 of us. Benji was ultimately so bad at his job that the Handler got another dog.

I can't recall the replacement animal's name, but it was equally useless, again due to the abysmal training from his untrained handler, a fine selection of sandwiches and Giles' glove puppet. The dogs were used in many searches, in the main as a public relations exercise. It was good for the public to see them scurrying about sniffing in all the necessary corners, but little did they know that they were seeking a fur lined glove and not a controlled substance.

We had a detective constable named Bill Kerr, who was totally dedicated to the job. He believed in what he was doing and had a few informants in the cannabis ring operating around the city. He often had search warrants and the information was usually very accurate. We would search houses, flats, and shops on these warrants. Often there were 10 of us, including Benji and the Handler. While I continued to have above average success at finding the drugs – the dog team would have better luck at Crufts with an exhibition of disobedience. This happened much to the mirth of every man and his dog in the team, except for the Handler, the man with the dog at the fore of our squad search in each and every venue.

I often found narcotics heavily wrapped in the fridge, or freezer, to prevent the dog smelling it, or so they thought. Had they seen Benji and his pal on any given raid, they might not have gone to all the trouble. They could have put it on the floor and he still wouldn't have found it.

With that in mind I recall when we raided a large house in a nice residential area of Salford. This was not the norm by any stretch of the imagination, but it was Bill's informant who had come up with address so we felt it had a chance. The bosses were nervous of this and urged particular caution, especially with regard to looking like policemen and not the usual down and out look we preferred. There was not to be any kicking of the subject and farting was to be kept to the minimum.

The occupier was a 40-year-old Jewish businessman in the clothing trade. In true Jewish fashion on reading our search warrant, he went ballistic, screaming and demanding his wife call his solicitor. He was going to have us all sacked as he knew the Chief Constable. This was now a trifle worrying for us, but for Bill it was a seriously bottom twitching moment with real squeaky bum time if the informant had fed him a dud as it was his tip, his warrant and above all his spotless reputation. He took little comfort from our comradeship in showing the support we did and pretending to phone the A Division to find him a point duty posting.

As we walked through the front door, we congregated in the large hallway and looked around in disbelief at the quality of the place and thinking Bill must have had a brain storm and had made a terrible mistake, worse still the kind of cock-up from which his career would never recover. Benji in his usual friendly fashion was running around saying 'Hello' to everyone, including the yelling householder and his wife who complicated the issue by having what appeared to be an asthma attack in the middle of all the shouting as it transpired she was allergic to dogs. It may have been a ploy, but the Handler had never experienced intelligent and 'connected' people coming up with such a tirade of complaints with possibly fatal consequences for any career. Benji, oblivious to the noise, was still actively seeking Giles and his glove puppet in the middle of this pantomime.

Incredibly and within three yards of Benji and indeed all of us - who were still gaping at the furnishings and curtains together with the fine paintings and impressive ornaments as we felt more and more like we'd made a terrible error – there was about a kilo of cannabis resin, all black and shiny, with a gold seal and no wrapping, whatsoever. To a dog trained to find resin, this would smell like the room was full of the stuff, as indeed it proved to be when we opened the hall cupboard where it was not even concealed, amongst some letters. Even the smokers among us could smell this enormous stash, as it was sweating in full view as now was the householder, who not surprisingly had quietened down. Benji on the other hand blanked the stash, still wagging his tail in the direction of Giles and his trusty glove puppet. The search immediately transformed into the fun they usually where, as the odd expletive, the loud laughter and the echoing fart filled the room. Poor old Benji once more showed his true worth – here was one highly misinformed and misplaced hound.

At the end of the day the information was great and Bill had another notch to his credit from his very impressive secret source. For Benji, it was looking more and more like early retirement. I spoke to Bill Kerr a few years ago and he was then the superintendent in charge of the Drug Squad. It was a promotion he well deserved above everyone else.

One of the Handler's other duties was the inspection of the prescribed controlled substances book and methods of secure storage at chemists. There were many registered addicts, and what a mess they were. They were emaciated, covered in bruises and spots on their typically grey skin. They were a disgrace to the human race and treated accordingly. Chemists, often Asian, tended to treat them a little too casually and were always looking for a quick earner. They were sometimes suspected of selling the heroin substitutes and barbiturates under the counter. But it remained an area where proof was at the minimum.

Another of the Handler's duties was to keep all seized drugs in a secure room and when there were enough, take them to the incinerator in Salford and have them all destroyed. Bill Kerr and the rest of us saw a flaw in this system, namely, we had no ideas how many people held a key to the store and what happened at the incinerator. Whenever we seized the full blocks, as in Salford, we would keep them as exhibits and then put them through the so-called 'system' for destruction. In storing the cannabis blocks we would engrave a mark into these blocks, perhaps an undetectable group of pin holes. We would wait and then perhaps only a week later they would appear again in another raid, usually in possession of one of the Jamaicans from Moss Side, usually one who had claimed to be an informant in the past. We used to make a lot of noise if such a situation arose, but there must have been a security issue at the incinerator and the drugs were leaking from that direction.

The bosses knew we were not happy, they couldn't fail to notice as we mentioned some jibe at every opportunity. There was no doubt in their minds that it was an internal matter and we wouldn't go elsewhere with our thoughts. How could we really, everyone was at it in their own little way, across the Force. The real pain with us was that we were not getting our share. Having already seen blocks of cannabis, secretly marked, back on the streets we knew it was not all being destroyed and said so. We wanted to see the incinerator process, but we never got to go and the bosses never picked up on our jibes or suspicions.

TICs and Stones

A couple of years ago I was at the funeral of 'Stoker' Potts – another legend in GMP. It was a light-hearted affair as he would have wished. A funeral director at the crematorium asked for six volunteers to carry the coffin. Of course, six friends jumped forward as an ex-detective inspector, loudly retorted: "You can sod off! I carried him all his service!"

I travelled there with an ex-CID colleague, John Schumsky, a mountain of a man, Judo 5th Dan and wrestling champion, but now, unfortunately, dead as are so many of my past colleagues. During the journey we were recounting old times when he referred to the recycling without any prompting. John had arrested a Jamaican dealer with a piece of cannabis, on which were lines, marking deals to be cut from the block. The block had been sent to the police laboratory to verify it was genuine. To do this, a small piece is cut from the block to complete the test. The practice was then, and still is, to return the entire block back to the officer to keep as an exhibit. When the case was closed the cannabis was locked in a room and taken for destruction by the intrepid Handler, via headquarters for the appropriate paperwork before ending up at the incinerator. Schumsky, believing this exhibit to have been destroyed, was amazed to find the same piece in the possession of another dealer some weeks later. The block was still marked out, and now bore the laboratory mark as well. This put John in a difficult position. The lab would recognise the block and, if they reported the circumstances, it would appear that the prisoner had been planted with the same piece by him. Therefore, he had no alternative other than to release the prisoner with no charge, rather than face the accusations. He had a very firm view on how it happened to get back on the street.

It became the general belief in the office that a little recycling of our own wouldn't do too much damage. Bush, which was dried cannabis leaves and stalks, was the favourite. It was common practice by the dealers to wet the bush, so that it weighed heavier and so the office stock became so wet you could wring it out. It weighed double. The buyer didn't like it, but had to look on it as rent, because he could carry on undeterred with the full protection of the law. It was a common sight in the office, usually on a Friday, to see many of the cannabis crowd weighing out and soaking the contraband and even adding a little formula to make up the weight. Formula was the term for 'copy' cannabis. It was made up from plants, which looked like cannabis when dried and then mixed with cannabis seeds to give it some apparent authenticity.

Few of the other officers in the drug squad were particularly memorable. They had been transferred there, perhaps to get them off their individual division, for any reason. While they took part in all the hooky elements, they didn't do much police work and merely joined in as back-ups to the many search warrants we were having issued. They did, however, lock up students with their little pound deals. Fifty per cent of these were usually found to be in possession of formula, which looked like cannabis, but as described previously, consisted of leaves and stalks picked up in Platt Fields Park and dried.

Formula was a common element in the drugs retail market and was aimed at the first year student population who didn't know any better. It looked and was made to smell exactly the same by adding a few cannabis seeds. The naive little bastards even thought they were getting high on it and used to be found giggling and lurching about at parties and music venues we raided. They were arrested with the bush they were smoking, and behaved like Che Guevara waving the V sign about as they were herded into the police van. They were now the big shots. "Gosh, I am now in the drug scene. Aren't I clever?" The antics of Rik Mayall in the TV series entitled 'The Young Ones' certainly comes to mind. They were bailed for laboratory reports and the bush was usually found to be formula. God knows what embarrassment they suffered with their 'revolutionary brothers' when the truth was known. From arresting so many of these, we found the common denominator for the purchases was the Bold Street Café in the centre of Moss Side. The café was already known as a stronghold of 'Black Power', which was in its infancy in those days.

We paid a visit, a heavy visit, and took the premises apart and the patrons too, for that matter. They were treated very roughly in an effort to have them react and be arrested for the 'good old' police assault. The café itself was a corner shop with a counter and a few tables and chairs littering the floor and, later, some of the clientele who had decided to fight for their 'black' rights. The walls had flock wallpaper with a couple of Jamaican posters and the Jamaican flag, which was upside down.

This had no political significance. It was just that these honest Jamaican citizens had no idea which way their flag should appear, despite the revolution they were to start. The customers were all black. They sat about in their fetching woolly hats in the middle of summer, without a cup of coffee to be seen.

We found quite a bit of cannabis in various forms. A realistic amount had been dropped on the floor, by the customers amid the blood and snot which quickly accumulated as the raid progressed. Some was found behind the counter, all tied up in tidy pound deals and some in coat pockets hanging on the cloakroom hooks. A not too original hiding point was also discovered as a table was thrown at someone, and a few deals were found Sellotaped beneath the Formica surface.

I searched a long leather coat (it was my size and quite fetching) and I found a large bag in one of the pockets. It was later found to be formula. I asked for the owner, but of course the coat was not claimed. I took the coat and continued to wear it every day as I swaggered about Moss Side doing my own impression of the famous film detective Shaft. It was a tasteful burgundy colour and very well made. The purchaser must have been a big man, because on me, at six foot one, the bottom went to below my calves. The coat was very well known and must have been the recognizable trademark of the owner. I wore this coat and attempted to trace the owner for many months. It caused some considerable amusement amongst the black populace and confusion from the white students who were obviously told to look out for the coat.

As I said the Bold Street Café was known to the Special Branch as the base for a militant black group, a group funded by drug sales. Our attention had upset the fundraising and so it continued for the rest of my Drug Squad service. It was the practice to inflict our own style of justice on the unfortunate students and today there must be many amongst the professional spheres who now appreciate the heavy hand used at the time. I was stopped once on Market Street, Manchester, by a very smartly dressed, pinstriped individual who described to me how he had been bounced about our office to frighten him and discourage him from other visits. It certainly worked and he was now working hard and had passed the exams he was happy to drop out from at the time. There must be many such individuals in Manchester and, indeed, such treatment is only an extension of the clip around the ear by the beat officer of long ago, so fondly referred to by today's pensioners. The fact that a smiling Dixon of Dock Green was substituted by a crowd of stinking psychopaths is merely an adaptation of a theme. We would arrest these terrified kids and treat them like the biggest dealer in the city. Then release them on police bail to return to the station a month later, to allow time for the pound deal to be tested by the forensic laboratory in Preston. They were told in that month they had to find somebody with more cannabis than them, preferably a dealer.

One such terrified little individual was on the phone almost daily, protesting he couldn't find anyone. Each time he was reminded of the long term of imprisonment he was facing. Prison was the child of his own imagination, so we didn't like to disappoint him. The day came and into the office came this trembling little white face, eyes wide open, but with a faint smile. He said: "I can't get you any drugs, but I have found a drinks still in Moss Side on Claremont Road." At first we laughed, and then one by one we realised we may have the makings of a party.

We already had some American NAAFI duty free rum from another raid which, didn't find its way to normal 'destruction' and this would dovetail nicely with whatever proceeds we got from the fresh raid. He explained that it was in the rear of a shop operated by an elderly Jamaican male. We were not accepting the information at face value and took him to the shop, sent him in with some readies and out he came with a stone jug containing the wildest hooch I had ever tasted. We all forensically tested the liquid, in the interests of law enforcement of course, and it really was one hell of a drink. The terrified little student was released with a warning and an unblemished record to accompany his academic achievement. The cannabis he had been found with was formula in any case, so he would have gone free. Of course, he was none the wiser.

The shop itself was a typical small terraced building. It was supposed to be an off-licence, but certainly it had the minimum of stock. The shelves were empty and the only alcohol that could be seen was in a few bottles of rum and a few cans of beer. It was not clear at this time how he could make a living from this business.

Bruche training school had taught us all about sheep dipping, incest, buggery, and indeed sheep shagging, but missed the law concerning the manufacture of alcohol with illegal stills. We had no choice but to inform the Inland Revenue with whom we crossed paths occasionally with drugs intelligence when we were all watching the same dealer. To me they were like the Fire Brigade. They had an air of efficiency. They knew they were the experts and treated everyone else like idiots, with an attitude bordering on superiority and condescension you could not quite put your finger on. Before we entered we were told the dangers of drinking this stuff. The manufacture is reliant on several factors and should they not all come together, the end result is poison. This knowledge would have come in handy two nights earlier when we were testing the jug. But we all seemed fine - except for experiencing a little short-sightedness, a trace of blurred vision, and the raging headaches. Just fine.

Some of us, perhaps those still suffering from the Pennine Way rigours, or two, or three, early pints in the Royal Oak, rushed straight back into the room, whilst the athletic amongst us in true Elliot Ness fashion vaulted the counter. The three earlier pints clearly took their toll on these also and on tripping, collapsing, or whatever the excuse they found themselves facing 30 stone jugs, hidden under the counter and awaiting sale.

In the rear room was a sight from the Beverly Hillbillies – that hit 1960s American sitcom starring the shapely Donna Douglas as delectable Elly May Clampett. The sparse brick walls, plaster falling off in various patches contrasted with the fetching pale green emulsion, usually favoured in police stations. The collapse of the plaster and the humidity in the room had caused damp and mildew everywhere. Whatever window there had been was covered with a large wooden board, plywood and separating due to the damp. Water was literally dripping off every smooth surface including the light bulbs, which could easily have caused a very interesting explosion.

The centre piece of the room was a large copper container, bulbous at the base and rising about five feet to a pointed end. The copper vessel was standing on a strong metal frame, which lifted it above the floor allowing for a large gas ring to be slid underneath. The ring was connected to a large red Calor gas cylinder. The gas ring was fully lit and burning brightly beneath the vessel, which was vibrating slightly due to the liquid inside, bubbling and boiling. From the top of the vessel was a curly copper pipe of some considerable size, at least eight feet long, which curled its way to a transparent plastic five gallon container which caught the constant flow of drips falling with regularity from the end of the copper pipe. In truly knowledgeable yet hardly scientific fashion every joint and even the odd leak in the length was sealed to an airtight standard with a mash of raw potato mixed with something that very effectively sealed the joints and stopped the leaks. Clearly, the strong alcohol being generated and forced through the pipe by the boiling mash had a corrosive effect on the innards of the pipe – let alone the drinker. Occasionally, a fresh leak occurred, whistling and blowing steam in the fashion of Thomas The Tank Engine, until yet again gripped by the do it yourself 'Bostick'. The entire apparatus was professionally manipulated by an elderly Jamaican who certainly appeared worse the wear from either the fumes or a joint. There were evidently many hand rolled reefer ends on the floor.

The information was perfect and the booze was unlike the Irish Pochin made from ordinary spuds, but instead concocted from the Jamaican sweet potatoes – which of course improved the general strength because of the natural sugar already in the ingredients. The smell alone was fabulous and without doubt replaced the giddiness of the three earlier pints, which were by now wearing off. Despite the various visions of parties and another free piss up, the search continued to the upstairs where we found several five gallon containers full of the transparent liquid. The sight was just too much for the in-house pissheads among us and we opened one of the containers to sniff the contents. By now the Customs boys had realised the truth of the matter – they were surrounded by a suicidal crowd of drunken psychopaths whose main aim was to try the interesting looking liquid. Customs were frantic in stopping us taking some because of the threat of poisoning, but couldn't be everywhere in the building as yet more interesting containers were found. I foolishly ignored all advice, opened a container and took a deep breath inward through my nose. The end result was quite alarming. The undiluted hooch gave off fierce fumes, which immediately attacked the back of my throat, my nostrils, my sight and I even suffered an intense twitching feeling in my bowels. I staggered back, peering through the black spots in my sight and unable to speak. Not from shock, but from the fact that the fumes had had an instant corrosive effect on my vocal chords. My voice was affected for the rest of the day, I sounded like Lee Marvin. It was immediately clear that this was likely to be a very interesting 'cocktail' if diluted a little perhaps even to the standard sold over the counter. Anyway, onwards and upwards, who dares wins and all that as we were able to slide one of the five gallon containers out and into the car.

Being a cross between a social enterprise and a police department we often had 'do's' in the rear rooms of pubs. The landlords were happy to oblige as for a change they didn't have to supply the booze. Sandwiches were regarded as the cheaper option. The rear room was booked, the butties were laid on and I really don't remember much more. I can't remember the pub, where it happened all night or even where in Manchester it was. I do remember my wife putting eye makeup on her lips - quite fetching really as she flashed a smile as she reeled about absolutely smashed.

I remember somehow getting home. Now the wife was as sexually experienced as I was when we met – which put us both in the enthusiastic amateur bracket rather than experienced. Though after this firewater she was certainly at her best and I tried out a variety of porn film poses and antics with little resistance until the pain and unnatural positions forced sensibility back and romance ended with a boot in the balls. At the time I was able to get Carlsberg Export into her and the Scandinavian porn positions would follow about half-an-hour after getting her home for some much appreciated extras. It ended up with me canning the Carlsberg Export as some of the deviations she introduced proved too much even with my appetite for the obscene.

Apart from the excesses of alcohol, we had normal daily duties which often consisted of executing search warrants at about 7am. We got the victims out of bed before their first fix, or their first cigarette. This helped make any detailed questioning come to a conclusion much speedier. Having found drugs of whatever classification, we would then take the prisoner to Whitworth Street where he would be questioned. There was none of this "you are not obliged to say . . ." (the caution). We sat him in a chair, and generally knocked him about until he was sufficiently terrified. There are ways to tell these things.

Skilled interrogators could spot a certain trembling about the body, occasionally resulting in an involuntary bowel movement, or the odd twitch about the eye and, clearly, the profuse sweating that generally accompanies terror. Then the suspect met the wet towel, which makes one unbelievably miserable. Having an existing headache from his drugs come down, exacerbated the pain additionally generated from the visit to our office. He was generally deprived of everything necessary for him to tackle the fun-filled day ahead. Eventually he agreed to co-operate and it was at this stage the lie detector was used.

The lie detector was not a complicated piece of equipment. An officer would stand behind the prisoner whilst a colleague asked a question, a question he already knew the answer to. Should the so-called co-operation prove to be a lie, the lie detector, our second officer, standing at attention, would suddenly go "beep beep" and slap the unfortunate off his chair with a blow to his already throbbing head. The poor wretch would pick himself up to prevent his balls being attacked by the wet towel. By this time, of course, the 'lie detector' would be poised and standing at attention once again. The entire procedure continued until we had the desired result, a volunteered statement. Life on Mars, eat your heart out.

This confession ensured that the court appearance would be short and sweet, and with a guilty plea. In the office we also had a very large syringe which was filled with milk. All junkies knew a quick jab with milk resulted in horrendous stomach cramps. It was rumoured that this was to be expected and there was no reason they should disbelieve it. The mere sight of this syringe struck fear and instant confessions were the norm.

The difficulties of the taped interviews of today in sterile, well illuminated rooms means that prisoners are now 'interviewed' in police vans and cars prior to arrival at the police station, so there is not really room to swing a wet towel. I was always very much in awe, but professionally annoyed by Bill Kerr's sources of information and was constantly using various means to try and cultivate my own. After the warrants were executed, we used to visit the haunts of the daytime junkies. These were the hippies, the registered addicts and the idiots who took the big sleepers and then fought sleep. They were in such a state they could barely stand. They simply lurched about, slurring and hurling abuse at all and sundry, until they could keep their eyes open no longer. They also fought the stairs of the Eighth Day, especially if we were on the same staircase. The Eighth Day was a shop with its own coffee lounge. They also sold paraphernalia - incense, pipes, long hippy clothes, and everything else that was totally useless to the general population except the regulars and the student populace who seemed to admire these freakish styles as children did with a comic book hero.

We often visited the Eighth Day and searched a few of the regulars. The stupid bastards knew this was always a possibility, but still carried the gear on their person. A few of the clever ones hid the gear under the seat they were sitting on, so we couldn't find them in possession. This little ruse had a fault. We always found their gear in the pocket of the person sitting nearest to the stash. The slightly more intelligent, or at least those with a less drug addled brain, would sit two chairs away, unknowing of the existence of someone else's under that particular chair, they were sitting on. This was a kind of a druggie form of Russian roulette, though less fatal we found it fun. Having had a joint on top of a sleeping tablet within an hour of Methadone always affected the thinking processes and being thrown into a game of musical chairs with nick as the prize, often proved much too confusing for the unfortunate brain-deads sitting about the café area. It was always amusing watching them staggering to the police van, shaking their befuddled heads in disbelief. They just couldn't understand how drugs they didn't know they possessed had jumped into their pockets. As part of our community work and our version of Save the Children, we would grab a couple of students, for just being there, throw them in the van with the other flotsam of life and take them to Bootle Street, where, despite the fact they were over 18, we would tell their parents of the situation. Even the most liberal of parents were concerned to hear their little child, away in the big bad world, may have caught something at the Eighth Day which moved and nibbled.

The Eighth Day was owned by Brian Livingstone, a solicitor who also represented his customers at court. He was a good man and, I think, he changed to follow Buddhism. He felt all his flock had a good side but, certainly, had difficulty finding it in many cases. He knew of all the violence and there was little he could do about it. We built up a good working relationship. He would accuse us and make a lot of noise at court, usually before John Bamber, the Stipendiary Magistrate, where the client was always convicted. That is unless we had made a terrible faux pas and committed perjury (though this rarely sent any of us to prison). The fact Brian had long flower power hair past his shoulders didn't really help, despite his black suit and Marks and Spencer's tie.

Brian no longer practices and has, apparently, retired to a smallholding in Hebden Bridge. He remains a friend, I think. I hope his furbishing skills have improved since the attempt at the Eighth Day wall coverings, which only provided a good back drop for LSD takers.

Cooking Benji

A body was dumped at the Jewish Hospital in the Cheetham area of Manchester, by some long-haired individuals with covered faces. The dead man appeared to have suffered a drug overdose. A murder (or suspicious death) was declared and a squad formed under Superintendent Harold Malone. Harold knew nothing about drugs or for that matter much about detecting murders as far as I was concerned. He was an old-school detective. He was also Chief Superintendent Charlie Horan's YES man. He drank with journalists, as senior CID officers did. There was, of course, the undoubted expertise of the murder squad team which, while having an exciting title, actually meant the men from the CID of that division. The 'squad' was lead by Malone, who generally played little part until the culprit was discovered and arrested. He then came into his own with press conferences and the like, most unofficial at the George and Dragon. At this time of the investigation and more so after the trial and imprisonment of the accused, Malone was always disgruntled at the number of private photographs from the family album which appeared in various newspapers with reporters who were not part of the 'inner circle' at the George and Dragon. Photographs were an excellent source of additional income and eventually I was to be the victim of such a sale as I became famous as Kevin Taylor's criminal associate.

Being the men on the ground with our fingers on the 'drug pulse' we were told to liaise and attend at the murder squad office. We were treated like the scum we were deemed to be. I had a beard and long hair, flared pants and a flowery tie. The rest of them had just as bizarre dress tastes. Griffiths in particular looked like a vagrant and smelt like a sewer. It appeared he had fallen foul of a good goat curry. Malone told us to ask around. That was about all he trusted us with. He clearly thought that such a motley crew could never undertake a serious murder investigation.

We decided to leave him to it, and see how far he got. We looked at the body in the morgue. We didn't even know him and, therefore, the victim must have been from out of town and a rare visitor. It was clear to us that this investigation was going to be uphill for the pipe smoking Malone, amongst the druggie cesspit of Manchester whose occupants would not have known this man.

Malone must have had a guardian angel because out of the blue, I got a phone call to meet a lad in his mid-20s, who I will call 'Dave', for the sake of anonymity. He must still be wanted by the underworld for the quality of information he gave us and the terms of imprisonment he caused. Dave was totally different in appearance and demeanour than the usual druggie but, incredibly, he knew all the details of the body and the location of the three men who delivered it. They had started to drive the man, while still alive, to the Jewish Hospital to put us totally off the trail. Unfortunately he was pronounced dead on arrival. They returned to Hattersley, 20 miles away, where they lived and remained in the house until the newspapers were out to report the incident the following day.

Malone thought he knew it all, so we told him nothing. We were taking a risk going to Hattersley and locking the three up. They were terrified to be accused of murder as the journalists had reported it. On the journey back to Manchester we got the confessions from all three. We handcuffed them together and marched them into the Murder Squad Office. The appearance of the three made Griffiths look like a Ralph Lauren model. Malone, the short-arsed little know-it-all he was, shouted: "Get those bags of shit out of my office! We have a murder to deal with." We weren't sure if Malone was referring to us or the prisoners but we laughed and retorted: "It is not a murder, and these men will tell you why. They dropped the body at the Jewish."

Malone was clearly upset. His embarrassment was obvious and we just walked out, leaving him to it. We sat in the canteen and had a brew, which was long overdue, having watched the house for a day and night to ensure it had occupants, before showing our hand. We even had Dave, the informant, sitting in the back of a van, which was hardly identification parade evidence. It was always the practice to charge your own prisoner. There was no extra money in it, but it helped the personal CV of every officer. Malone was having none of it and stole the glory for himself.

Malone was to appear again in my service and clearly he had not forgiven me. Members of his squad told me he was blazing at the embarrassment. Malone even tried to pin a murder on the three lads we arrested, because they had driven past the Manchester Royal Infirmary. The facts appeared immaterial to Malone as was the post mortem result that even Jesus couldn't have saved him, even if he could walk on water. The deceased was full of a mixture of drugs, which had poisoned his renal system and caused a heart attack. The overdose was so significant that the hospital was of the opinion that even a life support machine could not have helped his failing body. Again, failure was Malone's only option and he was left with some concealment of death charge, or something equally as wet.

I met Dave again and thanked him for the information. I was able to draw a few quid from our fund as Malone was still sulking. I had a five star informant who came with so much information it was embarrassing. I will not go into how I thanked him and how our working relationship blossomed suffice to say he always had an unending supply of dexis which he sold at the Twisted Wheel without fear of arrest. There was not a chemist's shop 'break-in' we did not detect. Dave came to our regular meetings and outlined the next shop to be burgled, before it was burgled. He gave me the opportunity to have a search warrant in place by telling me also the address where the proceeds would be concealed. Stipendiary Bamber showed the necessary theatrical concern for the issue of a search warrant before the offence had been committed. Obviously, such a situation tends to indicate that the informant is in on the job, from the detail of the information. He was not, but he was always in the company of the so-called planners. I never really asked him certain obvious questions, but the fact that chemists' shops would be burgled, that all the drugs, barbiturates and Speed, were kept off the streets was sufficient cause to celebrate and all possible through his co-operation.

With such a lack of stock on the streets, more shops were burgled and during my service, all chemist burglaries were detected as I have said. Barbiturate freaks and junkies were leaving Manchester as the arrest rate rose. The statistics involving street thefts to purchase drugs were falling, as was other petty crime in the city associated with the drug fraternity. Having such quality information we didn't have to put much effort into any other investigations and continued with our unending research of public houses about the city.

This research was not always for the social aspect, as it was an excellent way of being seen and seeing who was about, how they were dressing, and the cars they were driving. One thing about Jamaicans: they had to show what they had and, if they were on the inevitable dole, their 'chattels' stood out like a sore thumb. This sort of thinking appeared to go back to their African ancestry when whoever had the most wives and cows was considered the big shot, and later it might have been who had the shiniest bike.

At this time, there were many Jamaican clubs. Even in my day, blacks were allowed too much leeway and it was never clear if some of them were licensed or not. One such club on a first floor appeared to be licensed and even had an unreadable white license plate on the doorway. In a quiet spot close to the bar stood a round table and a chair and no one occupied it unless Chief Superintendent Dougie Nimmo visited. Many of the clubs had strange little foibles like this. I accepted drinks and mutton curries in these clubs but never cash bribes, which were offered regularly. As I was about to join the Drug Squad, Harry Kite, an experienced PC who had served in the unit, told me never to accept cash from anyone. He also told me to watch older colleagues. I took his advice on both counts. It appeared that we were sending a chill through the drug sellers and club owners.

As well as Moss Side, we spent a great deal of time in the main student residential areas. There were many cannabis dealers. Many of the junkies and hippies also resided in the Clyde Road area. And it was there one day that the Handler was sitting in his van when somebody threw a petrol bomb under it, nearly cooking Benji. Hoagy Carmichael was not amused. We all hit Didsbury, a popular student area, and pulled in everyone we knew to be connected to the drugs and local scene. They were arrested on the strength of planted drugs. They were kicked about the office until we had exhausted every avenue. Eventually, we put the pieces together and knew who was responsible. The arrest took place at the top of three flights of stairs in a large old Victorian house. Well actually, it took place in the cellar, but the prisoner was then taken, screaming and kicking to the top of the house, before 'attempting to escape' and falling down all three flights of very steep stairs. Mr Bamber chose to ignore the Technicolor features of the prisoner's face, as a dog lover he was not amused at the circumstances of the offence. He liked Labradors and sent Benji's potential chefs to prison.

Epilogue

Isn't it strange how fate operates? It is always a surprise and often difficult to deal with. There I was in the Drug Squad, arresting, seizing and even testing the gotten gains. I spent a great deal of time in Didsbury. It was a quaint little village, very lively with quite a few single ladies, but especially the divorced variety and those that wished they were.

Those of us who preferred such a snooty area to Cheetham Hill and Moss Side quickly became acquainted with the local female populace with the added bonus of illicit sex on demand, in flats with the 'singles', houses the proceeds of lucrative divorces and cars with those still entertaining husbands at home.

My time in this wonderful squad whilst I spent more time in this quaint little enclave was coming to an end. Service in the drug squad was limited to about a year to prevent friendly relationships in all areas especially with the drug dealing populace. It should actually have been fourteen days and even then that was too much. I had reached my 12 months and was considering my return to Bootle Street CID, with its free pints and clubland food during the evenings and, of course, the shoplifters in the day time. A few accessories in the kitchen needed replacing, so I was quite looking forward to it.

I could not have planned it, I was sent back to Didsbury as a full blown member of the CID. How was I to know or even imagine the wonders of this suburban playground and all it had to offer as a real detective rather than the dirty long haired 'hippy' I pretended to be, usually having never been home for a couple of days, smelly and unshaven and only meeting the druggie types of the area with regular monotony if I didn't branch out with a couple of 'silver grannies' out of the Didsbury Lodge on Barlow Moor Road, or a barmaid from the Royal Oak.

Now I had a source of frustrated females as I visited burglaries, all needing a shoulder to cry on in between a few arrests, not from detection practices but again confessions and TICs. It was easy, it was fun and again very lucrative, but in so many different ways.

Oh and I almost forgot my diplomatic and Royal protection duties – Prince Phillip was safe and Prime Minister Ted Heath was another sailor who washed up in Manchester.

But I'll shine the light of truth on that in my next book The Beat Goes On and then I'll try and take the reader on a journey through that and on to my third book Cop Out about my remarkable time as a private detective.

I turned the business into the multi-million pound money-spinner lots of people dream about and enjoyed all the trappings of wealth, celebrity friends and high rolling acquaintances.

It's funny how when fate takes a hand that things can actually go from being very bad to being very good indeed.

And then there's the John Stalker 'Shoot to Kill' inquiry into the goings on in Northern Ireland and the antics of God's Cop James Anderton.

The Happy Mondays even named a song after him when he was in office as Chief Constable of Greater Manchester, but the serving officers never had many happy Mondays during his time in charge. I even recall Ricky Tomlinson lampooning him as some sort of American Evangelical preacher ranting on about 'poofs' and 'pinkos', but I'd like to think the real version of events is even more interesting.

I really hope you join me on the journey through my next couple of books – I've already had interest from a movie producer. Now I've got to worry about Daniel Craig, or Tom Cruise, landing the starring role and I'm really looking forward to checking out the leading ladies.

And nobody has yet mentioned the casting couch…I for one cannot wait.

Lightning Source UK Ltd.
Milton Keynes UK
UKOW03f1915200314

228528UK00001B/2/P